Study Guide

to accompany

PSYCHOLOGY
the Science of Behavior

Fourth Edition

R. H. Ettinger

BVT
PUBLISHING

Study Guide to accompany PSYCHOLOGY, THE SCIENCE OF BEHAVIOR, Fourth Edition

ISBN: 978-1-60229-885-9

Contents

HOW TO USE THIS STUDY GUIDE

"Miracles do not happen. People work to accomplish what seems to be miraculous."

from the Chanukah Blessing

Students beginning a course in general psychology have varying preconceptions. Some students believe that because psychology is a science, it will be difficult for them to understand. Other students believe that because psychology is about people, it will be an easy course simply because they are a person and the course is about them. Most students fall somewhere in between these two extremes. This Study Guide is designed to assist all types of students to successfully complete their general psychology course. Students who feel (for whatever reason) that the course will be easy or difficult for them will benefit from the structure of and exercises included in this Study Guide. If, as you read this introduction at the beginning of the semester (or you just bought this Study Guide after performing poorly on your first exam), you believe that it would take a miracle for you to receive an A, B, or C (choose one) in this course, reread the quote at the top of the page. The quote is about work, not miracles. This Study Guide will help you work to master the material covered in your general psychology course. If you work by reading the text, attending class and taking notes, reading and doing the exercises in the Study Guide, and incorporating all of this information in your studying, your work will be rewarded with considerable knowledge concerning psychology. Further, this knowledge should be reflected in your course grade.

The introduction to the Study Guide has two main sections. The first section describes the major features of the Study Guide and provides information on how to effectively use it. The second section presents general information on effective studying and test-taking that is relevant for all your courses. You may have already noticed from the Table of Contents in the textbook that psychologists study such topics as learning, thinking, and memory. The second section of this introduction will refer you to specific sections of the textbook that are directly relevant to study and problem-solving skills that would be helpful for you to read at the beginning of the semester.

– ORGANIZATION OF EACH CHAPTER –

Each chapter in this Study Guide is divided into nine parts:

I.	Learning Objectives
II.	Overview
III.	Key Terms/Matching Exercises
IV.	True-False Statements
V.	Multiple-Choice Questions
VI.	Summary Tables
VII.	Thought Questions/Critical Thinking
VIII.	Applications
IX.	Summary Tables Solutions

This organization uses a number of methods to assist you in mastering the information presented in the textbook: highlights of or introduction to the material (Part I. and Part II.); questions to assess your basic knowledge of the material (Part III.–Part V.); and exercises designed to encourage critical thinking, by stimulating or challenging you to analyze, evaluate, and apply the principles discussed in the textbook in a variety of ways (Part VI.–Part VIII.). For your convenience, Part I.–Part V. are divided into sections that correspond to the major sections in the textbook. Let's look at each part individually.

PART I. LEARNING OBJECTIVES

The learning objectives highlight all the major topics discussed in the chapter, and should be used in three different ways. First, read the learning objectives before reading the text and attending class lectures so that you will be aware of the important topics, concepts, and terms upon which you should be focusing. Second, after reading the chapter and attending class lectures, you should be able to discuss each learning objective. Page references follow each learning objective. If you are having difficulty with a particular learning objective, refer to the textbook and reread the appropriate pages. Third, the learning objectives are phrased in a way that is suitable for essay questions; in studying for an exam, practice composing answers to each. It is useful to put an asterisk(*) beside those learning objectives your instructor emphasized in class and devote extra attention to those learning objectives. Similarly, if your instructor did not assign the entire chapter, you should cross off any learning objectives associated with the material in the text that was not assigned. (Caution: Do not cross off learning objectives that your instructor assigned but did not emphasize in class lectures. You are still responsible and may be questioned concerning that material.)

PART II. OVERVIEW

The overview contains a brief summary of the material presented in the chapter. The overview serves two functions. As with the learning objectives, you should read the overview before reading the text and attending class to prepare for the material that will be presented. The second function of the overview is that, because it is brief, it presents a concise overview (or global view) of how the different topics in the chapter relate to each other. Thus it is helpful to reread the overview after reading the chapter and when studying for your exams.

PART III. KEY TERMS/MATCHING EXERCISES

The matching exercises are designed to assess your knowledge of the basic concepts (and for some chapters, individuals) discussed in the text. The matching questions are organized by topic; therefore the terms are often closely related. The matching exercises focus your attention on subtle similarities and differences between related terms. Check your answers against the Answer Key. If you have difficulty with some of the concepts, the Answer Key includes page references to assist you in accurately learning each. You might want to consider first answering the matching exercises (and also the true-false statements and multiple-choice questions) on a separate sheet of paper, enabling you to go back over these exercises to give yourself a retest of the material.

PART IV. TRUE-FALSE STATEMENTS

True-false statements are included to assess your knowledge concerning definitions, facts, and concepts and also to focus on distinctions between related concepts. Many students find true-false items (where there is a 50 percent probability of guessing correctly) more difficult than multiple-choice questions (where there is only a 25 percent chance of guessing correctly). In multiple-choice questions the correct answer is directly stated, and the student's task is to select it from among the choices presented. You can visualize a true-false item as a multiple-choice question that only provides one choice (a). The student has to decide for himself or herself what choices b, c, and d would be and then decide which choice is correct. Carefully examine all terms in each true-false item before answering. Check your responses against the Answer Key. Space is provided for you to go back to the false statements and supply a revised statement that is true. This part of the true-false exercise can be very helpful in "fine-tuning" your knowledge of the material. For false items there are usually a number of ways to change the statement into a true statement: For example, if the statement is basically a definition, you could either change the term so that it matches the definition provided or change the definition so that it matches the term. The Answer Key supplies a page reference for each item. Those that are true are described on the referenced page. The page reference for false statements supplies at least one correct (or true) version of a related statement.

PART V. MULTIPLE-CHOICE QUESTIONS

Many instructors include some multiple-choice questions on their exams. The multiple choice questions in this Study Guide are similar to the type of multiple-choice questions you may encounter on your exams. Some of the multiple-choice questions are straightforward and refer specifically to the terms, facts, and concepts described in the text, whereas other questions require you to apply information from the text to new situations or examples. Answering these questions should give you a good estimate of how well prepared you are for the exam. You might want to take this "practice" multiple-choice test after you have started to review for the exam. Check your answers against the Answer Key, which has page references included. Allow yourself enough study time to be able to review the material related to those questions you missed or were unsure of the correct answer. For each chapter five multiple-choice questions have annotated answers provided. These annotations contain detailed information explaining why the correct answer is correct and also explain why the remaining choices are incorrect. The questions that receive the annotated answers are not necessarily the trickiest or even most difficult questions. Rather they are questions selected to cover a variety of topics from each chapter and to illustrate a number of different styles of multiple-choice questions.

PART VI. SUMMARY TABLES

Each chapter in the Study Guide has between one and four Summary Tables for you to complete. These tables take a variety of forms including listing and describing related concepts, summarizing a number of related theories, and summarizing a large body of information from the chapter in a concise manner. The Summary Tables serve two purposes. First, in order to complete these tables you will need to think about the information in the textbook and organize your thoughts. If you have carefully prepared for your exam, you should be able to fill in the information without constantly referring to the text and your notes for "hints." If you encounter difficulty with a Summary Table (or a substantial part of a table) it indicates an area of weakness that you should review. Part IX. Summary Tables Solutions, at the end of the chapter, provide completed tables for you to compare with your completed tables. Second, the completed tables are well suited for use to quickly review the material.

PART VII. THOUGHT QUESTIONS/CRITICAL THINKING

Research has shown that memory for material is enhanced through critical thinking. Critical thinking involves analyzing, evaluating, reorganizing, and relating information to a larger body of information. These questions ask you to really think about the principles of psychology that are discussed in the textbook. Perhaps not many of the thought questions included in the Study Guide will appear on your exams. However, by thinking about and preparing answers to these questions you will gain an increased understanding of the principles of psychology discussed in the textbook.

PART VIII. APPLICATIONS

To encourage you to continue to think critically, each chapter typically concludes with two applications. These applications fall into two general categories: research-based applications and everyday-life applications. Research-based applications ask you to examine your own behavior (for example, keep a sleep diary), examine the behavior of others (for example, the strategies they use to solve problems), and design experiments to illustrate or test some of the concepts discussed in the textbook. Everyday-life applications ask you, for example, to suggest possible diagnoses for individuals with psychological disorders, develop a stress test to determine the amount of stress experienced by college students, and evaluate television commercials. It is strongly suggested that you do at least one of the applications for each chapter in the Study Guide. These exercises will help you to master the material in the textbook and will also give you a more complete "feel" for the science of psychology and how it relates to the behavior and mental processes of individuals.

– HOW TO STUDY AND TAKE EXAMS –

SQ3R METHOD

The SQ3R method developed by educational psychologist Francis Robinson is a well-known and effective strategy for studying written material. There are five steps in the SQ3R method: Survey, Question, Read, Recite, and Review.

Survey   Before you begin to read and study a chapter, quickly scan or survey the chapter in order to get a general outline of the material to be discussed. Look at the main headings and subheadings and examine the tables and figures. The purpose of the survey is to provide you with general information concerning the chapter that you will expand upon later. Reading the learning objectives and chapter overview in this Study Guide would also be part of your survey.

Question   Before beginning to read the chapter, stop and write questions concerning the results of your survey. You could start by turning each chapter heading into a question (use key words such as who, what, when, where, why, and how). You might add to your list of questions after you begin to read the chapter. Asking a number of questions prepares you for the next step.

Read   Actively read the chapter, searching for the answers to the questions you formulated. Your comprehension of the chapter will be increased because your active reading has a purpose (answering specific questions). This approach is very different from passive reading ("Only 10 more pages to go") which often is not associated with gaining an understanding of the information.

Recite   After you have read the first section of the chapter, stop. Close your textbook or look away from it and recite (mentally, out loud, or in writing) the main points of the section. These main points should be the answer to the first questions you asked. After checking your recited answer with the text, make any necessary corrections to your answer and recite it again. Then proceed to read and recite for the next section of the chapter.

Review   After you have read all the new information (whether it is a chapter or a shorter daily reading assignment), go back over all the new material and review it and the material from previous assignments. This review step increases your retention of the information and also helps to clarify how the individual sections of the chapter relate to each other.

HELPFUL HINTS FROM YOUR TEXT

Three short sections in the text provide specific information directly related to studying and taking exams in your general psychology course and other classes. You should read the following sections of the text now.

1. In your classes it is frequently necessary to memorize information. The chapter on memory discusses six different mnemonic devices or memory systems to enhance your retention of specific information.

2. The memory chapter also includes a section titled "Improving Academic Memory," which discusses nine different strategies to improve the efficiency of your studying.

3. The chapter on intelligence discusses six steps involved in solving multiple choice-type problems, and the characteristics of students who perform poorly and well on these types of problems. The text outlines strategies for how to improve your performance on multiple-choice problems.

CLASS NOTES

Attending class lectures is good, listening attentively is better, and taking a good set of class notes is best. We will discuss notetaking from two perspectives, during class and after class.

In Class

1. Keep all of your notes for one class in a large notebook. Begin each day's notes with the date and topic or chapter that will be discussed.

2. Do not try to save money by conserving paper. When the instructor starts to lecture on a new chapter start a new page in your notebook. Write only on the front of each sheet. Do not write on every line and do not write across the entire length of any line. Do leave plenty of blank space so that you can add information later or make notes on your notes.

3. Do not try to write down everything the instructor says (it's impossible and not everything is important). Do try to summarize in your own words what the instructor says. When you study, your "own words" will make more sense to you than the instructor's.

4. Take notes in an outline format. Make certain that major topics or concepts stand out and are not buried within smaller details. List details under major topics in an orderly fashion.

5. If the instructor cares enough to write or draw something on the chalkboard, include it in your notes. Frequently, information presented on the chalkboard appears on exams.

6. Include examples in your notes. One of the main advantages an instructor has over a textbook author is that the instructor can supply many more examples to illustrate a concept than would be possible for the author. Don't just listen to these "extra examples or stories;" write them down in your notes. Often examples are well remembered, and by writing the example in your notes you will hopefully not only remember the example but also remember what concept it was designed to illustrate.

After Class

1. Review your notes as soon after class as possible, while the lecture is still relatively fresh in your mind. Fill in information or details (remember all that blank space you left) to supplement the notes you wrote down during class, rephrase information that is unclear, copy over words that are illegible (if you can barely read it today, it will be incomprehensible when studying for an exam). Also review your notes for accuracy and, if necessary, correct them.

2. Develop a system to cross-reference your class notes, text, and this Study Guide. There are a number of possibilities to accomplish this. For example, if your instructor gives a novel example to illustrate a concept (about his grandfather in World War I), note "Grandfather's war story" at the appropriate place in the text. You may find it helpful to write down in the text which days' lectures go with which sections of the text (and vice versa). You might also find it helpful to write in your notes which chapter learning objective is related to each section of the lecture material.

TEST-TAKING STRATEGIES

General Strategies

Before you begin to answer the test questions:

1. If there is no clock in the classroom, wear a watch on exam days.

2. Read all instructions for the entire test. If instructions are not clear to you, ask your instructor to explain.

3. Note how many points each question (and each section of the exam) is worth.

4. Decide how much time you will need to complete each section of the test and budget your time accordingly. You will want to devote more time to a 20-point essay question than to a 5-point short-answer question.

During the test:

1. Periodically check the time to see if you are "on schedule." Do not allow yourself to spend too much time on any particular question. At times it is necessary to "move along." If you spend too much time staring at a difficult question at the beginning of the test, you might not have time to answer the easy questions at the end.

2. Use all of the time you are allotted. If a few minutes are left after you finish the test, use this time to double-check that you answered all questions, to look for careless mistakes, to proofread your written answers, and to ponder those difficult questions.

Strategies for Multiple-Choice Tests

1. Do not jump or skip around through the questions. Answer all questions in order. If you are unsure of an answer, make an educated guess and mark that question so that you can go back and devote more attention to evaluating it carefully after you have finished the remainder of the test.

2. Read the main body of each question (the question stem) carefully and try to supply the answer before you read the choices. This prepares you to read the responses intelligently. Then read all the alternative responses to find the one best answer to the question. Examine each alternative and eliminate those that are obviously incorrect first.

3. Questions using words such as not and least likely may be tricky. Use extra care in reading these questions and the alternative responses.

4. Finally, your first "guess" on a multiple-choice question is usually correct. If you change your answer, have a good reason for doing so.

Strategies for Essay Tests

1. For exams that contain both essay and objective questions, read the essay questions first, but answer them last. You will probably find some information that will help you on the essay questions in the other sections of the test.

2. Read the questions carefully. Pay close attention to key words such as define, evaluate, and illustrate. Make sure that you answer the question that your instructor asked.

3. Answer the essay questions that you know best first, then answer the remaining questions.

CHAPTER 1
THE ORIGINS OF PSYCHOLOGY

– PART I. LEARNING OBJECTIVES –

When you finish studying this chapter, you should be able to do the following:

DEFINITION OF PSYCHOLOGY

1. Give a complete definition of psychology.

2. Explain why psychology is a science.

3. Explain why psychology studies behavior.

4. Discuss five reasons why psychology studies animal as well as human behavior.

PSYCHOLOGY'S HISTORY

5. Discuss the two roots (philosophy and physiology) of psychology. What did each contribute to the new science of psychology?

6. Describe how Wundt, Titchener, and other structuralists defined psychology and discuss their approach to the study of psychology.

7. Describe how James's approach—functionalism—would define and study psychology.

8. Discuss Freud's psychoanalytic approach, and explain how it fundamentally differed from the other early approaches to psychology.

9. Discuss why Watson and other behaviorists objected to the study of structuralism and functionalism. Describe the approach to psychology supported by behaviorists.

10. Discuss why Gestalt Psychology (Wertheimer, Köhler, Koffka) objected to structuralism and behaviorism, and describe this approach to psychology.

11. Describe the approach to psychology taken by humanistic psychologists. Discuss how this approach differs from that of Freud and the behaviorists.

CONTEMPORARY PSYCHOLOGY

12. Describe and give examples of the types of questions or fields of study that would interest cognitive psychologists.

13. Describe and give examples of the types of questions or fields of study that would interest developmental psychologists.

14. Describe and give examples of the types of questions or fields of study that would interest social psychologists.

15. Describe and give examples of the types of questions or fields of study that would interest personality psychologists.

16. Describe the work of experimental psychologists, and explain why it is misleading to consider experimental psychology to be a separate field.

17. Describe and give examples of the types of questions or fields of study that would interest biological psychologists.

18. Describe the work of clinical and counseling psychologists, and discuss the differences between clinical psychologists, counseling psychologists, and psychiatrists.

19. Discuss the difference between educational and school psychology, and give examples of the types of questions or fields of study that would interest educational and school psychologists.

20. Describe and give examples of the types of questions or fields of study that would interest industrial/organizational psychologists.

21. Describe and give examples of the types of questions or fields of study that would interest engineering psychologists.

22. Describe and give examples of the types of questions or fields of study that would interest health psychologists.

23. Describe and give examples of the types of questions or fields of study that would interest psychologists in the field of positive psychology.

24. Describe and give examples of the types of questions or fields of study that would interest forensic psychologists.

25. Describe and give examples of the types of questions or fields of study that would interest psychologists involved in artificial intelligence and connectionism.

26. Discuss the changing face of psychology and the current tension between scientifically oriented and health-care provider oriented psychologists.

THE GOALS OF PSYCHOLOGY

27. Name and discuss the three goals of psychology.

28. Discuss how theories and empirical tests contribute to our current understanding of psychology.

– PART II. OVERVIEW –

Psychology is the scientific study of the behavior of humans and other animals. The subject matter of psychology includes both observable behavior and complex mental processes such as perceiving, memory, and thinking. The goals of psychology are to understand, predict, and control or influence behavior.

The combined influence of two distinct fields led to the beginning of psychology in the late 1800s. Philosophers were concerned with the mind and attempted to understand it through the application of logical reasoning. Physiologists, on the other hand, relied on the scientific method to study bodily processes.

The new science of psychology had many different beginnings or approaches. Structuralism (Wundt and Titchener) tried to identify the basic elements of conscious experience through the use of introspection. Functionalism (James) was concerned with the adaptive functions of different conscious processes. While the structuralists were interested in the parts, or structure, of the mind, the functionalists were more interested in what the mind was capable of doing. Freud's psychoanalytic approach emphasized the role of the unconscious mind in the development of human personality. Behaviorism (Watson) took a very different approach and rejected mental processes from study and concentrated on observable behaviors. Gestalt psychology (Wertheimer, Köhler, and Koffka) believed that "the whole is different from the sum of its parts" and was interested in how people organize experiences and perceive patterns. More recently, Humanistic psychology (Maslow and Rogers) emphasized the role of free will and man's striving for self-actualization.

A large number of areas of specialization exist in psychology today. Some psychologists perform activities that help individuals cope with difficulties in their daily life (clinical, counseling, and school) or maintaining good health (health psychology), whereas others are concerned with making the work environment more satisfying (industrial/organizational) or well designed for efficiency (engineering). Educational psychologists are involved in the study and application of teaching methods. In many of the other areas of specializations, psychologists concentrate on studying basic psychological processes (developmental, biological, personality, and social). Positive psychology focuses on determining the factors that contribute to self-fulfillment and happiness.

– PART III. KEY TERMS/MATCHING EXERCISES –

Match the following concepts and/or individuals with the appropriate descriptions. Check your answers against the Answer Key.

DEFINITION OF PSYCHOLOGY

Concepts	Descriptions
_____ 1. psychology	a. Involve manipulating conditons or behaviors and observing the results
_____ 2. scientific method	b. An activity of an organism that can be observed
_____ 3. behavior	c. Provides reliable information as opposed to subjective opinions
_____ 4. theories	d. Tentative attempts to organize and explain a body of data, facts, or observations
_____ 5. American Psychological Association (APA)	e. The scientific study of the behavior and mental processes of humans and other animals
_____ 6. American Psychological Society (APS)	f. Organization with the stated purpose of representing the academic and research interests of psychology
_____ 7. empirical tests	g. A large and well-established organization that today is more closely aligned with applied, as opposed to academic, psychology

Answer Key

1. e   2. c   3. b   4. d   5. g   6. f   7. a

PSYCHOLOGY'S HISTORY

Concepts	Descriptions
_____ 1. behaviorism	a. Believes the relationship between the parts is more important than the individual parts
_____ 2. functionalism	b. Rejected the study of mental processes and emphasized the study of the relationship between stimuli and responses
_____ 3. Gestalt psychology	c. Emphasized the role of the unconscious mind and sexual urges in influencing human behavior
_____ 4. humanistic psychology	d. Attempts to reduce conscious experience to its basic elements
_____ 5. psychoanalysis	e. Emphasizes the practical nature of the mind
_____ 6. structuralism	f. Emphasizes the role that free choice and conscious rational choices have on human behavior

Answer Key

1. b   2. e   3. a   4. f   5. c   6. d

Individuals	Descriptions
_____ 1. Freud	a. Was strongly influenced by Darwin's Theory of Natural Selection
_____ 2. James	b. Developed his approach as a result of treating emotionally disturbed individuals
_____ 3. Maslow and Rogers	c. Pioneered the stimulus–response approach to psychology and emphasized objectively verifiable phenomena
_____ 4. Watson	d. Used introspection to study mental processes
_____ 5. Wertheimer, Köhler, and Koffka	e. Believed that people have a natural tendency to strive for self-actualization or the attainment of their fullest potential
_____ 6. Wundt and Titchener	f. Believed that the whole of an experience was different from the sum of its parts

Answer Key

1. b   2. a   3. e   4. c   5. f   6. d

CONTEMPORARY PSYCHOLOGY

Concepts	Descriptions
_____ 1. artificial intelligence	a. Concerned with the relationship between the working environment, equipment, and people
_____ 2. biological	b. Would be interested in topics such as interpersonal attraction, conformity, and group processes
_____ 3. clinical	c. Focuses on adjustment problems that are not serious psychological problems
_____ 4. cognitive	d. Concerned with the diagnosis and treatment of serious psychological problems
_____ 5. counseling	e. Focuses on the relationship between physiological processes and behavior
_____ 6. developmental	f. Concerned with using psychological concepts to make the workplace a more satisfying environment for employees and management
_____ 7. educational	g. Focuses on the study and application of teaching methods and learning
_____ 8. engineering	h. Focuses on the uniqueness of individuals and the key elements that provide the foundation of human personality
_____ 9. experimental	i. Concerned with evaluating and resolving learning and emotional problems as they relate to school activities
_____ 10. forensic	j. Concerned with factors that influence behavior and development throughout the life cycle
_____ 11. health	k. Resulted in renewed interest in mental processes such as thinking, problem solving, and creativity
_____ 12. industrial/organizational	l. Develops computer models that simulate complex human cognitive processes
_____ 13. personality	m. Concerned with how psychological and physical factors relate to the treatment and prevention of illness
_____ 14. social	n. Primary activity is conducting research
_____ 15. school	o. Works with the legal system in a variety of ways

Answer Key
  1. 1   2. e   3. d   4. k   5. c   6. j   7. g   8. a   9. n   10. o   11. m 12. f
13. h   14. b   15. i

– PART IV. TRUE-FALSE STATEMENTS –

Fill in the blank before each statement with either a T (true) or an F (false). Check your answers against the Answer Key. Then go back to the items that are false and make the necessary change(s) to the statements to convert the items into true statements.

DEFINITION OF PSYCHOLOGY

_____   1. Psychology is a science because it deals with both animal and human behavior.

_____   2. One reason why psychologists study animal behavior is that, occasionally, ethical considerations would prohibit the use of human subjects in a research project.

PSYCHOLOGY'S HISTORY

_____   3. One of the main benefits that the science of psychology received from its roots in philosophy is that philosophy emphasizes the use of observation to acquire knowledge.

_____   4. According to Wundt and Titchener, psychology should attempt to study the structure of the conscious mind.

_____   5. Although they were in general agreement with the principles of behaviorism, Gestalt psychologists had major disagreements with the principles of structuralism.

_____   6. Humanistic psychology emphasizes the role of the unconscious processes in determining human behavior.

CONTEMPORARY PSYCHOLOGY

_____ 7. Biological psychologists might investigate the effects of both drugs and brain damage on behavior.

_____

_____

_____ 8. Counseling psychologists focus on relatively minor psychological problems; clinical psychologists focus on more serious psychological problems.

_____

_____

_____ 9. In order to increase employee productivity, an industrial/organizational psychologist would likely assist in the design of a new fast-food restaurant.

_____

_____

_____ 10. Health psychology is a new area of specialization in psychology that has received widespread interest and is recognized as an important field of study.

_____

_____

THE GOALS OF PSYCHOLOGY

_____ 11. The goals of psychology are to understand, predict, and control (or influence) behavior and mental processes.

_____

_____

Answer Key
  1. F   2. T   3. F   4. T   5. F   6. F   7. T   8. T   9. F   10. T   11. T

– PART V. MULTIPLE-CHOICE QUESTIONS –

Choose the best answer to each question. Circle your choice. Check your answers against the Answer Key. Questions marked with an asterisk (*) include annotated answers.

DEFINITION OF PSYCHOLOGY

1. Which of the following terms or phrases is not included in the definition of psychology?
    a. Behavior
    b. Subjective study
    c. Scientific study
    d. Humans and other animals

2. Today psychologists are interested in studying _____.
   a. behavior
   b. mental processes
   c. both behavior and mental processes
   d. neither behavior nor mental processes

*3. You want to study the effects of the presence of red-filtered background lighting on resting heart rate. Originally, why might you choose to perform the study with animals rather than humans?
   a. Ethical considerations would prohibit the use of human subjects in this experiment.
   b. You could obtain information about the genetic background of animals but not of humans.
   c. Animals can be obtained at very little expense.
   d. Animal studies allow you to have more control.

4. The roots of modern psychology may be traced to _____.
   a. philosophy and physics
   b. philosophy and physiology
   c. psychoanalysis and physiology
   d. physics and philanthropy

5. The "root" of psychology that used logical thought processes to reach conclusions was _____.
   a. philosophy
   b. psychoanalysis
   c. physiology
   d. physics

6. An approach to psychology that attempted to break down experience into its basic elements was _____.
   a. structuralism
   b. psychoanalysis
   c. functionalism
   d. behaviorism

7. If you take a sip of a soft drink and concentrate on what you are experiencing (cold, bubbly, sweet, etc.), you would be utilizing the technique of _____.
   a. empiricism
   b. functionalism
   c. behaviorism
   d. introspection

8. The approach to psychology that emphasized the practical nature of the mind and believed that processes such as consciousness helped people adapt was _____.
   a. Gestalt psychology
   b. functionalism
   c. humanistic psychology
   d. structuralism

9. The introduction of observations of behavior and the use of animals into psychological research was originally done by _____.
   a. Wundt
   b. Skinner
   c. Watson
   d. James

10. Why has the psychoanalytic approach been widely criticized?
    a. Psychoanalysis does not help patients.
    b. Its assertions cannot be tested in the laboratory.
    c. It ignores mental processes.
    d. It does not include the study of animals.

11. You act impulsively, then wonder why. Freud would tell you that your behavior was influenced by your _____.
    a. irritation
    b. unconscious mind
    c. immaturity
    d. inability to think fast

12. "An empirical, objective science of behavior that has no need for theories of mind or personal freedom" characterizes _____.
    a. Gestalt psychology
    b. humanistic psychology
    c. structuralism
    d. behaviorism

13. Which individual is incorrectly paired with an approach to psychology?
    a. Titchener—structuralism
    b. Maslow—humanistic psychology
    c. Watson—Gestalt psychology
    d. James—functionalism

14. On what does Gestalt psychology focus?
    a. the most basic elements of our experiences
    b. gaining an understanding of the unconscious mind
    c. the relationship between environmental stimuli and an organism's response to them
    d. the perception of the whole

*15. Which approach to psychology could explain why some individuals interpret "IX" as the letters "I" and "X," and other individuals interpret it as the number 9?
    a. Humanistic psychology
    b. Functionalism
    c. Gestalt psychology
    d. Structuralism

*16. Which of the following is a *false* statement?
    a. Humanistic psychologists emphasize the role of free choice.
    b. Humanistic psychologists view people as being controlled by events in their environment.
    c. Humanistic psychologists have interest in topics such as self-esteem and personal fulfillment.
    d. Humanistic psychologists de-emphasize the influence of unconscious processes.

FIELDS OF SPECIALIZATION IN PSYCHOLOGY TODAY

17. Internal mental processes are of interest to _____ psychologists.
    a. biological
    c. cognitive
    b. developmental
    d. forensic

*18. You see an article titled "The Effect of Peer Pressure on Alcohol Consumption by Teenagers." The psychologist who conducted this research was most likely a(n) _____ psychologist.
   a. social
   b. educational
   c. organizational
   d. personality

19. You are studying to be a psychologist. The chances are greater than 50 percent that you will specialize in _____ psychology.
   a. experimental
   b. industrial
   c. educational
   d. clinical or counseling

20. You are interested in studying what makes people feel fulfilled and happy. You would most likely specialize in the field of _____ psychology
   a. health
   b. social
   c. positive
   d. enrichment

*21. Which of the following types of psychologists would be *least* likely to study the development of the ability of children to work appropriately on group projects in school?
   a. School psychologist
   b. Educational psychologist
   c. Developmental psychologist
   d. Social psychologist

22. Educational psychologists differ from school psychologists in that educational psychologists are more likely to _____.
   a. assist students with special problems
   b. help students with learning problems
   c. engage in research
   d. consult with parents and teachers

23. An _____ psychologist would be concerned with the workplace being organized for optimal efficiency; an _____ psychologist would be concerned that the workplace provided a satisfying environment.
   a. engineering / environmental
   b. engineering / industrial/organizational
   c. industrial/organizational / engineering
   d. industrial/organizational / environmental

24. You see an article titled "The Effect of Hawaiian Vacations on the Remission of Cancer." The psychologist who conducted this research was most likely a(n) _____ psychologist
   a. forensic
   b. medical
   c. developmental
   d. health

25. John Hinkley's (President Reagan's attempted assassin) psychological profile would probably have been performed by a(n) _____ psychologist.
   a. personality
   b. forensic

c. social

d. organizational

26. Computer hardware that is similar to the "wiring" of the neurons in the brain are

   a. connectionist machines

   b. biological computers

   c. artificial intelligence

   d. PCs

27. In recent years, what has happened to the number of individuals receiving doctorates in psychology?

   a. increased in social, personality, and biological psychology and decreased in clinical, counseling, and school psychology

   b. increased in clinical, counseling, and school psychology and decreased in social, personality, and biological psychology

   c. increased dramatically in all areas of psychology

   d. not changed since the 1950s

THE GOALS OF PSYCHOLOGY

28. The goal of psychology that is sometimes perceived as controversial is _____ behavior.

   a. understanding

   b. generating

   c. controlling

   d. predicting

29. _____ generate predictions or _____ that may be subjected to empirical tests.

   a. observations / beliefs

   b. hypotheses / theories

   c. theories / hypotheses

   d. facts / theories

Answer Key

1. b	2. c	*3. d	4. b	5. a	6. a	7. d	8. b	9. d	10. b	11. b	12. d
13. c	14. d	*15. c	*16. b	17. c	*18. a	19. d	20. c	*21. a	22. c	23. b	24. d
25. b	26. a	27. b	28. c	29. c							

Annotated Answers

3. The correct choice is **d**. With human subjects it would be more difficult to control the activities subjects engaged in prior to the experiment that could have an effect on resting heart rate.

   a. It would be ethical to conduct this experiment with human subjects.

   b. While there may be a potential genetic influence on resting heart rate, it does not appear to be a major consideration in this research.

   c. The cost of doing this research with human subjects would not be a major consideration in this experiment.

15. The correct choice is **c**. Gestalt psychology is concerned with the perception of the "whole." Different individuals might perceive the "I" as combined of two different types of symbols that would combine to give two different meanings.

   a. Humanistic psychology is concerned with topics such as personal fulfillment and self-esteem and not perception.

b. While functionalism is concerned with topics such as perception and learning, the specific example in the question is of "the whole is more than the sum of its parts" variety and therefore is more appropriately matched with Gestalt psychology.

d. The structuralist approach using introspection would probably be unsuccessful in explaining how the stimulus "I" could be broken down into two different sets of basic elements.

16. The correct choice is **b**. Behaviorists support this statement.
    a. Humanistic psychologists emphasize that people have free choice.
    c. Humanistic psychologists are very interested in topics such as self-esteem and personal fulfillment.
    d. Because humanistic psychologists emphasize conscious choices, they de-emphasize the influence of the unconscious.

18. The correct choice is **a**. Social psychology is interested in topics such as conformity and group processes and would examine the influence of these factors on drinking behavior.
    b. While teenagers are often of interest to educational psychologists, their focus is on learning and teaching methods.
    c. Organizational psychologists focus on the workplace.
    d. While personality psychologists might be interested in teenage drinking, their chief focus would be on the individual personality traits of teenagers who drink and not on the effect of peer pressure.

21. The correct choice is **a**. School psychologists are primarily interested in helping individual children resolve learning and emotional problems. Additionally, they typically do not conduct research.
    b. An educational psychologist might study this behavior from the perspective of gaining insight into how to best organize or coordinate group projects.
    c. A developmental psychologist might study this behavior from the perspective of discovering at what age children can appropriately handle group projects.
    d. A social psychologist might study this behavior from the perspective of observing the dynamics of group processes and the social roles involved in group projects.

– PART VI. SUMMARY TABLE –

To test your understanding of the material discussed in this chapter, complete the following table. Check your answers with those supplied in Part IX.

APPROACHES TO PSYCHOLOGY

Approach	Individuals	Area of Study	Methods of Study and/or Specific Areas of Interest
Structuralism			
Functionalism			
Behaviorism			
Gestalt psychology			
Psychoanalysis			
Humanistic psychology			

– PART VII. THOUGHT QUESTIONS/CRITICAL THINKING –

Prepare answers to the following discussion questions.

1. Many people would argue that psychology is not really a science but just common sense. These individuals might say that we all know that "Opposites attract," "You should look before you leap," and "Absence makes the heart grow fonder." How would you explain to these people that a science of psychology is necessary? Would your argument be strengthened if you mentioned that we also know "Birds of a feather flock together," "He who hesitates is lost," and "Out of sight, out of mind"?

2. If you had been an aspiring young psychologist when psychology was first becoming established, which school of psychology (structuralism, functionalism, behaviorism, Gestalt psychology, or psychoanalysis) do you think you would have been *most likely* to join and *least likely* to join? Explain your choices.

3. Imagine that Wundt, James, Watson, Wertheimer, and Freud are members of a panel at the First International Convention of Psychology. The topics on the agenda for discussion include: How should psychology be defined? What methods should psychologists use to gain information? What are two or three critical issues for psychology to address? The discussion would probably be very lively. On the different issues, who are the psychologists with opinions that are in general agreement? With opposing opinions? After the panel discussion is over do you think that any of the five panel members would leave together to discuss their similarities over lunch? If so, who and why? Would any of the psychologists be likely to eat lunch alone? If so, who and why?

4. The text distinguishes between empirically based or academic psychologists and applied or human-service provider psychologists. The differences between the two groups led to the founding of a new organization (APS) in 1988 that broke off from APA. Do you think it is a good idea or a bad idea (or doesn't it matter) for there to be more than one major national organization of psychologists?

– PART VIII. APPLICATIONS –

1. The areas of specialization in psychology overlap with other disciplines. If you were interested in a specific area of psychology but did not want to go on to graduate school in a psychology department, where else could you continue your education?

Field of Psychology	Related Field(s)
clinical	Medical School (Psychiatrist)
industrial/organizational	
forensic	
biological	
engineering	
positive	
health	
educational	

2. Imagine that you are the head of a major corporation. You have assembled a group of psychologists (clinical, cognitive, developmental, educational, engineering, health, industrial/organizational, personality, and social) to participate in a roundtable discussion to address the following issues or problem areas:
   a. You desire to implement a no-smoking policy in the office and manufacturing areas of your corporation.
   b. Your corporation manufactures VCRs. You are aware that many people (the stereotype would be grandparents) have difficulty learning to operate VCRs. You are also aware that young children (who are not hesitant to operate VCRs) frequently experience problems in operating the VCR. You believe that if you can develop a "Grandma-proof" and/or "child-proof", VCR your company's profits will increase dramatically.
   c. Although most of your managers do not report any difficulties with the weekly staff meetings they have with the employees, 20 percent of the managers report that these meetings generally are not productive and that the employees seem to enter the meetings with a negative attitude.
   d. It will be necessary for a group of your employees to travel to an isolated work site for two weeks where they will work in a cramped, temporary facility (a house trailer) under the supervision of a recently hired female employee who is quickly moving up the corporate ladder.
   e. At the recent company picnic you observed that while many of your employees and their families wore seatbelts, a significant number did not. It appeared that there might be some age-related (for example, individuals over age 50 were less likely to wear seatbelts than those under age 30) and sex-

related (women were more likely to wear seatbelts than men) differences in seatbelt use. You think 100 percent seatbelt use is a worthy task for your company to encourage.

    f.   Due to safety concerns, you feel it is necessary to start a random drug-test program for some of your employees. Obviously you want your employees to accept the testing program; therefore, you do not want the results of a positive drug test to be excessively punitive in nature.

What would the individual psychologists identify as critical features to be addressed in each example? What action would they recommend taking to accomplish your goals? For each example, which psychologist(s) would you put in charge of overseeing the accomplishment of your goals?

– PART IX. SUMMARY TABLE SOLUTION –

APPROACHES TO PSYCHOLOGY

Approach	Individuals	Area of Study	Methods of Study and/or Specific Areas of Interest
Structuralism	Wundt Titchener	Identify the basic elements of conscious experience	Introspection
Functionalism	James	The practical nature of conscious experience	How mental processes help people adapt
Behaviorism	Watson	Relationships between environmental events (stimuli) and responses	Objective phenomena (behavior)
Gestalt psychology	Wertheimer Köhler Koffka	How basic sensory elements are combined to form our perception	Perception
Psychoanalysis	Freud	How the unconscious mind and sexual urges influence personality	Subjective study from treating emotionally disturbed individuals
Humanistic psychology	Maslow Rogers	Role of free choice in determining human behavior	Self-actualization and topics such as love, self-esteem, personal fulfillment

CHAPTER 2
THE METHODS OF PSYCHOLOGY

– PART I. LEARNING OBJECTIVES –

When you finish studying this chapter, you should be able to do the following:

THE SCIENTIFIC METHOD AND BEHAVIOR

1. List and discuss the three reasons for conducting research.

RESEARCH METHODS

2. Describe the case-study method, and discuss the advantages of this research method.

3. Discuss three limitations of the case-study method of research.

4. Describe the survey method, and discuss the advantages of both interviews and questionnaires.

5. Define sample and explain the difference between representative and random samples.

6. Discuss three limitations of the survey method of research.

7. Describe the observational method, and discuss the advantages of this research method.

8. Discuss two potential drawbacks of the observational method.

9. Describe the correlational method, and explain the terms positive correlation and negative correlation.

10. Discuss why the correlational method does not allow for conclusions concerning cause-and-effect relationships.

11. Describe the experimental method, and discuss the advantages of this research method.

12. Define independent variable and dependent variable, and explain how the two terms are related.

13. Describe and explain the functions of experimental and control groups in research.

14. Discuss two limitations of the experimental method.

15. Discuss the APA's ethical guidelines for conducting research.

STATISTICAL CONCEPTS FOR RESEARCH

16. Explain the function of descriptive statistics.

17. Discuss the function of measures of central tendency, and define the mean, median, and mode.

18. Discuss the function of measures of variability, and define range and standard deviation.

19. Explain the function of inferential statistics and the difference between descriptive and inferential statistics.

20. Define operational definition, and discuss why operational definitions are essential in scientific communication.

21. Discuss several questions that should be considered when critically evaluating a research study.

– PART II. OVERVIEW –

This chapter discusses three reasons for conducting scientific research: (1) to test a hypothesis or tentative explanation concerning a possible relationship between variables; (2) to solve a specific problem; and (3) to replicate or confirm the results of previous research. Replication studies allow researchers to have more confidence in research findings if results are consistent with the results of other studies.

Psychologists use a variety of research methods. The choice of which method to use in a particular study depends in large part on the type of information desired. Case studies are used to provide detailed information concerning a specific individual. Frequently, individuals who provide a "good example" of a particular problem behavior are used for case studies. Survey methods, which include questionnaires and interviews, allow the researcher to describe and summarize the behaviors, attitudes, and values of large groups of people. Because every member of the population of interest cannot be included in a survey, the researcher selects a smaller number of individuals (a sample) to survey. Observational methods allow researchers to directly observe and describe the behaviors of individuals. Often individuals are observed behaving in their normal environment. Correlational studies allow the researcher to determine if there is a consistent relationship between two variables. Additionally, the researcher can determine the strength of the relationship between the variables. If two variables show a positive correlation, an increase in one variable would be accompanied by an increase in the second variable. In a negative correlation, an increase in one variable would be accompanied by a decrease in the second variable. Correlational studies do not allow the researcher to infer a cause-and-effect relationship between the two variables.

Because the experimental method offers the most control over conditions that might influence the behavior being studied, it is often the method selected in psychological research. When conducting an experiment, the researcher changes or manipulates one factor (the independent variable) and then observes whether there is a corresponding change in a second factor (the dependent variable). The simplest experiments contain two groups of subjects. The experimental group receives or is exposed to the independent variable, while the control group is not. By comparing the two groups' behavior (as measured by the dependent variable), the researcher may infer a cause-and-effect relationship between the independent variable and the change in the dependent variable.

Psychologists conducting research abide by a number of ethical guidelines. Ethical guidelines cover topics such as informed consent, protection of the subject's confidentiality, and treatment of subjects. Ethical guidelines also describe when it is appropriate to use deception in experiments.

The results of research are analyzed using statistics. Descriptive statistics help to reduce the data to a form that is more easily understood. The three measures of central tendency (mean, median, mode) provide different methods to describe the typical score. Measures of variability (range, standard deviation) provide information about how closely together or spread out the scores are. Inferential statistics are typically more sophisticated mathematical techniques that allow the researcher to infer or conclude whether the results obtained in the experiment are a result of the experimental manipulation (independent variable) or a result that could have been obtained by chance alone.

– PART III. KEY TERMS/MATCHING EXERCISES –

Match the following concepts with the appropriate descriptions. Check your answers against the Answer Key.

RESEARCH METHODS (OVERVIEW)

Concepts	Descriptions
_____ 1. case study	a. Allows for conclusions about cause-and-effect relationships
_____ 2. correlational method	b. Provides information concerning attitudes and behaviors
_____ 3. experimental method	c. Eliminates the possibility of inaccurate reports supplied by the subjects either intentionally or unintentionally
_____ 4. observational method	d. Commonly focuses on a specific individual
_____ 5. survey method	e. Provides information concerning the relationship between two variables

Answer Key

1. d   2. e   3. a   4. c   5. b

RESEARCH METHODS

Concepts	Descriptions
_____ 1. independent variable	a. Used because it is usually impossible to study all members of the group or population of interest to the researcher
_____ 2. dependent variable	b. Allows the researcher to clarify confusing questions
_____ 3. coefficient of correlation	c. Subjects who do not receive the independent variable
_____ 4. experimental group	d. Varies between −1.00 and +1.00
_____ 5. control group	e. Subjects who receive the independent variable
_____ 6. ethical guidelines	f. Condition or factor that the researcher manipulates
_____ 7. naturalistic observation	g. Indicates that an increase in one variable is accompanied by a decrease in a second variable
_____ 8. observer bias	h. Indicates that an increase in one variable is accompanied by an increase in a second variable
_____ 9. sample	i. May not accurately reflect or "mimic" the characteristics of the entire population of interest to the researcher
_____ 10. representative sample	j. Associated with deception, debriefing, and the protection of confidentiality
_____ 11. random sample	k. Assesses behavior in a natural setting
_____ 12. observer effect	l. Involves an individual answering a written list of questions
_____ 13. questionnaire	m. Tendency of a researcher to misinterpret behavior
_____ 14. interview	n. The tendency of individuals to modify their behavior because of the researcher's presence
_____ 15. positive correlation	o. Measure of behavior in an experiment
_____ 16. negative correlation	p. Would include individuals who reflect or "mimic" the characteristics of the entire population of interest to the researcher

Answer Key

1. f   2. o   3. d   4. e   5. c   6. j   7. k   8. m   9. a   10. p   11. i   12. n
13. l   14. b   15. h   16. g

STATISTICAL CONCEPTS FOR RESEARCH: OVERVIEW

Concepts	Descriptions
_____ 1. descriptive statistics	a. Specifies the procedures or techniques used to measure or observe a variable
_____ 2. measures of central tendency	b. Mathematical methods used to draw conclusions about the meaning of data
_____ 3. inferential statistics	c. Reflect the distribution of scores from a group of scores
_____ 4. measures of variability	d. Reflect the middle, average, or typical score from a group of scores
_____ 5. operational definition	e. Mathematical methods used to describe and interpret data
_____ 6. statistics	f. Reduce a quantity of data to a form that is more understandable

Answer Key

1. f   2. d   3. b   4. c   5. a   6. e

STATISTICAL CONCEPTS FOR RESEARCH: DESCRIPTIVE STATISTICS CONCEPTS

Concepts	Descriptions
_____ 1. mean	a. Exists when the three measures of central tendency are close together
_____ 2. median	b. Takes into account all scores in a group of scores and indicates how closely individual scores are clustered around the average score
_____ 3. mode	c. Most frequently occurring score in a group of scores
_____ 4. normal distribution	d. Mathematical measure that allows the researcher to determine, with a high level of confidence, if the independent variable was responsible for the difference in scores between the experimental and control group
_____ 5. range	e. Arithmetic average of a group of scores
_____ 6. standard deviation	f. Difference between the highest and lowest scores in a group of scores
_____ 7. statistical significance	g. Score that falls in the middle of a distribution of a group of scores
_____ 8. skewed	h. Exists when the three measures of central tendency are very different

Answer Key

1. e   2. g   3. c   4. a   5. f   6. b   7. d   8. h

– PART IV. TRUE-FALSE STATEMENTS –

Fill in the blank before each statement with either a T (true) or an F (false). Check your answers against the Answer Key. Then go back to the items that are false and make the necessary change(s) to the statements to convert the items into true statements.

RESEARCH METHODS

_____ 1. A replication study would be conducted in order to solve a problem.

_____

_____

_____ 2. The research method that allows the researcher the greatest amount of control over relevant factors is the case study method.

_____

_____

_____ 3. In the experimental method, the control group does not receive the experimental manipulation (the IV).

_____

_____

_____ 4. The ethical guidelines for conducting research with humans state that it is never appropriate to deceive the subject.

_____

_____

_____ 5. A main consideration for researchers conducting survey research involves the manner by which subjects are selected from the population to participate in the survey.

_____

_____

_____ 6. Observer bias relates to the potential drawback of observational studies characterized by participants altering their behavior as a result of the researcher's presence.

_____

_____

_____ 7. One major limitation of case studies is that it is often difficult to generalize findings from the individual used to other individuals.

_____

_____

_____ 8. If you are interested in uncovering cause-and-effect relationships between two variables, you would use the correlational method.

_____

_____

STATISTICAL CONCEPTS FOR RESEARCH

_____ 9. Descriptive statistics involve measures of central tendency, measures of variability, and measures of significance.

_____

_____

_____ 10. The standard deviation is a more sensitive measure of variability than the range.

_____

_____

_____ 11. Inferential statistics allow researchers to draw inferences of conclusions concerning the effect of the experimental manipulation.

_____

_____

Answer Key
1. F   2. F   3. T   4. F   5. T   6. F   7. T   8. F   9. F   10. T   11. T

– PART V. MULTIPLE-CHOICE QUESTIONS –

Choose the best answer to each question. Circle your choice. Check your answers against the Answer Key. Questions marked with an asterisk(*) include annotated answers.

THE SCIENTIFIC METHOD AND BEHAVIOR

1. Which of the following is *not* a reason to conduct research?
   a. To confirm previous findings
   b. To uncover serendipity
   c. To solve a problem
   d. To test a hypothesis

2. Because results of a study may vary considerably depending on the exact experimental conditions and research method used, _____ studies serve an important purpose.
   a. experimental
   b. redundant
   c. replication
   d. control

3. The results of previous research and the psychologist's observations of behavior are two common sources of _____.
   a. operational definitions
   b. serendipity
   c. hypotheses
   d. theories

RESEARCH METHODS

4. What is one problem with research methods used in psychology—with the exception of the experimental method?
   a. they take too long.
   b. they require too much effort.
   c. they cost a lot of money.
   d. they do not allow for precise control over factors influencing the outcome.

5. If a researcher is interested in an in-depth study concerning the long-term consequences physical disabilities have on psychological adjustment, this researcher would most likely use the _____ method.
   a. case-study
   b. interview
   c. observational
   d. experimental

6. If a researcher is interested in the relationship between birth order (first, second, third born) and popularity, this researcher would most likely use the _____ method.
   a. experimental
   b. survey
   c. correlational
   d. observational

7. Normally, which scientific method of research is used to learn about people's opinions, attitudes, and values?
   a. Survey
   b. Experimental
   c. Naturalistic observation
   d. Case study

8. A number of techniques such as observation, questionnaires, interviews, and experimentation may be utilized by a researcher using the _____ method.
   a. clinical
   b. survey
   c. inferential
   d. case-study

9. A researcher is interested in the effects of vitamin W on physical endurance. The control group would _____.
   a. receive a different vitamin (for example, vitamin C)
   b. not receive vitamin W
   c. receive vitamin W
   d. not be measured on the dependent variable

*10. In the example described in the last question, the what does the researcher need to do?
   a. Identify the research method used.
   b. Correlate physical endurance with the dependent variable.
   c. Measure the behavior of both the experimental and control groups on the independent variable
   d. Supply an operational definition of physical endurance.

11. Which of the following pairs of terms do not belong together?
   a. Independent variable, control group
   b. Independent variable, experimental group
   c. Dependent variable, control group
   d. Dependent variable, experimental group

12. The condition or factor that an experimenter manipulates is the _____ variable.
   a. representative sample
   b. dependent
   c. independent
   d. critical

*13. In Milgram's obedience to authority study described in the text, what was the dependent variable?
   a. whether or not the subjects had sadistic personalities
   b. whether or not the subjects really believed they were administering shocks to the other individual
   c. whether or not the subjects experienced stress when administering the shocks
   d. how many painful shocks the subjects administered

14. The most controversial of the ethical guidelines for conducting research with humans concerns _____.
   a. debriefing

b. deception

c. the protection of confidentiality

d. informed consent

15. What does survey research include?
    a. public opinion polls and case studies
    b. interviews and case studies
    c. questionnaires and interviews
    d. questionnaires and observational studies

16. Which type of sample would *least* likely be demographically biased?
    a. Representative sample
    b. Natural sample
    c. Random sample
    d. All of the above would show demographic bias.

17. What is one advantage the survey method of questionnaires has over interviews?
    a. Questionnaire studies are more flexible.
    b. Questionnaire studies usually provide more detailed information about an individual subject.
    c. Questionnaire studies allow the researcher to clarify confusing questions.
    d. Questionnaire studies usually take less time to complete.

18. When researchers want to explore a question concerning a large population, what must they do?
    a. Use every individual in the population.
    b. Select a research sample of the population.
    c. Use only a correlational approach.
    d. Use the help of census takers.

19. Secretly observing people in a fast-food restaurant and noting each time someone bites into a hamburger is an example of the _____ method.
    a. experimental
    b. case-study
    c. naturalistic observation
    d. survey

20. If correctly used, what does the observational method frequently results in the researcher doing?
    a. calculating the coefficient of correlation
    b. developing hypotheses to be examined more completely through the use of other research methods
    c. interpreting why the observed behaviors occurred
    d. concluding that his or her original hypothesis was correct

21. Children assigned arbitrary labels of normal, emotionally disturbed, or intellectually impaired were rated by their teachers. These ratings were clearly influenced by the labels applied to each child. This problem is called _____.
    a. observer bias
    b. observer effect
    c. human nature
    d. case study

22. Which of the following is *not* a limitation of the case-study method?
    a. The research project may last for months or even years.
    b. The researcher lacks investigative control over all potentially relevant variables.

c. Not all relevant data or information are directly observed by the researcher.

d. The potential of bias by the researcher

*23. Which of the following pairs of variables would you expect to show the highest positive correlation?

a. The stock market / interest rates

b. How many semesters a student has been at college / a student's overall grade-point average (GPA)

c. The age of a child / his or her height

d. The amount of allowance a child receives each week / how old the family car is

24. What does high correlation (either positive or negative) indicate?

a. The scores on the two variables are nearly identical.

b. A change in one variable caused a change in the second variable.

c. A third factor or variable was always responsible for the observed relationship between the variables.

d. There was a high level of consistency in the relationship between the two variables.

STATISTICAL CONCEPTS FOR RESEARCH

*25. In addition to your test score, your professor will give you only one piece of information concerning your test performance relative to that of your classmates. Which of the following statistics would give you the most useful information?

a. mean

b. percentile

c. standard deviation

d. median

26. Which of the following terms does not belong with the others?

a. range

b. mode

c. measures of central tendency

d. mean

27. A distribution of scores in which most scores fall relatively close to the mean score would have a _____.

a. low standard deviation

b. high standard deviation

c. low range

d. There is not enough information given to allow for a conclusion

28. In the following distribution of scores—1, 4, 4, 5, 6, 8, 8, 8, 10—the median score is _____.

a. 6

b. 7

c. 8

d. 9

29. In the distribution of scores listed in the previous question the mode is _____.

a. 6

b. 7

c. 8

d. 9

30. The distance between extreme measures of scores is referred to as the _____.

a. average

b. range

c. mean

d. median

31. What does inferential statistics allow the researcher to do?
    a. determine measures of variability
    b. calculate correlations
    c. determine if differences between groups of subjects are due to experimental manipulation or to chance
    d. reduce a quantity of data to a form that is more easily understood

*32. What is the most important question to ask when evaluating a survey study?
    a. Was there a control group?
    b. Was there bias in the selection of subjects?
    c. Have there been other surveys that confirm the results of this study?
    d. Did a reputable professional conduct the survey?

Answer Key

1. b	2. c	3. c	4. d	5. a	6. c	7. a	8. d	9. b	*10. d	11. a	12. c
*13. d	14. b	15. c	16. a	17. d	18. b	19. c	20. b	21. a	22. a	*23. c	24. d
*25. b	26. a	27. a	28. a	29. c	30. b	31. c	*32. b				

Annotated Answers

10. The correct choice is **d**. The researcher needs to specify exactly how physical endurance will be measured.
    a. The research will obviously be an experimental study because there is a control group.
    b. Physical endurance is the dependent variable and would not be correlated with itself.
    c. The independent variable is the experimental manipulation; it is the dependent variable that is the measure of behavior.

13. The correct choice is **d**. Milgram recorded the number and severity of shocks administered.
    a. The personalities of the subjects were not examined in this study.
    b. Although some of the subjects may have had doubts concerning whether or not they were really administering painful shocks, Milgram did not address this issue in this experiment.
    c. Milgram did notice that many of the subjects experienced stress, but this stress was neither the central feature of the experiment nor the behavior Milgram measured.

23. The correct choice is **c**. Because children become taller not shorter as they get older, there has to be a positive correlation. To get a feel for how strong or high the correlation would be, think of a typical newborn, 2-year-old, 6-year-old, and 10-year-old, and compare their heights.
    a. As was described in the text, the correlation between the stock market and interest rates is a negative correlation.
    b. While there probably is a positive correlation between semesters of college and GPA, it does not seem likely to be as strong a relationship as that between age and height.
    d. Most likely there is a negative correlation between allowance and how old the family car is. The less money a family has the smaller the allowance and older the car.

25. The correct choice is **b**. Your percentile would indicate your relative class standing by supplying information concerning what percentage of classmates received scores lower than yours.
    a. The mean would only allow you to know if your score was above or below average.

c. The standard deviation tells you how closely together scores in the distribution are to the mean, but if you do not know what the mean is (as is the case in this example), the standard deviation would provide no useful information.

d. The median would only allow you to know if your test score was in the top half or bottom half of the class.

32. The correct choice is **b**. If there was significant bias in the sample it would invalidate the results of the study. For example, if a researcher was surveying sexually active teenage girls to determine if they used a form of birth control regularly, he or she would get very different results if the survey was only given to girls (1) at an abortion clinic, (2) at a planned parenthood office, or (3) to a representative sample.

a. Control groups are not used in survey studies.

c. Although the existence of other surveys with comparable results might give more credibility to this survey's findings, it is not the most important question to ask in this example.

d. Who conducted the survey is a relevant question to ask, but it is not the most important consideration. A very good survey study could be conducted by an individual without extensive scientific training.

– PART VI. SUMMARY TABLES –

To test your understanding of the material discussed in this chapter, complete the following tables. Check your answers with those supplied in Part IX.

RESEARCH METHODS

Method	How Conducted	Advantages	Limitations
Experimental			
Survey			
Observational			
Case study			
Correlational			

DESCRIPTIVE STATISTICS

| | (Place a Check Mark in the Correct Column) Measure of | | How Is It Calculated? |
	Central Tendency	Variability	
Mean			
Median			
Mode			
Range			
Standard deviation			See Research Appendix in the text

– PART VII. THOUGHT QUESTIONS/CRITICAL THINKING –

Prepare answers to the following discussion questions.

1. Different research methods vary greatly in the way information is gathered, the type of information collected, and how the information is compiled or interpreted. Frequently a researcher has some degree of choice in selecting the appropriate method. For example, if a researcher was interested in studying "helping behavior," what might he or she do?
   a. Design an experimental situation in which one person would need help and then measure under what conditions other people would be most likely to give assistance.
   b. Conduct a survey asking people about how frequently and under what circumstances they have helped others in the past.
   c. Use the observational method to observe helping behaviors.
   d. Conduct a case study with "good samaritans".
   e. Correlate helping behavior with certain personality traits.

   Identify some of the critical features of a research topic that would argue for and/or against the selection of each of the research methods used by psychologists.

2. If you had a choice of research methods to use in order to study a particular problem, which research method would you select? (Do not automatically select the experimental method because it offers the researcher greater control.) Select the method that you feel would supply the most useful or relevant information or the method that would be most satisfying or interesting for you to conduct. Explain the reasons for your selection.

3. Some adolescents and adults are more popular than others. Imagine that you are interested in asking if "popularity" is also an appropriate concept to use to describe young children. You have unlimited access to a class of third-graders. You have made the following list of questions to study:
   a. What, if any, factors are related to popularity in third-graders?

b.   Do children differ in popularity?

c.   What effect does popularity (and unpopularity) have on a child's schoolwork?

In what order (first, second, third) would you address these questions? Which research method would you use to study each question?

4.   Many people do not like complex mathematical calculations. These people might say, "Since descriptive statistics give a researcher a lot of information, we don't need inferential statistics." How would you explain to these people why scientific research needs inferential statistics?

– PART VIII. APPLICATIONS –

1.   You would like to lose 25 pounds. In the local newspaper you see advertisements for two weight-loss programs:

a.   The "Say Goodbye to Fat, Inc." ad explains that their medically approved diet supplement (which is eaten before each meal) plan results in rapid weight loss when used along with a vigorous exercise program. The ad quotes a woman who says she lost over 100 pounds in the past year as a result of the diet supplement and two hours of exercise each day.

b.   The "Quick Weight Loss, Limited" ad explains that by using hypnosis and posthypnotic suggestions your desire to eat will be cut in half and the pounds will fade away. The ad quotes a woman who says that since her first orientation session last week she has lost 11 pounds and can't wait to see the results after four or six months.

You decide to check out each of the programs before you decide to sign up with one. At the "Say Goodbye to Fat" meeting you overhear someone say that, in addition to the diet supplement and exercise, she has also stopped having her traditional bedtime snack. You also notice one of the assistants telling a group member that she had "better shape up" or she would lose her deposit. At the "Quick Weight Loss" meeting you overhear someone say that they have also started to eat a commercially available instant breakfast.

Evaluate each of the programs for strengths and weaknesses. Which program would you be more likely to join? It would be a hard decision to make solely on the information provided. In order to make the best-informed decision possible, prepare a list of questions that you would ask the director of each of the programs.

2.   The text notes that the experimental method is often the research method of choice for psychologists. Imagine that instead of being a student in general psychology, you are a lab assistant in charge of the laboratory sections of the general psychology class. Periodically throughout the semester you would like to use the students in the lab sections as subjects in experiments designed to illustrate the different topics discussed in class. You decide to introduce the experimental method by conducting an experiment on either the effect of amount of time studying a list of Spanish vocabulary words on how much information is learned or the effect of exercise on heart rate.

a.   What is your hypothesis?

b.   Write a paragraph explaining exactly what procedure you will use to conduct the experiment.

c.   Identify the independent variable.

d.   Identify the dependent variable and explain how it will be measured.

e.   Identify the experimental group(s).

f.   Identify the control group.

g.   Explain how you would assign subjects to the experimental and control groups.

h.   Provide any necessary operational definitions.

i. Evaluate your experiment with regard to the APA's ethical guidelines. Even though this experiment is only a classroom exercise and not a "real" experiment, you must adhere to the guidelines.

j. How would you compare the experimental and control groups on their performance on the dependent variable? Using only descriptive statistics, how would you present the results (that is, would you calculate means, percentiles, etc.)?

k. Predict what differences in behavior you would find if your hypothesis was confirmed by the results of the experiment.

– PART IX. SUMMARY TABLE SOLUTIONS –

RESEARCH METHODS

Method	How Conducted	Advantages	Limitations
Experimental	Manipulate IV and look for a change in the DV	Precise control Can infer cause and effect	Artificial situation Not all variables can be manipulated.
Survey	Use questionnaires and interviews to ask people about attitudes, behaviors, and values	Supplies a lot of information with relative ease	Sample may be biased. Accuracy of reports Can't examine individuals in detail
Observational	Observe ongoing behavior frequently in a natural setting	Behavior is not "artificial" Direct observation by researcher	Observer bias Observer effect
Case study	In-depth study of one individual (or group of individuals)	More insight into individual is possible.	Lack of experimental control Bias by researcher May be difficult to generalize to other individuals
Correlational	Measure relationship between two variables	Can study variables that would be impossible to manipulate in an experiment	Cannot infer a cause-and-effect relationship

DESCRIPTIVE STATISTICS

| | (Place a Check Mark in the Correct Column) Measure of | | |
	Central Tendency	Variability	How Is It Calculated?
Mean	X		Add up all scores and divide by the number of scores.
Median	X		Arrange all scores in order from lowest to highest and select the score that falls in the middle of the distribution.
Mode	X		Select the most frequently occurring score.
Range		X	Subtract the lowest score from the highest score.
Standard deviation		X	See Research Appendix in the text

CHAPTER 3
THE BIOLOGY OF BEHAVIOR

– PART I. LEARNING OBJECTIVES –

When you finish studying this chapter, you should be able to do the following:

OVERVIEW OF THE NERVOUS SYSTEM: ORGANIZATION AND FUNCTION

1. Briefly describe the major components and functions of the central nervous system (CNS) and peripheral nervous system (PNS).

NEURONS: BASIC UNITS OF THE NERVOUS SYSTEM

2. Define neuron and describe the three types of neurons.

3. Identify four main parts of a neuron, and describe the functions of each part.

4. Define resting potential and graded potential. Describe how graded potentials result in the neuron reaching a threshold value.

5. Once a neuron reaches its excitatory threshold at the axon hillock, what happens to completely depolarize the neuron?

6. Describe the action potential, and discuss the all-or-none law.

7. Discuss the transmission of a neural impulse from one neuron to another. Include in your discussion the following terms: synapse, neurotransmitter, neural excitation, neural inhibition, EPSPs, and IPSPs.

8. List a number of neurotransmitters, and describe the part of the nervous system where each is found and the types(s) of behavior each influences.

THE PERIPHERAL NERVOUS SYSTEM

9. Discuss the components of and functions of the somatic and autonomic nervous systems.

10. Compare and contrast the functioning of the sympathetic and parasympathetic nervous systems.

THE CENTRAL NERVOUS SYSTEM

11. Describe the overall appearance of the human brain.

12. Describe the structure and functions of the spinal cord and spinal nerves.

13. Describe the functions of and location in the brain of the medulla, pons, cerebellum, and reticular formation.

14. Identify the general functions of the limbic system, and describe the specific functions of the amygdala, hippocampus, and septal area.

15. Describe the location and functions of the hypothalamus.

16. Describe the location and functions of the thalamus.

17. Describe the functions and components of the basal ganglia.

18. Describe the physical structure and primary functions of the cerebral cortex, and identify the sensory, motor, and association cortex.

19. Name and identify the location of the four lobes of the cortex, and indicate the specialized functions of each lobe.

20. Discuss differences between the brains of males and females.

21. Define lateralization of function, and describe the amount of lateralization of function that exists in the cortex.

22. Describe the split-brain procedure, and discuss the effects this procedure has on the overall functioning of the brain.

23. Name and describe four invasive techniques used to study the brain.

24. Name and describe four noninvasive techniques used to study the brain.

THE ENDOCRINE SYSTEM

25. Define endocrine gland and hormone, and describe the functioning of the endocrine system.

26. Identify the functions of the pituitary gland, thyroid gland, adrenal glands, and the gonads.

DRUGS AND BEHAVIOR

27. Define psychoactive drugs.

28. Describe the physiological and psychoactive effects of depressants (sedatives, opiates, and alcohol), giving examples of each type of drug.

29. Describe the physiological and psychoactive effects of stimulants (caffeine, nicotine, amphetamines, and cocaine).

30. Describe the physiological and psychoactive effects of hallucinogens (LSD).

– PART II. OVERVIEW –

The basic unit of the nervous system is the neuron. The main parts of the neuron are the dendrites (which receive impulses from other neurons); the cell body (which handles the cell's metabolic functions); the axon (which transmits the impulse away from the cell body toward other neurons); and at the end of the axon, the terminal buttons (which release neurotransmitter into the synapse). The process by which a neuron "decides" to transmit a neural impulse is electrical in nature. A neuron that is not receiving any neural impulses is at its resting potential. As a neuron receives input (its excitatory threshold), electrical changes or graded potentials occur. When the neuron receives a critical amount of excitatory input, the electrical state of the neuron again changes and the neuron fires its action potential or impulse down the axon to the terminal buttons. The process that allows the impulse to cross the synapse from one neuron to stimulate the next neuron is chemical in nature and controlled by the release of neurotransmitters from the terminal buttons.

The nervous system has two main divisions. The peripheral nervous system (PNS) consists of the somatic nervous system, which controls the major skeletal muscles and transmits information to and from the CNS. The autonomic nervous system, which controls the internal organs and glands, is further divided into two parts that have opposing effects. The sympathetic nervous system (which assumes control in emergency situations) tends to influence a number of organs to operate at their upper limits (for example, heart rate is increased) to help deal with an emergency situation. The parasympathetic nervous system tends to influence organs to operate at reduced or "normal" levels of functioning.

The central nervous system (CNS) consists of the brain and spinal cord. The location and functions of a number of brain structures (medulla, pons, cerebellum, reticular formation, limbic system, hypothalamus, thalamus, and basal ganglia) are described. The cerebral cortex is responsible for higher mental processes and is described in detail. The frontal lobe contains the motor cortex and Broca's area. The parietal lobe contains the somatosensory cortex. The occipital lobe contains the visual cortex. The temporal lobe contains the auditory cortex and Wernicke's area.

The endocrine system consists of a number of glands that influence internal physical responses by secreting hormones into the bloodstream. These hormones affect specific organs or functions of the body. The pituitary gland is an important endocrine gland that exerts an influence on many other endocrine glands. The functioning of the pituitary gland is controlled by the hypothalamus in the CNS. The text also describes the functions of the thyroid gland, adrenal gland, and gonads.

Psychoactive drugs alter consciousness by interfering with the normal functioning of neurotransmitter in the CNS. These drugs may result tolerance, dependance, and/or addiction depending on their mechanisms of action. There are three major groups of psychoactive drugs. Depressants decrease the activity of the CNS. Depressants include sedatives, opiates, and alcohol. Stimulants increase the transmission of nervous impulses in the CNS. Stimulants include caffeine, nicotine, amphetamines, and cocaine. Hallucinogens produce changes in sensory perceptions, thinking processes, and emotions. Hallucinogens include LSD, ecstacy, and very high doses of marijuana.

– PART III. KEY TERMS/MATCHING EXERCISES –

Match the following concepts with the appropriate descriptions. Check your answers against the Answer Key.

OVERVIEW OF THE NERVOUS SYSTEM

Concepts	Descriptions
_____ 1. peripheral nervous system	a. Present in the spinal cord and brain
_____ 2. sympathetic nervous system	b. Plays a central role in coordinating and integrating all bodily functions
_____ 3. central nervous system	c. Consists of the somatic and autonomic nervous systems
_____ 4. parasympathetic nervous system	d. Activated in emergency situations and causes heart rate and breathing to increase
_____ 5. interneuron	e. Counteracts the responses described in **d**
_____ 6. motor (efferent) neuron	f. Relays or sends messages from the body to the spinal cord and brain
_____ 7. sensory (afferent) neuron	g. Relays or sends messages from the brain and spinal cord to the muscles and glands

Answer Key
   1. c   2. d   3. b   4. e   5. a   6. g   7. f

NEURONS: BASIC UNITS OF THE NERVOUS SYSTEM

Concepts	Descriptions
_____ 1. action potential	a. Controls the metabolic functions of the neuron
_____ 2. axon	b. Receives information from other neurons
_____ 3. cell body	c. Sends the action potential toward other neurons
_____ 4. dendrites	d. Composed of insulating glia cells
_____ 5. EPSPs	e. Exposed or uninsulated areas of the axon
_____ 6. graded potentials	f. Release neurotransmitter
_____ 7. IPSPs	g. Electrical state that occurs in an all-or-none manner
_____ 8. myelin sheath	h. Chemicals that move between two neurons
_____ 9. neurotransmitter	i. Vary in relation to the intensity of stimulation and distance from the point of stimulation
_____ 10. node of Ranvier	j. Polarized electrical state of a neuron when it is not receiving information or impulses from other neurons
_____ 11. resting potential	k. Relates to where neurotransmission is primarily a chemical process
_____ 12. terminal buttons	l. Occurs when positive charged ions enter the postsynaptic membrane
_____ 13. synapse	m. Occurs when negative charged ions enter or positive charged ions exit the postsynaptic membrane

Answer Key

1. g   2. c   3. a   4. b   5. l   6. i   7. m   8. d   9. h   10. e   11. j   12. f   13. k

THE CENTRAL NERVOUS SYSTEM: BRAIN STRUCTURES

Concepts	Descriptions
_____ 1. cerebellum	a. Involved in basic motivation, emotional expression, and control of the endocrine system
_____ 2. cerebrum	b. Contains the amygdala, hippocampus, and septal areas; involved in emotional expression
_____ 3. corpus callosum	c. Controls vital functions such as breathing, heart rate, and blood pressure
_____ 4. hypothalamus	d. Nerve fibers that connect the two cerebral hemispheres
_____ 5. limbic system	e. Controls species-specific behaviors and influences facial expressions
_____ 6. basal ganglia	f. Composed of the "gray matter" and "white matter"
_____ 7. pons	g. Directs sensory information to the appropriate areas of the cortex
_____ 8. reticular formation	h. Plays a critical role in arousal or alertness
_____ 9. thalamus	i. Provides fine-tuning or control of body movements
_____ 10. medulla	j. Contains the caudate nucleus, putamen, and substantia nigra; involved in control and initiation of motor movement

Answer Key

1. i   2. f   3. d   4. a   5. b   6. j   7. e   8. h   9. g   10. c

THE CENTRAL NERVOUS SYSTEM: CEREBRAL CORTEX

Concepts	Descriptions
_____ 1. temporal lobe	a. Involved in higher mental functions and consists of 75 percent of the cortex
_____ 2. parietal lobe	b. Contains the visual cortex
_____ 3. association cortex	c. Degree to which a particular function is controlled by only one side of the cortex
_____ 4. frontal lobe	d. Contains the motor cortex, Broca's area, and is involved in emotional expression
_____ 5. lateralization of function	e. Contains the auditory cortex and Wernicke's area
_____ 6. occipital lobe	f. Contains the somatosensory cortex

Answer Key
  1. e   2. f   3. a   4. d   5. c   6. b

THE ENDOCRINE SYSTEM

Concepts	Descriptions
_____ 1. adrenal gland	a. Chemicals secreted into the bloodstream that influence target organs
_____ 2. endocrine system	b. Secretes hormones that act in association with the sympathetic nervous system and also increases metabolism
_____ 3. gonads	c. Releases a number of hormones that influence other glands
_____ 4. hormones	d. Another way, along with the nervous system, that the body governs behavior
_____ 5. pitituary gland	e. Regulates metabolism
_____ 6. thyroid gland	f. Secrete estrogens and/or androgens

Answer Key
  1. b   2. d   3. f   4. a   5. c   6. e

DRUGS AND BEHAVIOR

Concepts	Descriptions
_____ 1. psychoactive drugs	a. Include sedatives, opiates, and alcohol
_____ 2. depressants	b. Result in changes in sensory perceptions, emotions, and thinking processes
_____ 3. stimulants	c. Increase the transmission of nerve impulses in the CNS
_____ 4. hallucinogens	d. Alter perceptions and behavior

Answer Key
  1. d   2. a   3. c   4. b

– PART IV. TRUE-FALSE STATEMENTS –

Fill in the blank before each statement with either a T (true) or an F (false). Check your answers against the Answer Key. Then go back to the items that are false and make the necessary change(s) to the statements to convert the items into true statements.

NEURONS: BASIC UNITS OF THE NERVOUS SYSTEM

_____ 1. The terminal buttons of one neuron secrete neurotransmitter into the synapse where it stimulates the axon of a second neuron.

_____

_____

_____ 2. Axons insulated with myelin sheaths conduct the action potential at a faster rate than uninsulated axons.

_____

_____

_____ 3. Neurotransmitters may have either an excitatory or inhibitory effect on the postsynaptic membrane.

_____

_____

THE PERIPHERAL NERVOUS SYSTEM

_____ 4. The somatic nervous system controls the smooth muscles, internal organs, and glands of the body.

_____

_____

_____ 5. Following the body's response to an emergency situation, the parasympathetic nervous system resumes control of bodily functions such as heart rate and digestion.

_____

_____

THE CENTRAL NERVOUS SYSTEM

_____ 6. Considerable damage to the frontal lobe would likely affect the emotional life of an individual.

_____

_____

_____ 7. The cerebellum is the brain structure responsible for higher mental processes such as perceiving, thinking, and remembering.

_____

_____

_____ 8. Approximately 75 percent of the human cortex consists of the motor and sensory cortex.

_____

_____

THE ENDOCRINE SYSTEM

_____ 9. The pituitary gland is considered the "master gland" because it secretes hormones that stimulate the hypothalamus to release additional hormones.

_____

_____

_____ 10. The activation of the endocrine system has a more immediate effect on behavior than does the activation of the nervous system.

_____

_____

_____ 11. Marijuana may have a sedative effect, stimulant effect, or hallucinogenic effect.

_____

_____

Answer Key
1. F   2. T   3. T   4. T   5. F   6. F   7. F   8. T   9. F   10. F   11. T

– PART V. MULTIPLE-CHOICE QUESTIONS –

Choose the best answer to each question. Circle your choice. Check your answers against the Answer Key. Questions marked with an asterisk(*) include annotated answers.

OVERVIEW OF THE NERVOUS SYSTEM

1. What are the two major divisions of the nervous system?
    a.   brain and spinal cord.
    b.   central nervous system and endocrine system.
    c.   central nervous system and peripheral nervous system.
    d.   central nervous system and autonomic nervous system.

NEURONS: BASIC UNITS OF THE NERVOUS SYSTEM

2. Afferent nerves send messages _____ the spinal cord and brain.
    a.   away from
    b.   toward
    c.   within
    d.   slowly away from

3. The part of the neuron that receives impulses from other neurons is the
    a.   axon
    b.   dendrites
    c.   synapse
    d.   terminal buttons

*4. Which is the last part of the neuron to be involved in the transmission of a neural impulse toward the next neuron?
   a. axon hillock
   b. cell body
   c. dendrites
   d. terminal buttons

5. The process by which neural impulses are transmitted within the central nervous system is _____.
   a. not chemical in nature
   b. seen only in the brain
   c. electrochemical in nature
   d. the same as electricity through a wire

*6. As a neuron is receiving an excitatory impulse from another neuron the cell membrane becomes _____.
   a. depolarized
   b. polarized
   c. impermeable to ions
   d. a graded potential

7. Which of the following follows the all-or-none law?
   a. graded potentials
   b. electrical potentials
   c. resting potentials
   d. action potentials

8. Two factors that relate to the perceived intensity of a stimuli are how many neurons are firing action potentials and _____.
   a. if the axons have myelin sheaths
   b. the voltage associated with each action potential
   c. the rate at which these neurons are firing
   d. whether the supply of neurotransmitter is exhausted

9. Which of the following would occur if IPSPs did not exist
   a. It would be "easier" for a neuron to fire its action potential.
   b. It would be "harder" for a neuron to fire its action potential.
   c. There would be no effect on the ease with which a neuron fires its action potential.
   d. It would be impossible for neural impulses to travel across the synapse.

10. Which of the following has an effect on the body similar to morphine?
   a. serotonin
   b. acetylcholine
   c. dopamine
   d. endorphins

THE PERIPHERAL NERVOUS SYSTEM

11. The two major divisions of the peripheral nervous system are the _____ nervous systems.
   a. afferent and efferent
   b. sympathetic and parasympathetic
   c. somatic and parasympathetic
   d. somatic and autonomic

12. Which of the following is not controlled by the autonomic nervous system?
    a. the major skeletal muscles
    b. digestion
    c. pupil size
    d. heart rate

13. If you hit your thumb with a hammer, which nervous system sends the pain message to your brain?
    a. somatic nervous system
    b. central nervous system
    c. autonomic nervous system
    d. corpus callosum

14. Our normal state (somewhere between extreme excitement and complete relaxation) is maintained by _____.
    a. the sympathetic nervous system
    b. the parasympathetic nervous system
    c. a balance between the sympathetic and parasympathetic nervous systems
    d. the reticular activating system

*15. One major difference between the sympathetic and parasympathetic nervous system is that the sympathetic nervous system _____.
    a. increases the level of functioning in all the affected bodily systems
    b. decreases the level of functioning in all the affected bodily systems
    c. stimulates the different parts of the body independently of one another
    d. simultaneously stimulates the different parts of the body

THE CENTRAL NERVOUS SYSTEM

16. Basic reflexive behaviors, such as the quick withdrawal of a hand from a hot stove, are controlled by the _____.
    a. lower brain centers
    b. spinal cord
    c. limbic system
    d. cortex

17. Sensory input from the eyes is relayed to the visual cortex by the _____.
    a. thalamus
    b. hypothalamus
    c. pons
    d. reticular activating system

18. If an animal's amygdala is electrically stimulated, that animal would _____.
    a. go into a blind rage
    b. experience a sensation that could be labeled "pleasure"
    c. become aroused or alert
    d. enter a comalike sleep

*19. If a person had an auto accident and suffered brain damage, and afterward had awkward, jerky, and uncoordinated movements, the damaged part of that person's brain would most likely be the _____.
    a. motor cortex
    b. spinal cord
    c. cerebellum
    d. myelin sheaths

20. In what does the reticular formation play a role?
    a. life-supporting functions such as breathing and heartbeat
    b. the fine-tuning of motor messages
    c. coordinating and regulating motor movements
    d. controlling levels of arousal and alertness

21. Over which of the following does the hypothalamus *not* exert control?
    a. the endocrine system
    b. emotional expression
    c. arousal and alertness
    d. basic motivations (eating, drinking, sexual behavior)

22. The association cortex is another name for what area?
    a. area of the cortex involved with higher mental processes and integrating sensory and motor messages
    b. area of the cerebrum that is underneath and directly associated with the cerebral cortex
    c. sensory and motor cortex
    d. frontal lobe

23. If you were to electrically stimulate a person's occipital lobe, what would that person most likely do?
    a. have difficulty recalling their phone number
    b. report a visual experience
    c. move a part of their body
    d. report an auditory experience

24. Individuals with damage to _____ have difficulty articulating speech, while individuals with damage to _____ have difficulty comprehending speech.
    a. cortex / reticular formation
    b. Broca's area / Wernicke's area
    c. Wernicke's area / Broca's area
    d. central fissure / corpus callosum

25. If a split-brain operated patient sees "airxplane" briefly while focusing on the "x," the patient would say that he or she saw the word _____.
    a. plane
    b. airplane
    c. air
    d. That patient would report that he or she did not see a word.

26. Research on lateralization of function suggests that the right hemisphere is better than the left in _____.
    a. tasks involving the use of logic
    b. spatial orientations
    c. math
    d. verbal ability

THE ENDOCRINE SYSTEM

27. The brain structure that most directly influences the endocrine system is the _____.
    a. thalamus
    b. hypothalamus
    c. temporal lobe
    d. limbic system

28. The pituitary hormones _____.
    a. have a variety of target organs
    b. have the thyroid as their only target organ
    c. directly influence the hypothalamus to begin secreting hormones
    d. become neuropeptides

29. The part of the endocrine system that is most closely associated with activation of the sympathetic nervous system is the _____.
    a. gonads
    b. pituitary gland
    c. adrenal medulla
    d. adrenal cortex

30. The thyroid gland secretes thyroxine, which _____.
    a. is also called growth hormone
    b. is associated with fear and rage
    c. regulates metabolism
    d. is responsible for the development of secondary sex characteristics during puberty

DRUGS AND BEHAVIOR

31. The three major types of psychoactive drugs are _____, _____, and _____.
    a. sedatives, opiates, and hallucinogens
    b. depressants, amphetamines, and cocaine
    c. depressants, stimulants, and hallucinogens
    d. alcohol, opiates, and hallucinogens

32. Taking a drug to maintain adequate levels in order to avoid withdrawal symptoms is referred to as
    a. physiological dependence
    b. psychological dependence
    c. tolerance
    d. prolonged dependence

33. In American society, the most widely used stimulant is
    a. diet pills
    b. caffeine
    c. cocaine
    d. nicotine

*34. The effects of cocaine are similar to the effects of
    a. heroin
    b. ecstacy
    c. amphetamines
    d. barbiturates

35. A person admitted to a hospital following a drug is experiencing hyperthermia, rapid heart rate, high blood pressure, muscle rigidity, and convulsions. Most likely he took which one of the following drugs?
    a. seconal
    b. heroin
    c. ecstasy
    d. cocaine

Annotated Answers

4. The correct choice is **d**. The terminal buttons on the transmitting end of the axon release neurotransmitter into the synapse.
   a. The axon hillock is a part of the cell body near the base or beginning of the axon.
   b. The cell body is in the middle of the neuron and therefore is not the last part of the neuron involved in neurotransmission.
   c. The dendrites are the first part of the neuron involved in the transmission of the neural impulse.

6. The correct choice is **a**. Depolarized relates to the cell membrane becoming less negative, which is what occurs when a neuron receives excitatory impulses.
   b. The membrane is said to be polarized when it is at the resting potential.
   c. If the cell membrane were to become impermeable to ions, the ions could not pass through the cell membrane and the electrical changes necessary for the neuron to fire its action potential could not occur.
   d. While the situation described in this question would result in a graded potential, the cell membrane does not become a graded potential.

15. The correct answer is **d**. Because the primary action of the SNS is to help us respond to emergency situations, it is important that the body react quickly; therefore, the SNS stimulates the different body parts simultaneously.
   a. The SNS does not increase the functioning of all the affected body parts; digestion is decreased.
   b. The PNS does not decrease the functioning of all the affected body parts; digestion is increased.
   c. It is the PNS that stimulates the different body parts independently.

19. The correct choice is **c**. The cerebellum functions to fine-tune muscle movements that are broadly under the control of higher brain centers.
   a. Damage to the motor cortex would leave the person paralyzed in the affected body parts and not just with a lack of smoothness of movement.
   b. First, the spinal cord is not part of the brain. Second, damage to the spinal cord would leave the person paralyzed in the affected body parts.
   d. Although the absence of myelin sheaths is associated with loss of motor control (as in MS), myelin is not a brain structure and would not be subject to damage in an auto accident.

34. The correct choice is **c**. Both cocaine and amphetamines are classified as stimulants.
   a. Heroin is classified as a depressant.
   b. Ecstacy is classified as a hallucinogen.
   d. Barbiturates are classified as depressants.

– PART VI. SUMMARY TABLES –

To test your understanding of the material discussed in this chapter, complete the following tables. Check your answers with those supplied in Part IX.

OVERVIEW OF THE NERVOUS SYSTEM

Fill in the following diagram to visualize the separate divisions of the nervous system. Two of the lowest-level components of the nervous system are described. (Hint: Work backward to complete the diagram.)

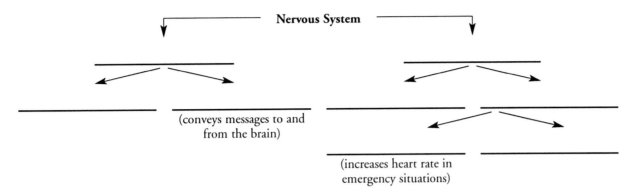

PARTS OF A NEURON

	Description	Location	Function
Dendrites			
Cell body			
Axon			
Terminal buttons			

BRAIN STRUCTURES

Structure	Location	Primary Function
Medulla		
Pons		
Cerebellum		
Reticular formation		
Limbic system		
Hypothalamus		
Thalamus		
Cerebral cortex		

TYPES OF PSYCHOACTIVE DRUGS

Class	Effect	Types	Neurotransmitters Affected by at Least Some Drugs of This Class
Depressants			
Stimulants			
Hallucinogens			

– PART VII. THOUGHT QUESTIONS/CRITICAL THINKING –

Prepare answers to the following discussion questions.

1. A computer model is frequently used to describe the functioning of the nervous system. Both a computer and the nervous system receive input, perform internal activities or decision-making functions, and provide output. Using a computer analogy (input, internal activities, output) describe what controls the decision-making process an individual neuron goes through when "deciding" whether to fire its action potential (or output).

2. Following brain damage, an individual may show a number of behavioral deficits and symptoms. For each of the following symptoms, identify which brain structure(s) or area(s) of the brain is (are) most likely to have been damaged. Explain or justify your choices.
   a. Following a stroke a person has difficulty performing tasks involving logical thought processes and is partially paralyzed on the right side of the body.
   b. A person is unable to effectively control or regulate his or her food intake and gains fifty pounds in a short period of time.
   c. A tiger is no longer capable of effectively stalking and killing its prey.
   d. A person undergoes a significant change in personality and has difficulty coping with simple problems associated with daily life.
   e. A person is in a comalike sleep for a period of weeks or months.
   f. A person who appears to be fairly normal goes on a violent killing spree.

3. Your body has two primary systems for sending messages: the nervous system and the endocrine system. If you wanted to get a message from one place to another quickly (or by "express mail" method), which system would you use? If you wanted to be constantly reminded of a message (or by "a string on your finger" method), which system would you use? Explain your answers.

4. Many people take psychoactive drugs because they desire a specific consciousness-altering effect: to relax, to reduce stress or anxiety, to reduce boredom, to heighten sensory experiences, to obtain pain relief, to alter their thinking, to increase their physical arousal or energy level, or to gain personal insight. Many of these effects may also be obtained without the use of psychoactive drugs. For each of the following activities indicate which drug(s) might also result in similar effects in a less natural manner. Explain your choices.
   a. Jogging or some other physical exercise
   b. Taking a long, warm bath
   c. Sky diving
   d. Reading a good book

e. Playing an intellectually stimulating computer game

f. Taking a "nature walk"

– PART VIII. APPLICATIONS –

1. At the beginning of a discussion on the nervous system, its functioning is often described by using an analogy to the electrical wiring of a house. However, because a message progresses through the nervous system via an electrochemical process and the wiring of a house is strictly electrical, the analogy is incomplete. The analogy is also incomplete for at least one other reason. Develop an analogy to the functioning of the nervous system that would describe the functioning of a house's electrical system as if it was controlled by a similar electrochemical process.

2. Neurologists use a variety of specialized techniques (EEG, CAT, PET, MRI) to diagnose the location and extent of possible brain damage. However, the neurologist can frequently isolate the areas in which they believe the brain damage is located by the behavioral deficits or symptoms shown by the patient. Try to develop simple behavioral tests that could be used to determine the location of damage to a variety of brain structures. (For example, if the individual has a problem memorizing and recalling a list of phone numbers, you might suspect damage to the hippocampus.)

3. We know that many parts of the cerebral cortex have specific functions (motor, somatosensory, visual, and auditory cortex); we also have data indicating lateralization of function regarding abilities such as language, perceiving spatial orientation, and math. It is appropriate to conclude that many areas of the brain are involved in specific functions. This idea—that different areas of the brain have specific "jobs"—is not a new idea. In the early 1800s a "science" of phrenology was developed by Joseph Gall with the intent of identifying the location of brain areas associated with specific personality traits or abilities. Gall believed that the brain was very similar to a muscle and if a specific area of the brain (associated with a specific function) received a lot of "exercise," that area would enlarge and become a detectable bump or bulge on the skull. Gall went around feeling the skulls of individuals known to show specific traits (pickpockets, people with high sex drives or sadistic personalities, etc.) in an effort to find bumps that could be associated with the specific "talents" of the individuals. Gall developed a complex map of the skull showing the areas associated with the different abilities. (For example, the tendency to steal was just above the ears, and sexuality was at the back of the skull.) For a time, phrenology was a very popular "science," but ultimately it fell into disfavor because it was not accurate. Based on the information from this chapter and the "Methods of Psychology" chapter, discuss why phrenology was a "bad science" and doomed to failure.

– PART IX. SUMMARY TABLES AND SOLUTIONS –

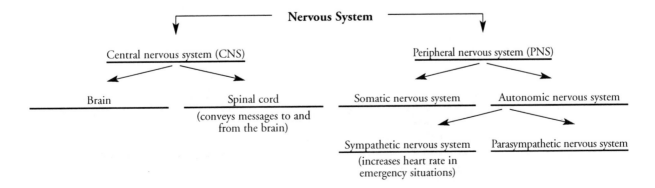

PARTS OF A NEURON

	Description	Location	Function
Dendrites	Resembles the branches of a tree	At one end of the neuron	Receives messages from other neurons
Cell body	Larger part of the neuron; contains nucleus	In the middle of the neuron	Handles metabolic functions of the neuron
Axon	Slender extended fiber length varies greatly	At end of neuron opposite dendrites	Transmits the action potential toward other neurons
Terminal buttons	Bulblike structures	At the transmitting end of the axon	Releases neurotransmitters into the synapse

BRAIN STRUCTURES

Structure	Location	Primary Function
Medulla	Directly above the spinal cord	Critical functions such as breathing, heart rate, blood pressure
Pons	Lower brain, directly above medulla	Fine tunes motor messages prior to cerebellum involvement in species-typical behaviors
Cerebellum	Under back part of cerebral hemispheres	Coordinates and regulates motor movements
Reticular formation	Fibers extend from lower brain (near spinal cord) to the thalamus	Controls arousal and alertness
Limbic system	Central core of brain along innermost edges of cerebral hemispheres	Emotional expression, motivation, learning, memory
Hypothalamus	Beneath cerebrum and thalamus	Homeostasis, motivations, emotions, controls endocrine system
Thalamus	Beneath cerebrum	Relays sensory messages to appropriate areas of cortex
Cerebral cortex	Outer layer of cerebrum	Responsible for higher mental processes

TYPES OF PSYCHOACTIVE DRUGS

Class	Effect	Types	Neurotransmitters Affected by at Least Some Drugs of This Class
Depressants	Decreases action in the CNS	Alcohol, opiates, sedatives	GABA
Stimulants	Increases activity in the CNS	Amphetamines, caffeine, cocaine, nicotine	Dopamine and norepinephrine
Hallucinogens	Changes in sensory perception, thinking processes, and emotions	LSD, ecstasy, and possibly marijuana	Serotonin

CHAPTER 4
SENSATION AND PERCEPTION

– PART I. LEARNING OBJECTIVES –

When you finish studying this chapter, you should be able to do the following:

PRINCIPLES OF SENSATION AND PERCEPTION

1. Define sensation and perception, and explain the relationship between the processes.

2. Describe the process of transduction.

3. Define absolute threshold and difference threshold, and discuss how Weber's law relates to the difference threshold.

4. Define attention and adaptation, and discuss how they prevent us from perceiving the occurrence of many stimuli or events.

5. Describe signal detection theory, and discuss how background noise and response criterion affect the detection of a stimulus.

VISION

6. Discuss how brightness, hue, and saturation are related to the physical properties of a light stimulus.

7. Describe the structure of and explain the functions of each part of the human eye.

8. Describe how visual information is transmitted to and interpreted by the visual cortex.

9. Differentiate between subtractive and additive color mixing.

10. Discuss two theories of color vision: the trichromatic theory and the opponent-process theory.

AUDITION

11. Describe how loudness, pitch, and timbre are related to the physical properties of a sound stimulus.

12. Describe the structure of and explain the functions of each part of the human ear.

13. Discuss two theories of pitch discrimination: the place theory and the frequency theory.

14. Explain the process by which we locate the source of a sound.

15. Describe the two major types of hearing loss: sensorineural and conduction.

GUSTATION AND OLFACTION

16. Describe how the sensation of gustation occurs, and identify the four different taste sensations.

17. Describe how the sensation of olfaction occurs, and summarize one widely held theory of olfaction.

THE SKIN SENSES

18. Describe the receptors for and briefly discuss the three different components of the sense of touch (pressure, temperature, and pain).

19. Explain why it is difficult to gain a scientific understanding of pain, and describe the gate control theory of pain and the role of neurotransmitters in the sensation of pain.

KINESTHESIS AND EQUILIBRIUM

20. Discuss the two body senses (kinesthesis and equilibrium), and describe the structures that are involved in each.

SYNESTHESIA

21. Explain the unusual phenomenon of synesthesia.

PERCEIVING THE WORLD

22. Explain what is meant by perceptual organization, and describe three principles that influence how people organize sensations.

23. Define selective attention and describe several characteristics of stimuli that influence which of a number of stimuli are attended to.

24. Describe several binocular and monocular cues that aid our perception of distance.

25. Describe the visual cliff, and summarize the results of experiments that show that depth perception is innate in many species.

26. Define perceptual constancy, and describe four types of perceptual constancies.

27. Describe several illusions, and discuss the mechanisms believed to be responsible for each.

28. Define perceptual set, and explain how a perceptual set influences our perception of a stimulus.

– PART II. OVERVIEW –

The processes of sensation and perception relate to how individuals become aware of stimulus events in the environment and how they interpret those events. The term sensation refers to the response of a sensory receptor cell to a stimulus. Receptor cells transduce physical energy from the environment into electrochemical energy. Perception involves how the nervous system interprets or gives meaning to a sensation. Psychophysics is concerned with the relationship between the physical attributes of the stimulus and our perception of the stimulus. Psychophysics studies topics such as thresholds (absolute and difference), attention, and adaptation. Signal detection theory describes how we perceive a stimulus (signal) from background noise.

Visible light is composed of electromagnetic radiation. Brightness, hue, and saturation are the three properties of light that are perceived. The structures of the eye can be described by an analogy to a camera and film. Structures such as the cornea, iris and pupil, and lens are comparable to a camera. The retina, which contains the photoreceptor cells (rods and cones), is comparable to the film. The trichromatic theory of color vision proposes that there are three types of cones (red, blue, green) in the eye that can be combined to produce the perception of all the colors. The opponent process theory proposes that color vision results from three types of receptors, each of which is sensitive to two colors (red-green, blue-yellow, black-white).

Sound waves consist of rhythmic changes in air pressure. Loudness, pitch, and timbre are the three properties of sound that are perceived. The ear consists of the outer ear (which collects the sound), the middle ear (which amplifies the sound), and the inner ear (which transduces the sound into electrochemical energy). The place theory of pitch discrimination (which is well supported for higher frequencies) states that pitch is determined by the location on the basilar membrane that is most displaced by the sound. The frequency theory states that for low frequencies pitch is determined by the frequency of the firing of the hair cells. Additionally, the two primary types of hearing loss are described.

The chemical senses (gustation, or taste, and olfaction, or smell), the skin senses (pressure, temperature, and pain), body senses (kinesthesis and equilibrium), and synesthesia (the ability to hear flavors or see sounds) are briefly described.

Gestalt psychologists identified a number of principles of perceptual organization including figure ground, perceptual grouping (proximity, similarity, and good continuation), and closure. Selective attention is the process that describes how we come to focus our attention on only some sensations while "screening out" others. Both binocular (two eyes) and monocular (one eye) cues that are used to perceive distance are described. Binocular cues include binocular disparity and convergence. Monocular cues include elevation, interposition, linear perspective, relative size, texture gradient, aerial perspective, and motion parallax. Perceptual constancy is the tendency to perceive an object as unchanging even if the sensations transmitted through the nervous system change. The four types of perceptual constancies are size, shape, color, and brightness. Perceptual sets (or subjective factors) may also influence our perceptions.

– PART III. KEY TERMS/MATCHING EXERCISES –

Match the following concepts with the appropriate descriptions. Check your answers against the Answer Key.

PRINCIPLES OF SENSATION AND PERCEPTION

Concepts	Descriptions
_____ 1. absolute threshold	a. Response of a sensory receptor to a stimulus event
_____ 2. difference threshold	b. Response of organizing or interpreting a stimulus event
_____ 3. perception	c. Studies the relationship between physical aspects of stimulus and our perceptions
_____ 4. sensation	d. Weakest intensity of a stimulus that can be perceived 50 percent of the time
_____ 5. signal detection theory	e. Equivalent to a just noticeable difference (JND)
_____ 6. psychophysics	f. Selective psychological process of being aware of some stimuli and not others
_____ 7. attention	g. Utilizes the concepts of noise and response criterion
_____ 8. transduction	h. Decrease in response of sensory neurons with unchanging stimulation
_____ 9. Weber's law	i. Occurs when sensory input in the form of energy is transformed into electrochemical energy
_____ 10. sensory adaptation	j. Quantifies the relationship between the intensity of a stimulus and the just noticeable difference (JND)

VISION

Concepts	Descriptions
_____ 1. brightness	a. Related to the intensity of a light stimulus
_____ 2. saturation	b. Related to the wavelength of a light stimulus
_____ 3. rods	c. Related to the proportion of chromatic to achromatic light present in a light stimulus
_____ 4. lens	d. Contains photoreceptor cells
_____ 5. trichromatic theory	e. Sensitive to low intensities of light and primarily responsible for peripheral vision
_____ 6. opponent-process theory	f. Concentrated in the fovea and responsible for color vision
_____ 7. subtractive color mixing	g. Functions to project a focused image of a visual stimulus on the back of the eye
_____ 8. cones	h. Occurs when lights of different wavelengths are combined
_____ 9. retina	i. Supported by evidence that different types of cones are most sensitive to one of three wavelengths
_____ 10. hue	j. Supported by the phenomenon of negative afterimages and cases of color blindness
_____ 11. additive color mixing	k. Occurs when pigments are combined

AUDITION

Concepts	Descriptions
_____ 1. place theory	a. Related to the intensity of a sound stimulus
_____ 2. sensorineural hearing loss	b. Related to the frequency of a sound stimulus
_____ 3. ossicles	c. Helps to explain why a musical note sounds different when played on a clarinet and a saxophone
_____ 4. pitch	d. Commonly referred to as the eardrum
_____ 5. tympanic membrane	e. Consists of the malleus, incus, and stapes
_____ 6. frequency theory	f. Contains the basilar membrane, the organ of Corti, and is filled with fluid
_____ 7. conduction hearing loss	g. Transduces sound stimuli into electrochemical energy
_____ 8. loudness	h. Explains the ability to discriminate pitches that are higher than 4000 Hz
_____ 9. timbre	i. Includes the volley theory of pitch discrimination
_____ 10. auditory hair cells	j. Would result from damage to the hair cells or auditory nerve
_____ 11. cochlea	k. Can be compensated for by the use of a hearing aid

GUSTATION AND OLFACTION AND THE SKIN SENSES

Concepts	Descriptions
_____ 1. olfaction	a. Greatly enhanced by our sense of smell
_____ 2. kinethesis	b. Researchers have not identified the most basic or primary sensations associated with this sense.
_____ 3. gustation	c. Found in the spinal cord, pons, and medulla
_____ 4. equilibrium	d. Proposes an explanation concerning the experience or perception of pain
_____ 5. synesthesia	e. Allows us to be aware of the relative placement or location of our body parts
_____ 6. gate control theory	f. Dependent on the semicircular canals and vestibular sacs
_____ 7. Substance P	g. A condition in which sensations from one modality cause perceptions in another

Answer Key

1. b   2. e   3. a   4. f   5. g   6. d   7. c

PERCEIVING THE WORLD

Concepts	Descriptions
_____ 1. binocular disparity	a. Principle that explains why some ambiguous figures may be perceived in more than one way
_____ 2. linear perspective	b. Includes proximity, similarity, and good continuation
_____ 3. perceptual grouping	c. Relates to the tendency to perceive incomplete figures as complete
_____ 4. figure–ground patterns	d. Based on the fact that each eye sees a slightly different view of the world
_____ 5. perceptual constancy	e. Results from the tension created by rotation (or crossing) of one's eyes
_____ 6. perceptual set	f. Observation that closer objects obstruct one's view of more distant objects
_____ 7. binocular cues	g. Observation that parallel lines appear to converge off in the distance
_____ 8. monocular cues	h. Observation that elements farther away appear more dense than elements that are closer
_____ 9. visual cliff	i. Has been utilized to suggest that depth perception is innate in many animals
_____ 10. closure	j. Require only the use of one eye
_____ 11. texture gradients	k. Require the use of both eyes
_____ 12. convergence	l. Tendency to perceive stimuli as unchanging even though the images projected onto the retina may change
_____ 13. interposition	m. States that the environment supplies all necessary information for depth perception
_____ 14. selective attention	n. Related to expectancies and selective perception
_____ 15. Gibson's Theory of Direct Perception	o. Influenced by factors such as contrast, novelty, and intensity

Answer Key
1. d   2. g   3. b   4. a   5. l   6. n   7. k   8. j   9. i   10. c   11. h   12. e
13. f   14. o   15. m

– PART IV. TRUE-FALSE STATEMENTS –

Fill in the blank before each statement with either a T (true) or an F (false). Check your answers against the Answer Key. Then go back to the items that are false and make the necessary change(s) to the statements to convert the items into true statements.

PRINCIPLES OF SENSATION AND PERCEPTION

_____   1. A stimulus sufficiently intense to be perceived 50 percent of the time is at the absolute threshold.

_____   2. The simplest explanation of why we become accustomed to a foul-smelling environment and after a while do not even notice it is offered by signal detection theory.

VISION

_____   3. The wavelength of a light stimulus is related to the hue we perceive the stimulus to be.

_____   4. Light energy is transduced into electrochemical energy by the lens.

_____   5. Additive color mixing relates to mixing or combining lights of different wavelengths.

AUDITION

_____   6. The function of the pinna and auditory canal is to amplify the intensity of a sound stimulus.

_____   7. The place theory of pitch discrimination proposes that high frequency sounds are detected or sensed near the oval window, whereas lower frequency sounds are detected farther from the oval window.

_____ 8. A person suffering from conduction hearing loss would still be able to hear through bone conduction.

_____

_____

PERCEIVING THE WORLD

_____ 9. The major principles of perceptual organization were identified by the humanistic psychologists.

_____

_____

_____ 10. The psychological principle that states that we would tend to focus on a stimulus that is complex is known as selective attention.

_____

_____

_____ 11. The two binocular depth perception cues are binocular disparity and interposition.

_____

_____

Answer Key
1. T   2. F   3. T   4. F   5. T   6. F   7. T   8. T   9. F   10. T   11. F

– PART V. MULTIPLE-CHOICE QUESTIONS –

Choose the best answer to each question. Circle your choice. Check your answers against the Answer Key. Questions marked with an asterisk (*) include annotated answers.

PRINCIPLES OF SENSATION AND PERCEPTION

1. The process of interpreting and organizing the nervous system's response to a stimulus is known as _____.
   a. adaptation
   b. sensation
   c. perception
   d. psychophysics

2. The process by which sensory organs transform mechanical, chemical, or light energy into the electrochemical energy of neural transmission is called _____.
   a. transduction
   b. sensation
   c. adaptation
   d. psychophysics

3. A hearing test that requires a child to respond when he or she can first hear a soft sound is determining the child's _____ threshold.
   a. auditory
   b. difference
   c. absolute
   d. intensity

4. When you were a teenager listening to the stereo at home, at some point your mother most likely told you to "Turn down that racket." After you turned down the volume your mom yelled at you for not doing what she told you to do. Why didn't your mother think you turned down the volume?
   a. Although you had adapted to the reduced volume, your mother had not.
   b. Because she is older, your mother's ears are less sensitive than yours.
   c. You probably did not lower the volume enough to exceed the auditory threshold.
   d. You probably did not lower the volume enough to exceed the difference threshold.

5. What is the discovery that the difference threshold tends to be a constant fraction of the original stimulus intensity called?
   a. Weber's law
   b. threshold consistency
   c. adaptation
   d. the attention factor

*6. What does signal detection theory state happen as noise increases?
   a. A just noticeable difference becomes smaller.
   b. It would be more difficult to detect a signal.
   c. "Hits" would probably increase.
   d. It would become less difficult to detect a signal.

VISION

*7. Which of the following terms does not belong with the others?
   a. saturation
   b. hue
   c. wavelength
   d. brightness

8. Which of the following structures does light energy pass through first?
   a. aqueous humor
   b. retina
   c. vitreous humor
   d. pupil

9. While _____ are responsible for color vision, _____ allow us to see in dim light.
   a. cones / rods
   b. rods / cones
   c. photoreceptor cells / bipolar cells
   d. rods / reels

10. A person with poor peripheral vision would most likely have a problem associated with his or her _____.
   a. lens
   b. optic nerve
   c. cones
   d. rods

11. A person whose lens cannot correctly focus an image on his or her retina has a problem associated with which of the following?
   a. maintaining the proper pupil size
   b. accommodation
   c. convergence
   d. adaptation

*12. To what are dual processes of dark and light adaptation related to?
   a. the activity of the cones
   b. the activity of the rods
   c. the chemical response of the photopigments in the photoreceptor cells
   d. pupil size

13. The one type of sight-destroying or sight-limiting problem that medical procedures cannot compensate for or overcome involves damage to the
   a. optic nerve
   b. visual cortex
   c. cornea
   d. lens

14. The three primary colors of additive light are
   a. red, white, and black
   b. blue, green, and yellow-green
   c. red, blue, and yellow
   d. red, blue, and green

15. The opponent-process theory is supported at the level of the _____; the trichromatic theory is supported at the level of the _____.
   a. lateral geniculate nucleus / cortex
   b. ganglion cells / cones
   c. cones / ganglion cells
   d. rods / optic nerve

16. The fact that we never perceive such shades as greenish-red or bluish-yellow supports which theory of color vision?
   a. the opponent-process theory
   b. the trichromatic theory
   c. the Young theory
   d. the Young-Helmholtz theory

AUDITION

17. What are sound waves really?
   a. changes in the concentration of photons
   b. changes in the complexity of air molecules
   c. changes in air pressure
   d. a bending of the cilia of hair cells

18. If the frequency of a sound stimulus changes, you would perceive a change in _____.
   a. timbre
   b. saturation
   c. loudness
   d. pitch

19. The retina of the eye is analogous to the _____ of the ear.
   a. hair cells
   b. cochlea
   c. organ of Corti
   d. oval window

20. The function of the middle ear is to _____; the function of the inner ear is to _____ __.
    a. amplify the sound / transduce the sound into electrochemical energy
    b. transduce the sound into electrochemical energy / ample the sound
    c. register the sensation / perceive the stimulus
    d. collect the sound / amplify the sound

21. The place theory of pitch discrimination best explains how _____ frequency sounds are sensed.
    a. low
    b. medium
    c. high
    d. No frequencies of sounds—the place theory is no longer accepted.

22. The _____ theory proposes a mechanism that combines with the more global _____ theory to account for the ability to distinguish tones in the 1000–4000 Hz range.
    a. frequency / volley
    b. volley / frequency
    c. place / frequency
    d. volley / place

23. The two factors that allow us to locate the place of origin of a sound stimulus are _____.
    a. frequency and complexity
    b. arrival time and closure
    c. intensity and kinesthesis
    d. intensity and arrival time

*24. What is the reason that you can hear sounds of higher frequencies than your parents and grandparents can?
    a. They have deterioration of the auditory nerve.
    b. They have sensorineural hearing loss.
    c. They have conduction hearing loss.
    d. They have poorer bone conduction.

GUSTATION AND OLFACTION

25. The chemical senses include _____.
    a. gustation and olfaction
    b. touch and pain
    c. vision and hearing
    d. kinesthesis and equilibrium

26. Which of the following is not one of the four main sensations that can be distinguished by our sense of taste?
    a. bitterness
    b. sourness
    c. saltiness
    d. spiciness

27. The receptor cells for smell are located in (on) the
    a. basilar membrane
    b. olfactory membrane
    c. organ of Corti
    d. auditory nerve

THE SKIN SENSES

28. Temperature receptors for cold _____ while the receptors for heat _____.
    a. are closer to the skin's surface / are farther away from the skin's surface
    b. are farther away from the skin's surface / are closer to the skin's surface
    c. use myelinated fibers / use unmyelinated fibers
    d. are stimulated by increasing pressure to the skin / are stimulated by decreasing pressure to the skin

29. What does the gate-control theory of pain suggest?
    a. Pain is inevitable.
    b. Acupuncture does not work.
    c. Chemicals induce the perception of pain.
    d. Competition from other sensations may block one's perception of pain.

KINESTHESIS AND EQUILIBRIUM

30. Astronauts experiencing weightlessness in space do not know when they are upside-down because the absence of gravity would disrupt their _____ sense(s).
    a. vestibular
    b. kinesthesis
    c. equilibrium and kinesthesis
    d. olfactory

SYNESTHESIA

31. It is believed that synesthesia is the result of what?
    a. cross wiring between cortical brain centers involved in sensory processing
    b. damage to free nerve endings
    c. the inability of certain stimuli to reach a threshold
    d. damage to the occipital lobe in the brain

PERCEIVING THE WORLD

32. The tendency to perceive a pile of change as being composed of pennies, nickels, and dimes is the result of
    a. closure
    b. similarity
    c. proximity
    d. selective attention

33. The processes of selective attention would most likely cause you to perceive which of the following while driving on a highway?
    a. the blue car that you have been passing and been passed by for the last hour
    b. the exit signs for the next city, which is not your destination
    c. a small airplane being towed by a truck
    d. a road sign that says you are 300 miles from your destination

34. The feeling of tension in the eye muscles provides a binocular cue for depth when attempting to focus on a nearby object. This is referred to as _____.
    a. retinal disparity
    b. size constancy
    c. convergence
    d. motion parallax

*35. When watching a travelogue video of the Grand Canyon, you perceive depth as a result of _____.
   a. only monocular cues
   b. only binocular cues
   c. both monocular and binocular cues
   d. relative size, aerial perspective, and motion parallax

36. A newly hatched chick would be likely to _____.
   a. "fall off" a visual cliff
   b. "fall off" only a visual cliff only one time
   c. not cross over from the shallow side to the deep side of a visual cliff
   d. cross over to the deep side of a visual cliff if food were available on the deep side

37. When you incorrectly perceive that two lines are the same length when they are not, you are experiencing _____.
   a. the Müller-Lyer effect
   b. a hallucination
   c. an illusion
   d. a delusion

38. Subjective factors (such as your expectancies and preconceived ideas) that influence your perceptions are referred to as _____.
   a. perceptual constancies
   b. perceptual set
   c. subjective perceptions
   d. objective perceptions

Answer Key

1. c	2. a	3. c	4. d	5. a	*6. b	*7. c	8. a	9. a	10. d	11. b	*12. c
13. b	14. d	15. b	16. a	17. c	18. d	19. c	20. a	21. c	22. b	23. d	*24. b
25. a	26. d	27. b	28. a	29. d	30. c	31. a	32. b	33. c	34. c	*35. a	36. c
37. c	38. b										

Annotated Answers

6. The correct choice is **b**. An increase in noise would have the effect of overshadowing the signal, and the signal would become less noticeable and more difficult to detect.
   a. According to Weber's law the JND would not change.
   c. Because a "hit" is defined as the correct detection of a signal, hits would tend to decrease.
   d. This choice is the exact opposite of the correct choice.

7. The correct choice is **c**. Wavelength is the unit of measurement used to describe a physical characteristic of a light stimulus; a, b, and d are all qualities related to how we interpret or perceive a light stimulus.

12. The correct choice is **c**. The photopigments in both the rods and cones respond to light energy. In dark adaptation, the resulting change is relatively slow to be completed; in light adaptation, the changes occur more rapidly.
   a. & b. are both incomplete because they each related to only one type of photoreceptor cell.
   d. Although pupil size does change when going from a light to a dark environment (and vice versa), changes in pupil size are not sufficient to account for the changes that occur in a light and dark

environment and could not explain why the process of dark adaptation takes 30 minutes to complete.

24. The correct choice is **b**. The most common form of sensorineural hearing loss is the gradual loss of the ability to hear high frequencies that occurs with aging.
   a. The auditory nerve does not typically deteriorate with age.
   c. Conduction hearing loss would typically result in a reduction of sensitivity to all frequencies—not just high frequency sounds.
   d. The effectiveness of bone conduction does not significantly change as a result of aging.

35. The correct choice is **a**. Because the video was shot with only one camera, the image on the screen is monocular in nature, and binocular cues would not be present.
   b. Binocular cues would not be available.
   c. This choice is incorrect because **b** is incorrect.
   d. The cues listed are monocular cues; other monocular cues, such as overlap and linear perspective, would also be available.

– PART VI. SUMMARY TABLES –

To test your understanding of the material discussed in this chapter, complete the following tables. Check your answers with those supplied in Part IX.

THEORIES OF COLOR VISION

Theory	Assumption	Supporting Evidence	Weaknesses
Trichromatic or Young-Helmholtz			
Opponent process			

THEORIES OF PITCH DISCRIMINATION

Theory	Assumption	Supporting Evidence	Weaknesses
Place			
Frequency			

PERCEPTUAL ORGANIZATION

Principle	Description	Number of Corresponding Figure in Textbook as Example
Figure-ground		
Proximity		
Similarity		
Good continuation		
Closure		

DEPTH PERCEPTION CUES

Cue	Monocular/Binocular	Description
Aerial perspective		
Binocular disparity		
Convergence		
Height of plane		
Linear perspective		
Overlap		
Relative size		
Texture gradient		
Relative motion		

– PART VII. THOUGHT QUESTIONS/CRITICAL THINKING –

Prepare answers to the following discussion questions.

1. Discuss the principles of sensation and perception that help explain each of the following observations.
   a. If you close your eyes and press on your eyelids, you "see lights."
   b. If the walls and/or the floors of a room (usually a bathroom) are composed of small rectangular tiles that form a repeating square pattern (such as shown), you almost cannot help but try to decide which group of "squares" go together to make up a larger piece or tile. Additionally, as soon as you think you have figured it out ("These four make a big tile"), you decide you're wrong ("No, it's those four").
   c. If you hit your thumb with a hammer and it hurts, when you hold your thumb and squeeze it your thumb doesn't hurt nearly as bad.
   d. You never mistake a car down the road for a toy car, but if you look down from the twentieth floor of a building the cars on the street below do look like toy cars.

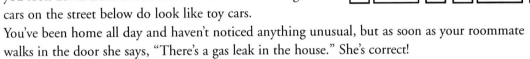

   e. You've been home all day and haven't noticed anything unusual, but as soon as your roommate walks in the door she says, "There's a gas leak in the house." She's correct!

2. Discuss how sensory thresholds, selective attention, and signal detection theory combine to influence our perceptions of the world.

3. a. Draw and label a diagram showing the structure of the eye and ear.
   b. For each of the following structures of the eye, identify the structure of the ear that has a comparable function.
      rods and cones _____
      retina _____
      cornea _____
      lens _____

4. When you're driving and hear a siren, sometimes you immediately know where the siren is coming from (usually the left or right); other times it's much harder to determine where the sound is coming from (usually the front or back). Explain why it is easier to locate a sound coming from the left or right than sound coming from the front or back (and also from above and below).

5. Irrespective of whether flying saucers exist or not, if two people see the same "flying saucer" they often give very different descriptions. One person might say, "It was huge, the size of a city block and about 3,000 feet above the ground." The second person might say, "Oh no, it was hovering just above the treetops and about the size of a small airplane." Explain why their descriptions differ so widely. (Hint: How big is a flying saucer? How high do flying saucers usually fly?)

– PART VIII. APPLICATIONS –

1. Imagine that in addition to the five major senses (vision, hearing, smell, taste, and touch) people have a sixth sense. Design this sensory system. What type of energy will be sensed? How would that energy be transduced into electrochemical energy? What would the receptor cells be like? How would different

qualities of that energy (such as loudness, pitch, and timbre) be sensed? How would the brain organize and interpret the sensation? Design one of the following sensory systems:

a. A temperature-sensing system that would be more complete than the cold and heat receptors in the skin we already have: This sensory system would allow people to know the exact temperature of their environment. If you decide that it would be beneficial for this sensory system to supply information concerning humidity and the wind-chill factor, how would these factors be incorporated into the functioning of the system?

b. An ultraviolet radiation–sensing system that would allow us to limit damage to our skin associated with excessive ultraviolet radiation

c. A bacteria- or virus-sensing system that would allow us to limit our exposure to health threats

d. A "sensory system" for a computer network that would allow the computer to detect the presence of a computer virus or unauthorized user

2. You are in charge of a lab section of general psychology, and it's time for you to design an experiment to illustrate the principles of sensation and perception. Decide whether the experiment will involve: a comparison of the relative effectiveness of monocular and binocular depth-perception cues, whether one's perception of taste is enhanced by his/her sense of smell, or whether people are better at locating a sound source from the left and right or front and back (see Thought Question #4). Answer and/or describe the following:

a. What is your hypothesis?

b. Write a paragraph explaining exactly which procedure you will use to conduct the experiment.

c. Identify the independent variable.

d. Identify the dependent variable, and explain how it will be measured.

e. Identify the experimental group(s).

f. Identify the control group.

g. Explain how you would assign subjects to the experimental and control group(s).

h. Provide any necessary operational definitions.

i. Evaluate your experiment with regard to the APA's ethical guidelines. Even though this experiment is only a classroom exercise and not a "real" experiment, you must adhere to the guidelines.

j. How would you compare the experimental and control group(s) on their performance on the dependent variable? Using only descriptive statistics, how would you present the results (that is, would you calculate means, percentiles, etc.)?

k. Predict what differences in behavior you would find if your hypothesis was confirmed by the results of the experiment.

– PART IX. SUMMARY TABLES SOLUTIONS –

THEORIES OF COLOR VISION

Theory	Assumption	Supporting Evidence	Weaknesses
Trichromatic or Young-Helmholtz	Three types of cones for red, blue, and green	Evidence of three types of cones most sensitive to blue, green, and yellow-green (Genes cones) genes have been identified for the three types of cones	Does not explain color blindness, negative afterimages
Opponent process	Three types of receptors each respond to pairs of colors: red-green, blue-yellow, and black-white	Cannot see reddish-green; color blindness; negative afterimages; and supported by the functioning of the ganglion cells and lateral geniculate nuclei	No major weaknesses when combined with the trichromatic theory

THEORIES OF PITCH DISCRIMINATION

Theory	Assumption	Supporting Evidence	Weaknesses
Place	Different frequencies displace different regions of the basilar membrane: high frequencies closest to the oval window	Predictions consistent with displacement of basilar membrane for high and medium frequencies	Predictions not supported for low frequency sound; cannot explain how very small differences in frequency can be perceived
Frequency	Frequency is determined by the frequency of impulses in the auditory nerve	For frequencies below 1000 Hz the firing of individual auditory nerve fibers match the frequency; with volley theory can explain frequencies between 1000–4000 Hz	Unnecessary for frequencies above 400 Hz, which can be explained by the place theory

PERCEPTUAL ORGANIZATION

Principle	Description	Number of Corresponding Figure in Textbook as Example
Figure-ground	When perceiving a stimulus, attention is focused on the figure and everything else becomes the ground (or background).	Figure 4.20
Proximity	Objects that are close to each other are perceived as belonging together.	Figure 4.21a
Similarity	Objects that are alike are perceived as belonging together	Figure 4.21b
Good continuation	Objects or elements that flow smoothly together are perceived as belonging together.	Figure 4.21c
Closure	We tend to perceive incomplete figures as closed or completed.	Figure 4.21d

DEPTH PERCEPTION CUES

Cue	Monocular/Binocular	Description
Aerial perspective	Mono	Distant objects appear hazy or fuzzy.
Binocular disparity	Bino	Each eye sees a slightly different view of the world.
Convergence	Bino	The awareness of tension in the eye muscles.
Height of plane	Mono	More distant objects appear to be higher than closer objects.
Linear perspective	Mono	Parallel lines appear to converge in the distance.
Overlap	Mono	Closer objects block the view of more distant objects.
Relative size	Mono	Closer objects appear larger than more distant objects.
Texture gradient	Mono	Closer objects appear less dense than more distant objects.
Relative motion	Mono	Nearby objects appear to move a greater distance and faster than more distant objects.

CHAPTER 5
SLEEP, DREAMING, AND CONSCIOUSNESS

– PART I. LEARNING OBJECTIVES –

When you finish studying this chapter, you should be able to do the following:

BIOLOGICAL RHYTHMS

1. Define circadian rhythms, and discuss how circadian rhythms are affected when there is no light-dark schedule.

THE SCIENCE OF SLEEP AND DREAMING

2. Describe the differences between REM (rapid eye movement) and NREM (nonrapid eye movement) sleep.

3. Explain the relationship between REM sleep and dreaming, and discuss changes in muscular activity and brain activity associated with REM sleep.

4. Describe the four stages of sleep and include how brain waves, eye movements, and muscular activity differ in each stage.

5. Describe the pattern of changes in stages of sleep a person experiences throughout a night's sleep (or the sleep cycle).

6. Discuss two major brain areas (the ascending reticular activating system and the raphe system) that are involved in sleep and wakefulness.

7. Describe the results of sleep-deprivation experiments with both humans and animals as subjects.

8. Outline theories that explain why we need to sleep.

9. Describe the results of dream-deprivation experiments with both humans and animals as subjects.

10. Outline Freud's theory of why we dream.

DISORDERS OF SLEEP

11. Define insomnia and differentiate between temporary and chronic insomnia. Discuss factors believed to be associated with insomnia and the treatment for insomnia.

12. Define sleep apnea, discuss factors believed to be associated with it, and examine the treatment for it.

13. Define narcolepsy, discuss factors believed to be associated with it, and examine the treatment for it.

14. Describe nightmares and sleep terrors, and note the stage(s) of sleep during which nightmares and sleep terrors typically occur.

15. Describe sleepwalking and sleep talking, and note the stage(s) of sleep during which sleepwalking and sleep talking typically occur.

16. Discuss the effects frequent travel or rotating shifts have on the sleep/wake schedule.

HYPNOSIS

17. Explain how a hypnotic state differs from a normal waking state, and discuss a number of phenomena that have been associated with hypnosis.

18. Describe the conflicting theories concerning hypnosis proposed by Hilgard and Barber.

– PART II. OVERVIEW –

Many physiological processes (such as activity, behavior, body temperature) vary according to circadian (24-hour) rhythms that are influenced by patterns of light and dark. In the absence of a day/night schedule, the individual's biological clock adjusts to a 25-hour day.

Sleep consists of two types of sleep. REM (rapid eye movement) sleep is associated with dreaming. During REM sleep, muscular activity is inhibited. NREM (nonrapid eye movement) sleep is further divided into four stages that differ in how "deep" the sleep is and in brain wave patterns. Throughout a night's sleep an individual goes through a complete sleep cycle (NREM and REM) every 90 minutes. When rats have been deprived of sleep for extended periods of time, they died within approximately one month. For obvious reasons, humans have not been sleep deprived for an equivalent length of time. Several theories of why sleep is necessary are discussed. Most of these theories are primarily focused on biological functions (to conserve energy, to avoid predation, and for restoration). Another theory focuses on a mental function (sleep as necessary to consolidate memory).

The function of dreaming is discussed by looking at deprivation studies. People deprived of REM (or dream) sleep increase the amount of time they spend in REM sleep when they are allowed uninterrupted sleep. Freud's theory of dreaming, stating that dreams are an expression of the unconscious, is explored.

A number of sleep disorders are discussed. People with insomnia have difficulty either going to sleep or frequently awakening. Sleep apnea is a disorder in which people awaken very frequently (perhaps hundreds of times a night) in order to breathe. A person with narcolepsy has sudden uncontrollable sleep attacks. Nightmares occur during REM sleep, while sleep terrors occur during stage 3 and 4 sleep. While sleep talking can occur at any point in the sleep cycle, sleepwalking occurs during stage 3 and 4 sleep. People have difficulty adjusting to changes in their sleep/wake cycle (jet lag).

Hypnosis is a state of relaxation during which the hypnotized individual is highly suggestible to the instructions of the hypnotist. Hypnosis is effective in relieving symptoms of some stress-related illnesses and in the control of pain. The neodissociation theory of hypnosis suggests that hypnosis involves the individual functioning on more than one level of consciousness at the same time.

– PART III. KEY TERMS/MATCHING EXERCISES –

Match the following concepts with the appropriate descriptions. Check your answers against the Answer Key.

THE SCIENCE OF SLEEP AND DREAMING

Concepts	Descriptions
_____ 1. ascending reticular activating system	a. Characterized by sleep spindles and K complex brain wave patterns
_____ 2. raphe system	b. Is commonly associated with dreaming
_____ 3. sleep	c. Consists of four stages of sleep
_____ 4. REM sleep	d. Occurs when delta waves are present 20–50% of the time
_____ 5. NREM sleep	e. Primarily responsible for the awake state
_____ 6. stage 1 sleep	f. Occurs when delta waves predominate; it is difficult to wake an individual
_____ 7. stage 2 sleep	g. Is associated with low-amplitude brain waves; individuals awaken easily
_____ 8. stage 3 sleep	h. Most active at time of sleep onset
_____ 9. stage 4 sleep	i. Characterized by reduced activity and responsiveness and distinctive brain wave patterns

Theories	*Descriptions*
_____ 1. to avoid predation	a. Suggests that sleep is a helpful mechanism to prevent exhaustion
_____ 2. to conserve energy	b. Suggests that sleep reduces interaction with the environment at times when the species is not well suited to function properly
_____ 3. as expressions of the unconscious	c. Supported by findings that people sleep longer after particularly tiring activities
_____ 4. to consolidate memory	d. Suggests that sleep promotes the storage of newly learned information
_____ 5. for restoration	e. Distinguishes between the manifest and latent content of dreams

Answer Key
   1. b   2. a   3. e   4. d   5. c

DISORDERS OF SLEEP

Concepts	*Descriptions*
_____ 1. insomnia	a. May occur during REM or NREM sleep
_____ 2. sleep talking	b. Occurs during NREM sleep; may be difficult to awaken individual
_____ 3. nightmare	c. Frightening experiences that occur during stage 3 and 4 sleep
_____ 4. sleep apnea	d. A "bad dream" that occurs during REM sleep
_____ 5. sleepwalking	e. Associated with the inappropriate loss of muscle tone and the immediate onset of REM sleep
_____ 6. narcolepsy	f. Associated with difficulty in falling asleep and/or frequently awakening during the night
_____ 7. sleep terror	g. Occurs when an individual frequently wakes up briefly in order to breathe

Answer Key
   1. f   2. a   3. d   4. g   5. b   6. e   7. c

– PART IV. TRUE-FALSE STATEMENTS –

Fill in the blank before each statement with either a T (true) or an F (false). Check your answers against the Answer Key. Then go back to the items that are false and make the necessary change(s) to the statements to convert the items into true statements.

BIOLOGICAL RHYTHMS

_____ 1. In an environment that is lighted 24 hours a day, a person's biological clock would adjust to a 25- hour free-running clock.

_____

_____

THE SCIENCE OF SLEEP AND DREAMING

_____ 2. During REM sleep there is more muscular activity than there is during NREM sleep.

_____

_____

_____ 3. After being deprived of REM sleep, people spend increased time in REM sleep, which is referred to as REM rebound.

_____

_____

_____ 4. Freud believed that people dream in order to solve problems.

_____

_____

DISORDERS OF SLEEP

_____ 5. Obesity is often associated with narcolepsy.

_____

_____

_____ 6. Nightmares occur during REM sleep; sleep terrors occur during stage 3 & 4 sleep.

_____

_____

HYPNOSIS

_____ 7. Currently there is increased interest in using hypnosis to enhance the memories of witnesses to crime.

_____

_____

_____ 8. Although the idea of hypnotized people acting out posthypnotic suggestions is commonly accepted, it has not been scientifically demonstrated.

_____

_____

_____ 9. The "hidden observer" is associated with the dissociation theory of hypnosis.

_____

_____

Answer Key
1. T   2. F   3. T   4. F   5. F   6. T   7. F   8. F   9. T

– PART V. MULTIPLE-CHOICE QUESTIONS –

Choose the best answer to each question. Circle your choice. Check your answers against the Answer Key. Questions marked with an asterisk (*) include annotated answers.

BIOLOGICAL RHYTHMS

1. A biological rhythm that is approximately one year in length is called a _____ rhythm.
   a. circumlunar
   b. diurnal
   c. circadian
   d. circumannual

2. The suprachiasmatic nucleus adjusts the biological clock by monitoring activity in the _____ system.
   a. ascending reticular activating
   b. raphe
   c. visual
   d. auditory

THE SCIENCE OF SLEEP AND DREAMING

3. A natural recurring state of rest characterized by reduced activity, diminished responsiveness to stimuli, and distinctive brain wave patterns describes _____.
   a. sleep
   b. meditation
   c. hypnosis
   d. dreaming

4. Which of the following bodily functions are reduced during REM sleep?
   a. muscular activity
   b. brain wave activity
   c. heart rate
   d. breathing

5. The atonia produced during REM sleep _____.
   a. is a result of a loss of sleep
   b. causes nightmares
   c. causes increased muscle activity
   d. keeps people from physically acting out their dreams

6. Theta waves, slow eye movements, irregular breathing, and muscle relaxation characterize _____ sleep.
   a. stage 1
   b. stage 2
   c. stage 3
   d. stage 4

7. What does the primary distinction between stage 3 and stage 4 sleep concerns?
   a. the proportion of rapid eye movements to nonrapid eye movements
   b. the relative proportion of delta waves to other brain waves
   c. the amount of muscular activity
   d. whether or not the person is experiencing a dream

*8. If you normally sleep eight hours each night, you probably experience _____ complete sleep cycle(s) each night.
   a. one
   b. three
   c. five
   d. eight

9. Generally speaking, we tend to have our longest dream period during the _____ part of the night.
   a. first
   b. middle
   c. last
   d. quietest

10. Electrical stimulation of the what causes animals to fall asleep?
   a. suprachiasmatic nucleus
   b. raphe system
   c. pontine reticular formation
   d. ascending reticular activating system

*11. Compared to adults, newborn babies sleep _____.
   a. the same amount of time, but their sleep is differently distributed throughout the day
   b. much longer, and spend the same amount of time in REM sleep
   c. much longer, and spend a smaller percentage of time in REM sleep
   d. much longer, and spend a greater percentage of time in REM sleep

12. Which of the following theories of why we need to sleep would be more applicable to a person barely surviving in a Third World country in the midst of a famine than to a typical American?
   a. to restore depleted resources
   b. to conserve energy
   c. to prevent boredom
   d. to consolidate memory

13. When people deprived of REM sleep for a number of days are allowed uninterrupted sleep, what do they do?
   a. experience sleep apnea
   b. show sleep cycles that are identical to people not deprived of REM sleep
   c. spend a greater percentage of time in REM sleep than they would normally spend
   d. sleep about 50 percent longer than they would normally sleep

14. According to Freud, the _____ is the "true" meaning of a dream.
   a. plot
   b. latent content
   c. manifest content
   d. analogy content

DISORDERS OF SLEEP

15. A serious sleep disorder in which a person stops breathing and frequently must waken briefly in order to breathe describes _____.
   a. lucid sleeping
   b. narcolepsy
   c. sleep apnea
   d. sleep terrors

16. A sleep disorder whereby a person falls asleep suddenly and uncontrollably is called
    a. sleep terrors
    b. somnambulism
    c. narcolepsy
    d. apnea

17. Sleeping pills like barbiturates disrupt the _____ portion of the sleep cycle by _____ the amount of time spent in this portion.
    a. NREM / increasing
    b. NREM / decreasing
    c. REM & stage 4 / increasing
    d. REM & stage 4 / decreasing

18. A person who is sleepwalking is _____.
    a. acting out a dream.
    b. in REM sleep.
    c. experiencing sleep terrors.
    d. in stage 3 or stage 4 sleep.

*19. Jet lag would be a problem of little concern following a 3,000 mile trip from _____.
    a. north to south
    b. west to east
    c. east to west
    d. Jet lag would be similar following all of the above choices

HYPNOSIS

*20. Which of the following statements does *not* describe a hypnotized person?
    a. He or she is highly suggestible to the hypnotist's instructions.
    b. He or she is passive.
    c. He or she has few, if any, independent thoughts.
    d. He or she is not alert.

21. Although hypnosis has been shown to be helpful in a number of medical applications, in what has it been effective?
    a. treating self-initiated behaviors such as smoking, alcoholism, and overeating
    b. treating stress-related illnesses such as asthma and ulcers
    c. reducing pain
    d. treating skin ailments such as warts and psoriasis

22. That people can selectively focus attention on one thing (the hypnotic suggestion) and still perceive other things "subconsciously" describes Hilgard's _____ theory.
    a. psychoanalytic
    b. dissociation
    c. role-playing
    d. meditation

Answer Key
   1. d   2. c   3. a   4. a   5. d   6. a   7. b   *8. c   9. c   10. b   *11. d   12. b
   13. c   14. b   15. c   16. c   17. d   18. d   *19. a   *20. d   21. a   22. b

8. The correct choice is **c**. Since the sleep cycle is 90 minutes, in 8 hours you should complete 5 cycles.
   a. One sleep cycle would result in 11/2 hours of sleep.
   b. Three sleep cycles would result in 41/2 hours of sleep.
   d. Eight sleep cycles would result in 12 hours of sleep.

11. The correct choice is **d**. Newborn babies sleep 16 hrs. a day (vs. 8 for young adults) and spend approximately 50 percent (vs. 20 percent for young adults) of their sleep time in REM sleep.
   a. Newborn babies sleep much more than adults.
   b. Newborn babies spend more time in REM sleep than adults.
   c. Newborn babies spend a larger percentage of time in REM sleep than adults.

19. The correct choice is **a**. Jet lag is caused by changes in the wake/sleep cycle. Since a north to south trip would not cross time zones, it should not result in jet lag.
   b. A west to east trip would result in the most jet lag, since the trip would "shorten" the traveler's day.
   c. An east to west trip would result in less jet lag than a west to east trip since it would "lengthen" the traveler's day, and our internal biological clocks "prefer" a slightly longer (25-hr.) day.
   d. Each of the above choices would result in a different effect on potential jet lag.

20. The correct choice is **d**. Even though the term hypnosis comes from the name of the Greek god of sleep, a hypnotized person is not drowsy, but very alert.
   a. One of the characteristics of hypnosis that allows it to be helpful in a variety of situations is that the individual is highly responsive to the hypnotist's instructions.
   b. Hypnotized individuals are passive in that they do not independently initiate activities.
   c. Similar to **b**, the hypnotized person does not tend to have independent thoughts.

– PART VI. SUMMARY TABLE –

To test your understanding of the material discussed in this chapter, complete the following table. Check your answers with those supplied in Part IX.

STAGES OF THE SLEEP CYCLE

Stage	Brain Wave Patterns	Eye Movements	Muscular Activity	Other
1				
2				
3				
4				
Stage 1 REM				

– PART VII. THOUGHT QUESTIONS/CRITICAL THINKING –

Prepare answers to the following discussion questions.

1. With the amount of research being conducted in all areas of psychology, do you think it is "just a matter of time" before sleep researchers have definitive information concerning the effects of long-term sleep (or REM sleep) deprivation on humans? Explain your answer.

2. You get home from class and are tired and decide to take a nap before dinner. Based on your knowledge of the sleep cycle, what would be the ideal length of time for a nap? Explain. What would be the worst length of time for a nap? Explain.

3. Which theory of why we sleep would best explain each of the following observations? Explain you choices.
   a. Why we sleep more when we are sick
   b. Why babies sleep more than adults
   c. Why babies have more REM sleep than adults
   d. Why a person might spend more time in REM sleep after attending a beneficial two-day workshop related to the performance of their job
   e. Why a person might sleep more after attending a useless two-day workshop related to the performance of their job
   f. Why pregnant women sleep more than they did before they were pregnant

4. Obviously, brain activity and dreaming are related. Which do you think comes first? Do you think brain activity causes dreams to develop, or does the dream result in changes in brain wave patterns? Explain your answers.

– PART VIII. APPLICATIONS –

1. This chapter describes a number of theories as to why we sleep and dream. It also presents information that supports some of the theories. For the next week to ten days, keep a diary of your daily activities and the number of hours you sleep. Note the time you go to sleep each night and the time you wake up. Note whether or not you were wakened by an alarm clock or if you "just woke up." If you wake up during the night, note the time. If you recall any dreams, write down what each dream was about. After you have completed your diary, examine it to answer the following:
   a. Is there evidence to support any of the theories as to why we sleep?
   b. Is there evidence to support Freud's theory as to why we dream?
   c. Was the length of time you slept each night (or length of time you slept before awakening in the "middle of the night") consistent with a 90-minute sleep cycle?

2. In the "Methods of Psychology" chapter of this text, it was noted that relatively similar experiments do not always yield similar results. From the information presented in the text concerning the effect of REM-sleep deprivation on rats, there appears to be conflicting results. The first study (Morden et al., 1967) found that REM-deprived rats did not show any significant behavioral or emotional difficulties, while in the second study (Kushida et al., 1989), all the REM-deprived rats died. Prepare a list of questions you would like to see answered concerning these two studies that would help you decide how to reconcile these seemingly conflicting results. The discussion of the two studies in the text was necessarily brief, and your questions might be answered by reading the original reports of the experiments published in scientific journals. The references for the two experiments are listed in the bibliography. If your college library subscribes to these journals, read the articles and decide if the

conflicting results and conclusions can be reconciled by a difference in the procedures employed in the two studies, or if additional research is needed to reach a conclusion concerning the effects of REM deprivation on rats.

– PART IX. SUMMARY TABLE SOLUTIONS –

STAGES OF THE SLEEP CYCLE

Stage	Brain Wave Patterns	Eye Movements	Muscular Activity	Other
1	Theta waves Low amplitude-low frequency (3–7 cps)	Slow	Relaxed	Easily wakened
2	Burst of sleep spindles (12–14 cps)	Minimal	Decreases	—
3	Delta waves 20–50 percent of the time High amplitude–low frequency (0.5–2 cps)	Virtually none	Movement; may sleepwalk	—
4	Delta waves over 50 percent of the time	Virtually none	Movement; may sleepwalk	Difficult to waken
Stage 1 REM	Beta waves Low amplitude–high frequency	Rapid (REM)	No movement Muscular inhibition	Dreaming Easily wakened

CHAPTER 6
LEARNING AND BEHAVIOR

– PART I. LEARNING OBJECTIVES –

When you finish studying this chapter, you should be able to do the following:

DEFINING LEARNING

1. Define learning and discuss the three elements of the definition.

2. Define associative learning, and briefly discuss the two forms of associative learning.

PAVLOVIAN CONDITIONING

3. Describe the four key terms involved in Pavlovian conditioning: unconditioned stimulus (UCS), unconditioned response (UCR), conditioned stimulus (CS), conditioned response (CR).

4. Describe how a response is acquired through Pavlovian conditioning.

5. Discuss the effects stimulus contingency and CS-UCS timing have on the acquisition of a conditioned response.

6. Describe conditioned taste aversions, and discuss the concepts of preparedness and selective associations.

7. Define extinction its adaptive function.

8. Define reinstatement and how this might make relapse back into addiction more likely in a familiar drug using environment.

9. Define generalization and discrimination, and explain how the two processes differ.

10. Describe second order conditioning.

OPERANT CONDITIONING

11. Describe the approach used by Thorndike to study operant conditioning, and discuss the Law of Effect.

12. Describe the approach used by Skinner to study operant conditioning, and discuss the concept of response selection.

13. Define reinforcement, and differentiate between positive and negative reinforcement in terms of response outcome.

14. Discriminate between primary and conditioned reinforcers, and explain how the latter acquire reinforcing properties.

15. Discuss the difference between continuous and partial reinforcement.

16. Describe and contrast the four schedules of partial reinforcement.

17. Describe four techniques that may be used to "encourage" the initial operant response.

18. Discuss the differences between negative reinforcement and punishment.

COMPARING PAVLOVIAN AND OPERANT CONDITIONING

18. Discuss three problems or limitations associated with the use of punishment.

19. Discuss some ways to make punishment more effective.

20. Explain two differences between Pavlovian and operant conditioning.

21. Describe how two-factor theory of avoidance combines elements of Pavlovian and operant conditioning.

COGNITIVE INFLUENCES ON LEARNING

22. Explain how the cognitive learning perspective differs from the associative learning perspective.

23. Describe Tolman's contributions involving latent learning and cognitive maps.

24. Explain how cognitive learning theorists interpret Pavlovian and operant conditioning.

25. Define observational learning, and identify the four key steps involved in observational learning.

BIOLOGICAL BASES OF LEARNING

26. Explain why researchers studying the biological mechanisms of learning use species such as the aplysia.

27. Briefly discuss Pavlovian conditioning of the aplysia.

– PART II. OVERVIEW –

Learning refers to a relatively enduring change in potential behavior that results from experience. Both associative and cognitive learning are described.

The first type of associative learning is Pavlovian conditioning, which involves learning an association between two stimuli. Before Pavlovian conditioning training, one stimulus (the unconditioned stimulus or UCS) naturally causes a specific response (the unconditioned response or UCR). During acquisition of Pavlovian conditioning, another stimulus (the conditioned stimulus or CS) is associated or paired with the UCS. The UCS is therefore contingent on the CS (the UCS never occurs unless the CS is presented). Eventually the CS will come to elicit a response (the conditioned response or CR) that may be similar to the UCR or, as we saw in drug conditioning, it may be opposite.

A number of processes that elaborate on the general features of Pavlovian conditioning are described. Extinction of the CR occurs if the CS is repeatedly presented without the UCS. However, following extinction of the CR and the passage of time, when the CS is again presented the CR will occur or show reinstatement. Stimulus generalization exists if the CR occurs to a stimulus that is similar to the original CS. If training with two CSs takes place, and one stimulus is associated with the UCS and the other is not, discrimination will develop and the subject will selectively respond to the two stimuli.

The second type of associative learning is operant conditioning, which involves learning an association between a behavior and the consequences of that behavior (response-outcome). If the consequences of a behavior result in an increase in the frequency of the behavior the consequence is termed a reinforcer. On the other hand, if the consequences result in a decrease in the frequency of behavior it is termed a punisher. There are two main categories of reinforcers: If the consequences is presented it is termed positive reinforcement. If the consequence is removed or terminated it is termed a negative reinforcer. Note, the terms positive and negative refer to the presentation or removal of the reinforcer, not its hedonic value. There are four schedules of partial reinforcement (fixed ratio, variable ratio, fixed interval, variable interval) that lead to different patterns of responding. A number of techniques (physical guidance, shaping, modeling, verbal instruction) may be used to facilitate the original learning of the operant response. There are a number of potential problems associated with the use of punishment. If punishment is used, it should be applied immediately, consistently, and at a low level of intensity.

Cognitive learning takes into account complex mental processes such as perception, thinking, and memory. Tolman studied latent learning (learning that occurs in the absence of reinforcement) and found that rats and other species are capable of learning cognitive maps of their environment. Social learning theory is concerned with observational learning in which an individual learns through observing another's behavior and imitating or modeling that behavior.

Finally, researchers interested in the biological bases of learning tend to focus on species with simple nervous systems (such as the aplysia). In these animals, specific changes in the nervous system following learning may be observed.

– PART III. KEY TERMS/MATCHING EXERCISES –

Match the following concepts and/or individuals with the appropriate descriptions. Check your answers against the Answer Key.

DEFINING LEARNING AND OVERVIEW

Concepts	Descriptions
_____ 1. learning	a. The learning process by which behavior is influenced by its consequences
_____ 2. associative learning	b. The learning process by which a connection is made between two events
_____ 3. Pavlovian conditioning	c. Learning that occurs as a result of modeling without the individual being reinforced
_____ 4. operant conditioning	d. A relatively enduring change in potential behavior that results from experience
_____ 5. two-factor learning	e. Learning theory that takes into account mental processes such as perception, thinking, and memory
_____ 6. template learning	f. Learning that occurs in the absence of reinforcement
_____ 7. latent learning	g. The learning process that combines both Pavlovian and operant conditioning
_____ 8. observational learning	h. Emphasizes the role of observation and imitation in learning
_____ 9. social learning theory	i. The learning process by which one stimulus becomes a signal associated with another stimulus

Answer Key
   1. d   2. b   3. i   4. a   5. g   6. e   7. f   8. c   9. h

Individuals	Descriptions
_____ 1. Pavlov	a. Developed the Law of Effect
_____ 2. Thorndike	b. Associated with positive reinforcement, shaping, and cumulative records
_____ 3. Skinner	c. Believed that animals could develop cognitive maps of their environment
_____ 4. Tolman	d. Studied learning that involved the association of two stimuli
_____ 5. Bandura	e. Emphasized learning through observation and imitation

Answer Key

   1. d   2. a   3. b   4. c   5. e

PAVLOVIAN CONDITIONING

Concepts	Descriptions
_____ 1. unconditioned stimulus (UCS)	a. Occurs when a CS is presented following extinction and the passage of time
_____ 2. unconditioned response (UCR)	b. The tendency for a new stimulus to elicit the same response as the original CS
_____ 3. conditioned stimulus (CS)	c. A response to a stimulus that does not require learning
_____ 4. conditioned response (CR)	d. A response given to a previously neutral stimulus
_____ 5. extinction	e. An originally neutral stimulus that eventually elicits a response
_____ 6. spontaneous recovery	f. A stimulus that elicits a response before Pavlovian conditioning training
_____ 7. generalization	g. Occurs when a second stimulus is associated with a CS
_____ 8. discrimination	h. Occurs if a CS is repeatedly presented without being followed by a UCS
_____ 9. second order conditioning	i. The tendency to respond to some stimuli while not responding to other similar stimuli

Answer Key

   1. f   2. c   3. e   4. d   5. h   6. a   7. b   8. i   9. g

OPERANT CONDITIONING

Concepts	Descriptions
_____ 1. Law of Effect	a. Involves the termination of an unpleasant stimulus following an appropriate response
_____ 2. discriminative stimulus	b. May be used to visualize an individual's rate of response
_____ 3. cumulative record	c. A stimulus that is presented following a response that increases the probability of that response occurring again
_____ 4. positive reinforcement	d. Reinforcement occurs following every specified number of responses.
_____ 5. negative reinforcement	e. Reinforcement occurs following the first response after an unpredictable or average amount of time.
_____ 6. punishment	f. Reinforcement occurs following the first response after a specific amount of time.
_____ 7. escape conditioning	g. Reinforcement occurs following an unpredictable or average number of responses.
_____ 8. avoidance conditioning	h. If an appropriate response is made, an unpleasant stimulus does not occur.
_____ 9. primary reinforcer	i. States that behavior followed by a satisfying consequence will be strengthened
_____ 10. conditioned reinforcer	j. A stimulus that terminates or avoids an unpleasant event and increases the probability of that response occurring again
_____ 11. continuous reinforcement	k. A stimulus, such as money or praise, that acquires reinforcing qualities
_____ 12. partial reinforcement	l. Involves reinforcing behaviors that are closer and closer to the desired operant response
	(continues)

Concepts (continued)	Descriptions (continued)
_____ 13. shaping	m. A stimulus, such as food or water, that satisfies a biological drive or need
_____ 14. fixed ratio (FR)	n. A stimulus that is presented following a response that decreases the probability of that response occurring again
_____ 15. variable ratio (VR)	o. A stimulus that signifies the availability of reinforcement
_____ 16. fixed interval (FI)	p. Should be used during acquisition of an operantly conditioned response
_____ 17. variable interval (VI)	q. If persistent responding is desired, this should be used after the behavior has been learned

Answer Key

1. i   2. o   3. b   4. c   5. j   6. n   7. a   8. h   9. m   10. k   11. p   12. q
13. l   14. d   15. g   16. f   17. e

– PART IV. TRUE-FALSE STATEMENTS –

Fill in the blank before each statement with either a T (true) or an F (false). Check your answers against the Answer Key. Then go back to the items that are false and make the necessary change(s) to the statements to convert the items into true statements.

DEFINING LEARNING

_____ 1. A new behavior that is acquired as a result of an individual's maturation is considered a learned behavior.

_____

_____

PAVLOVIAN CONDITIONING

_____ 2. Ideally, for Pavlovian conditioning to take place, the UCS must be presented before the CS.

_____ _____

_____ _____

_____ 3. When a CR that has been extinguished suddenly returns after an interval of rest, we say reinstatement has occurred.

_____

_____

_____ 4. Generalization describes the situation in which a CR is made to a stimulus that is different from the original CS.

_____

_____

OPERANT CONDITIONING

_____ 5. A positive reinforcer increases the probability of a response occurring again, whereas a punisher decreases the probability of a response occurring again.

_____

_____

_____ 6. Typically, a rat on a FR schedule of reinforcement has a higher rate of responding than a rat on a FI schedule of reinforcement.

_____

_____

_____ 7. Shaping involves the physical guidance of the subject to make the desired response.

_____

_____

_____ 8. While punishment usually suppresses an unwanted behavior temporarily, it does not necessarily extinguish the behavior.

_____

_____ 9. If you are using punishment in an appropriate manner, it is not important to also reward acceptable behaviors.

_____

_____

COGNITIVE INFLUENCES ON LEARNING

_____ 10. Cognitive learning suggests that cognitive factors such as expectancy provide the basis for the behavior changes observed in Pavlovian and operant conditioning.

_____

_____

_____ 11. Bandura's study involving children and a Bobo doll demonstrated modeling.

_____

_____

BIOLOGICAL BASES OF LEARNING

_____ 12. Research interested in the biological mechanisms of learning has focused on operant conditioning in the marine snail aplysia.

_____

_____

Answer Key
1. F   2. F   3. T   4. T   5. F   6. T   7. F   8. T   9. F   10. T   11. T   12. F

– PART V. MULTIPLE-CHOICE QUESTIONS –

Choose the best answer to each question. Circle your choice. Check your answers against the Answer Key. Questions marked with an asterisk (*) include annotated answers.

DEFINING LEARNING

1. To what does learning refer?
   a. a change in behavior that is demonstrated immediately
   b. a change in behavior that results from disease or maturation
   c. a relatively enduring change in potential behavior that results from experience
   d. all changes in behavior

2. Associative learning describes the process by which a connection or association is made between
   a. two stimuli
   b. a behavior and the consequences of that behavior

    c. a problem and the solution to that problem

    d. Both a and b are correct

3. After receiving a traffic ticket for not coming to a complete stop at a stop sign, you now very carefully stop at that intersection. According to learning theorists, you have experienced _____ learning.

    a. social

    b. associative

    c. motor-skill

    d. defensive

PAVLOVIAN CONDITIONING

4. If a dog salivates after hearing the sound of a bell, salivation would be a(n) _____.

    a. conditioned stimulus (CS)

    b. conditioned response (CR)

    c. unconditioned stimulus (UCS)

    d. unconditioned response (UCR)

5. Young children frequently cry when their mothers leave them. Sometimes they start to cry as soon as the babysitter arrives. Why does this occur?

    a. Babysitter is an UCS associated with the mother leaving.

    b. Babysitter uses negative reinforcement.

    c. Babysitter is a CS associated with the mother leaving.

    d. Child dislikes the babysitter.

6. Which of the following statements best describes the relationship between the UCR and CR?

    a. They are identical in all respects.

    b. The CR is generally more intense.

    c. The UCR is generally more intense.

    d. The CR only occurs following the presentation of the UCS.

7. Which of the following is *not* an important factor in the initial acquisition of a CR?

    a. the motivation of the individual to perform the CR

    b. the timing of the presentation of the CS and UCS

    c. that the CS is clearly different from other stimuli

    d. how frequently the CS and UCS have been paired

8. Rescorla's experiments examining stimulus contingency and Pavlovian conditioning showed that _____ relationship between the CS and UCS was necessary for conditioning to take place.

    a. a contingent

    b. a non-contingent

    c. either a contingent or a non-contingent

    d. neither a contingent nor a non-contingent

9. Conditioned taste aversions illustrate what concept?

    a. second order conditioning

    b. spontaneous recovery

    c. preparedness

    d. conditioned punishers

*10. What should you do to extinguish a CR?
   a. pair the CS with a second order stimulus
   b. repeatedly present the CS while not presenting the UCS
   c. withhold the UCR
   d. not present the CS for a period of several days

11. Years ago, a young woman's boyfriend broke up with her while they were watching the movie *Top Gun* starring Tom Cruise. Today, when the woman sees a Tom Cruise movie or sees him on TV, she starts to cry. Her behavior illustrates _____.
   a. generalization
   b. neurosis
   c. latent learning
   d. discrimination

12. When driving, I stop when the light turns red and go when the light turns green. My driving illustrates _____.
   a. spontaneous recovery
   b. generalization
   c. discrimination
   d. UCR

13. Teaching an organism to respond to only one of a series of similar stimuli is called _____.
   a. operant conditioning
   b. generalization
   c. extinction
   d. discrimination training

*14. What is necessary to demonstrate second order conditioning?
   a. pair the CS with a new UCS
   b. employ discrimination training
   c. pair a new stimulus with the CS
   d. repeatedly present the CS while not presenting the UCS

OPERANT CONDITIONING

*15. What is the most commonly used measure of the strength of an operant response?
   a. the rate of response
   b. the calculation from the Law of Effect
   c. the variety of stimuli that elicit the response
   d. how much generalization is shown

16. "Any event that increases the probability that a response will occur" is the definition of _____.
   a. primary reinforcers
   b. operant conditioning
   c. rewards
   d. reinforcement

17. A reinforcer that is reinforcing because it causes something unpleasant to end or not occur is called a _____.
   a. reverse reinforcer
   b. negative reinforcer

c. positive reinforcer

d. punishment

18. Your child gets a gold star on her perfect spelling test. The gold star is a(n _____.)

a. conditioned reinforcer

b. primary reinforcer

c. UCS

d. discriminative stimulus

19. What is true of conditioned reinforcers?

a. They satisfy biologically based drives, such as hunger and thirst.

b. They acquire reinforcing properties through association with primary reinforcers.

c. They are reinforced on partial or secondary schedules of reinforcement.

d. They are less important than primary reinforcers.

*20. Even after getting 20 doors in a row slammed in his face, a door-to-door salesman doesn't quit because his behavior has most likely been reinforced on a _____ schedule of reinforcement.

a. continuous

b. fixed

c. variable

d. gambler's

21. Immediately after being reinforced, a rat on which schedule of reinforcement would show the longest pause before its next bar press?

a. FR

b. VR

c. FI

d. VI

22. Which technique for obtaining an initial operant response would be most effective in teaching a rat to bar press?

a. shaping

b. modeling

c. physical guidance

d. verbal instruction

23. A mentally handicapped child is rewarded for each step of the dressing process until he is able to completely dress himself. This behavioral technique is called _____.

a. variable ratio schedules

b. shaping

c. variable interval schedules

d. modeling

24. Many human phobias are learned as a result of

a. Pavlovian conditioning

b. spontaneous recovery

c. punishment

d. operant conditioning

25. A child's punishment for raiding the cookie jar successfully suppresses the behavior until the grandparents babysit. Why does the child again raid the cookie jar?

a. Punishment suppresses but does not eliminate the behavior in many cases.

b. The child enjoys punishment.

c. The grandparents were not looking.

d. The punishment was not strong enough.

26. Which of the following is *not* a limitation or undesirable side effect of punishment?

   a. It may induce counteraggression against the punisher.

   b. Fear or anxiety may develop.

   c. Positive reinforcers lose their reinforcing properties.

   d. The results are often temporary.

27. For punishment to be effective, what it should occur?

   a. It should be administered every time the inappropriate behavior occurs.

   b. It should not be too severe.

   c. It should be administered immediately after the inappropriate behavior occurs.

   d. All of the above are correct.

COGNITIVE INFLUENCES ON LEARNING

28. Which line of research demonstrates the distinction between learning and performance?

   a. Bandura's observational learning

   b. Tolman's latent learning

   c. Thorndike's puzzle box

   d. Both a and b are correct

*29. A mother attempts to take her 5-year-old son to a birthday party at a bowling alley they have been to only once before. While the mother is frantically reading the directions, her son says, "You should have turned at the McDonald's and again at the church." He's correct. What most likely explains his behavior?

   a. latent learning

   b. Pavlovian conditioning

   c. modeling

   d. positive reinforcement

30. If you believe that Pavlovian conditioning develops because the CS provides information about the UCS, you agree with _____.

   a. Thorndike

   b. the cognitive learning perspective

   c. Pavlov

   d. Skinner

31. What is the basic premise of observational learning?

   a. Behavior learned through observational learning is never extinguished

   b. Insight into the model's motivation is gained.

   c. Learning may occur without physical responses or reinforcement.

   d. All learning results from modeling.

32. According to Bandura, the fourth and final step involved in observational learning concerns which of the following?

   a. performing the modeled response

   b. having our attention drawn to a modeled behavior

   c. the decision to perform the modeled response when we are able to do so

   d. whether we are reinforced for performing the modeled response

Answer Key

1. c   2. d   3. b   4. b   5. c   6. c   7. a   8. a   9. c   *10. b   11. a   12. c
13. d   *14. c   *15. a   16. d   17. b   18. a   19. b   *20. c   21. c   22. a   23. b   24. a
25. a   26. c   27. d   28. d   *29. a   30. b   31. c   32. d

Annotated Answers

10. The correct choice is **b**. This describes the procedure used to obtain extinction of a previously conditioned response.
    a. Pairing the CS with a second order stimulus (a bell with a light) would result in second order conditioning (or a CR to the light or bell).
    c. You could not withhold the UCR. If a UCS (food) is presented you will observe a UCR (salivation).
    d. Once a CR is conditioned, it should not extinguish with the passage of time.

14. The correct choice is **c**. An example of higher order conditioning is as follows: After a dog learns to salivate to the sound of a bell, you then present a light before sounding the bell. The light would become a CS (a higher order CS) for the original CS, the bell.
    a. This would result in the animal learning to give another CR to the original CS.
    b. Discrimination is not related to higher order conditioning.
    d. This would result in the extinction of the CR.

15. The correct choice is **a**. This measure quantifies the number of responses given in a specified amount of time, allowing a relative measurement of how strong a behavior is (stronger behaviors would result in higher rates of responding).
    b. There is no calculation from the Law of Effect. It merely states that a behavior that is followed by a satisfying consequence will be strengthened.
    c. This alternative relates to generalization and the term elicit implies Pavlovian conditioning.
    d. Generalization is relevant to operant conditioning as well as to Pavlovian conditioning, but it would be difficult to quantify as a measure of the strength of a behavior. For example, if the operant response is my dog sitting when I say "Sit," generalization would relate to both how frequently my dog sits when I say some other word or how frequently my dog sits when someone else says "Sit."

20. The correct choice is **c**. Because the salesman was reinforced on a variable schedule, he would continue to believe that he might make a sale at the next house and would persist in his behavior.
    a. If the salesman was reinforced on a continuous schedule, he would make a sale at every house.
    b. If the salesman was reinforced on a fixed schedule he, would make a sale after every specific number of houses (FR) or after every specific amount of time (FI).
    d. While gambling can be reinforced on a variable schedule, the term "gambler's schedule of reinforcement" does not exist.

29. The correct choice is **a**. The child learned a cognitive map of the relevant landmarks to the bowling alley on his first visit there.
    b. Even if you could justify the McDonald's as being a CS for the bowling alley, Pavlovian conditioning would not explain how the behavior was learned in one trial.
    c. Modeling is not appropriate for this question.
    d. This is similar to the logic involved for alternative **b**. A weak case could be made for the turn at McDonald's being reinforced. However, operant conditioning would not explain how the behavior was learned in one trial. Alternative **a** is clearly the best choice.

– PART VI. SUMMARY TABLES –

To test your understanding of the materials discussed in this chapter, complete the following tables. Check your answers with those supplied in Part IX.

COMPARISON OF POSITIVE REINFORCEMENT AND NEGATIVE REINFORCEMENT

| | Consequences of Behavior | | Probability of Response | Example |
	(Good/Bad)	What Occurs	(Increases/Decreases)	
Positive reinforcement				
Negative reinforcement				

SCHEDULES OF PARTIAL REINFORCEMENT

	Rate of Response (High/Low)	Pause After Reinforcement (Yes/No)	Length of Pause After Reinforcement (Brief/Extended)
Fixed ratio			
Variable ratio			
Fixed interval			
Variable interval			

COMPARISON OF PAVLOVIAN AND OPERANT CONDITIONING

	Which Two Elements are Associated?	Is Response Elicited or Emitted?	Does Subject Play an Active or Passive Role?	Is Presentation of UCS/Reinforcement Contingent on the Subject's Behavior?
Pavlovian conditioning				
Operant conditioning				

– PART VII. THOUGHT QUESTIONS/CRITICAL THINKING –

Prepare answers to the following discussion questions.

1. Based on the definition of learning presented in the text, is it appropriate to say a young baby learns to eat solid foods? Why or why not?

2. You want to teach your dog to fetch the remote control for your TV. Why should you first use continuous reinforcement and then switch to partial reinforcement?

3. How are Pavlovian and operant conditioning both involved in avoidance conditioning?

4. Extinction is commonly thought of as the unlearning or forgetting of a learned response. Which of the following statements concerning extinction is more appropriate? (a) All memory traces of the learned response are wiped out (or "out of sight, out of mind"). (b) Some learning remains (or "an elephant never forgets"). Explain your answer.

5. Think of one behavior that you would like someone you know to perform (for example, picking up his/her clothes, speaking English more grammatically, being on time). Based on the information discussed in this chapter, which approach would you use (Pavlovian conditioning, operant conditioning, punishment, cognitive learning) to "teach" that behavior? What specific steps would you use to accomplish your objective?

– PART VIII. APPLICATIONS –

1. The following situation (or one similar to it) is relatively common in homes with young children:

   It's 10 minutes before dinner and the child asks for a cookie. The mother says, "No, it will spoil your appetite." The child begins to plead, beg, scream, and cry for the cookie. Mom continues to say, "No, no, no," until the child wears her down and she says, "OK, but you'd better eat all your dinner." The child stops screaming and takes the cookie.

   In operant conditioning terms, what exactly is happening here?
   a. Is the child being reinforced? If so, in what manner?
   b. Is the mother being reinforced? If so, in what manner?
   c. What do you think will happen tomorrow 10 minutes before dinner?
   d. What should the mother do if she wants to eliminate this pre-dinner cookie-eating behavior?
   e. Why might B. F. Skinner say, "If you have the slightest doubt that you will give in and give the child the cookie, give it to the child when they first ask for it"?

2. Read each of the following descriptions of a behavior that you would like an individual to learn.
   a. A parent would like his/her child to say "please" and "thank you."
   b. You would like to teach your dog to "speak" on command.
   c. A parent would like his/her children to stop leaving their room a mess and start to make their bed each morning.
   d. You would like your dog to stop begging for food from the table while you are eating.
   e. You have just bought a telephone answering machine for your apartment. You want your roommate to learn how to operate it.

   What would be the most effective way to teach each behavior (Pavlovian conditioning, modeling, punishment, shaping, verbal instruction)? Explain how you would teach each behavior. Would another method also be effective in teaching the behavior? If your answer is yes, justify your original decision.

– PART IX. SUMMARY TABLES SOLUTIONS –

COMPARISON OF POSITIVE REINFORCEMENT AND NEGATIVE REINFORCEMENT

	Consequences of Behavior		Probability of Response	
	(Good/Bad)	What Occurs	(Increases/Decreases)	Example
Positive reinforcement	good	pleasant event starts	increaases	food
Negative reinforcement	bad	unpleasant event stops or is avoided	increases	terminates or avoids shock

SCHEDULES OF PARTIAL REINFORCEMENT

	Rate of Response (High/Low)	Pause After Reinforcement (Yes/No)	Length of Pause After Reinforcement (Brief/Extended)
Fixed ratio	high	yes	brief
Variable ratio	high	no	—
Fixed interval	low	yes	extended
Variable interval	low	no	—

COMPARISON OF PAVLOVIAN AND OPERANT CONDITIONING

	Which Two Elements are Associated?	Is Response Elicited or Emitted?	Does Subject Play an Active or Passive Role?	Is Presentation of UCS/Reinforcement Contingent on the Subject's Behavior?
Pavlovian conditioning	two stimuli (CS and UCS)	elicited	passive	not contingent
Operant conditioning	behavior and consequence	emitted	active	contigent

CHAPTER 7
MEMORY

– PART I. LEARNING OBJECTIVES –

When you finish studying this chapter, you should be able to do the following::

INFORMATION PROCESSING AND MEMORY

1. Define memory.

2. Describe the information-processing model of memory, including the three processes of encoding, storage, and retrieval.

A MODEL OF MEMORY

3. Explain the function of sensory memory.

4. Compare and contrast iconic and echoic memory.

5. Explain the function and capacity of short-term memory (STM), and explain the importance of rehearsal for STM.

6. Describe chunking, and explain how chunking increases the capacity of STM.

7. Describe how information is coded or represented in STM.

8. Describe the function and capacity of long-term memory (LTM), and identify two types of LTM.

9. Describe the dual-code model of how information is stored or represented in LTM.

10. Define mnemonic devices and describe six mnemonic devices that can be used to improve coding in LTM.

11. Explain how retrieval cues and association networks influence retrieval from LTM.

12. Describe three methods to measure long-term memory, and order the three methods from most sensitive to least sensitive.

13. Differentiate between and discuss explicit and implicit memories.

14. Describe how explicit memories might be investigated.

MEMORY AS A DYNAMIC PROCESS

15. Explain why memory is considered a constructive process, and describe how schemas are associated with memory being constructive.

16. Explain false memories and how they can be implanted.

17. Summarize the results of experiments on eyewitness testimony, and discuss why eyewitness reports may not be accurate.

18. Discuss how context, state-dependent memory, and extreme emotions influence memory.

FORGETTING

19. Describe the decay explanation of forgetting, and explain why this theory is nearly impossible to prove or disprove.

20. Describe the interference explanation of forgetting, and describe both retroactive and proactive interference.

21. Describe the serial position effect and explain why it occurs.

22. Explain forgetting from the retrieval failure perspective, and indicate two reasons why information may not be retrieved.

23. Describe the motivated forgetting explanation of forgetting, and relate it to Freud's concept of repression.

24. Define and describe three types of organic amnesia.

THE BIOLOGY OF MEMORY

25. Describe Hebb's conception of how STMs and LTMs are stored.

26. Discuss long-term potentiation, which involves how neurons change during the memory processes.

27. Describe how and where in the brain LTMs and STMs are stored and processed. What evedence supports your view?

IMPROVING ACADEMIC MEMORY

28. Describe a variety of strategies for improving academic memory.

– PART II. OVERVIEW –

According to the information-processing perspective, being able to remember a piece of information involves three processes: (1) the information has to be encoded or translated into a neural code or message that the nervous system can process, (2) the encoded information then has to be stored or retained by the nervous system; and (3) when one wishes to recall the information it must be retrieved from storage.

There are three different memory systems. First, sensory memory briefly holds an accurate "copy" of the sensory information to which people are exposed. Sensory memories are held only for a second or two. Information in sensory memory is only encoded at the level of the sensory systems. Next, short-term memory (STM), which is referred to as the working memory, is the bridge or transition for the flow of information from sensory memory to long-term memory and then back to awareness. STM can retain information for only about 20 seconds unless the information is actively rehearsed. The capacity of STM is limited to about seven pieces of information, but its capacity can be effectively increased through the process of chunking (or making each "piece" of information larger). Typically, STMs are encoded acoustically. Third, long-term memory (LTM) has an unlimited storage capacity and may retain information for extensive periods of time. Typically, information is stored in LTM in a verbal form. The efficiency of LTM is increased if information is stored in LTM in an organized or systematic manner that facilitates its retrieval at a later time.

Our memories may be explicit, readily available to our consciousness, or implicit, unavailable to conscious awareness. Psychologists have found ways to investigate implicit memories, and through PET imaging they have shown that implicit and explicit memory systems rely on different neural structures.

Because memory is a constructive process, LTMs may not be completely accurate accounts of the original event. We may omit or add information to "construct" a memory that seems more "correct" to us. The issue of false memories has become a matter of concern as reports of child abuse under hypnosis began to increase. In addition, we use schemas to try to make sense out of our world, but these schemas can lead to significant distortion in our memory processes. Studies of eyewitness testimony have confirmed that we reconstruct memories of events to fit our schemas. Finally, our memories are affected by our internal state—a concept known as state dependency. Extreme emotion can result in vivid, but not necessarily accurate, recall known as a flashbulb memory.

A number of explanations for why forgetting occurs have been proposed. Decay theory proposes that the memory trace fades with the passage of time. Decay theory is an appropriate explanation of forgetting from sensory memory and at times from STM. However, there is disagreement as to whether LTMs decay over time. The interference explanation states that information may not be recalled because of the presence of other information or memories that make it difficult to recall the intended information. Interference exists when either later learning affects recall of earlier information (retroactive) or earlier learning affects later learning (proactive). Information may also seemingly be forgotten from LTM when the information is merely inaccessible due to poor original encoding or the absence of sufficient retrieval cues. The motivated forgetting explanation states that some information may be forgotten or inaccessible to conscious awareness due to its unpleasant or threatening nature. Forgetting may also occur as a result of organic amnesia (physical illness, drugs and alcohol, or injuries that affect the brain).

STMs appear to be associated with activity within the nervous system, whereas the storage of LTMs is associated with physical changes in the nervous system. LTMs appear to be represented by large networks of neurons distributed over broad portions of the brain. From extensive study of individuals with specific types of brain damage and memory deficits, it has been shown that brain structures such as the hippocampus, amygdala, and thalamus are involved in the processing or transferring of memories between STM and LTM.

– PART III. KEY TERMS/MATCHING EXERCISES –

Match the following concepts with the appropriate descriptions. Check your answers against the Answer Key.

INFORMATION PROCESSING AND MEMORY
AND A MODEL OF MEMORY: THREE MEMORY SYSTEMS

Concepts	*Descriptions*
_____ 1. short-term memory (STM)	a. Process of perceiving a stimulus and establishing associations between the stimulus and other information
_____ 2. long-term memory (LTM)	b. Information is retained for no more than 20 seconds, unless it's rehearsed.
_____ 3. sensory memory	c. Visual sensory memory
_____ 4. chunking	d. Process of retaining information in the nervous system
_____ 5. storage	e. Holds visual information for 0.3 seconds and auditory information for 2 seconds
_____ 6. retrieval	f. Effective in increasing the capacity of STM
_____ 7. encode	g. Auditory sensory memory
_____ 8. echoic memory	h. Unlimited storage capacity (i.e., never fills up)
_____ 9. iconic memory	i. Process of recalling (or remembering) information

Answer Key
   1. b   2. h   3 e   4. f   5. d   6. i   7. a   8. g   9. c

A MODEL OF MEMORY: LONG-TERM MEMORY (LTM)

Concepts	Descriptions
_____ 1. dual-code model of memory)	a. Contains memories for how-to-perform skills
_____ 2. association networks	b. Contains memories for specific facts
_____ 3. serial position effect	c. Memories that are readily available to our consciousness
_____ 4. state-dependent memory	d. Involves associating items with a series of words that correspond to a sequence of numbers
_____ 5. mnemonic devices	e. Memory systems to improve meaningful organization of material
_____ 6. declarative memory	f. Consists of making up a sentence in which the first letter of each word is a cue for specific material
_____ 7. procedural memory	g. States that storage may be in either verbal or sensory codes
_____ 8. false memories	h. Memories that are unavailable to conscious awareness
_____ 9. schemas	i. Observation that items at the beginning and end of a list are more likely to be remembered than items in the middle
_____ 10. flashbulb memory	j. Relates to vivid memories for first learning about an emotional event
_____ 11. implicit memory	k. Involves organizing items to be remembered into a story
_____ 12. narrative story	l. Involves forming mental associations between items and locations along a familiar route
_____ 13. clustering	m. Memories of events that did not really occur
_____ 14. acronyms	n. Associated with the concept of spreading activation
_____ 15. peg-word system	o. Consists of a group of letters that are cues for specific material
_____ 16. explicit memory	p. Involves grouping items into categories
_____ 17. method of loci	q. Conceptual frameworks used to make the world seem more predictable
_____ 18. acrostics	r. Observation that one remembers information better when in a situation similar to that in which the information was first encode

Answer Key

1. g   2. n   3. i   4. r   5. e   6. b   7. a   8. m   9. q   10. j   11. h   12. k
13. p   14. o   15. d   16. c   17. l   18. f

FORGETTING

Concepts	Descriptions
_____ 1. proactive interference	a. May occur because information was poorly encoded or because of lack of appropriate cues
_____ 2. retroactive interference	b. Memory deficits resulting from some form of brain damage
_____ 3. retrograde amnesia	c. Proposes that the memory trace fades with the passage of time
_____ 4. anterograde amnesia	d. Memory loss in which old LTMs are accessible but new information cannot be retained
_____ 5. decay	e. Occurs when earlier learning disrupts memory for later learning
_____ 6. motivated forgetting	f. Related to Freud's concept of repression
_____ 7. retrieval failure	g. Occurs when a later event interferes with recall of earlier information
_____ 8. organic amnesia	h. Loss of memory of events that preceded an accident

THE BIOLOGY OF MEMORY

Concepts	*Descriptions*
_____ 1. distributed memory	a. A change in the strength of a synapse that is associated with memory processes
_____ 2. consolidation	b. Describes location where LTMs are stored
_____ 3. cell assembly	c. Hebb's conception of how STM is maintained
_____ 4. engram	d. Process in which LTMs are coded by physical changes in the nervous system
_____ 5. long-term potention	e. Lashley's term for the place where memories are stored

Answer Key

1. b 2. d 3. c 4. e 5. a

– PART IV. TRUE-FALSE STATEMENTS –

Fill in the blank before each statement with either a T (true) or an F (false). Check your answers against the Answer Key. Then go back to the items that are false and make the necessary change(s) to the statements to convert the items into true statements.

INFORMATION PROCESSING AND MEMORY

_____ 1. The first step in the processing of a memory is the storage of the information in the nervous system.

_____

_____

A MODEL OF MEMORY

_____ 2. Long-term memory is often referred to as our working memory.

_____

_____

_____ 3. Information in declarative memory is typically established more quickly but is more likely to be forgotten than information in procedural memory.

_____

_____

_____ 4. The peg-word mnemonic system involves pegging or hanging an item to be remembered onto a familiar location.

_____

MEMORY AS A DYNAMIC PROCESS

_____ 5. The observation that people tend to remember events and facts that are inaccurate is evidence for memory being a constructive process.

_____

_____

FORGETTING

_____ 6. The serial position effect describes the observation that beginning-list items are remembered better than middle-list items, which are remembered better than end-of-list items.

_____

_____

_____ 7. Interference, in which later learning makes it more difficult to recall previously learned information, is labeled "proactive interference."

_____

_____

_____ 8. It is a well-established fact that LTM traces decay or fade with the passage of time.

_____

_____

_____ 9. People suffering from anterograde amnesia are unable to adequately remember information received after the onset of their amnesia.

_____

_____

THE BIOLOGY OF MEMORY

_____ 10. Recently, substantial evidence has shown that STMs are stored or coded by structural or physical changes in the nervous system.

_____

_____

_____ 11. The mechanism underlying the Hebbian Rule is long-term potentiation.

_____

_____

_____ 12. Lashley's findings confirmed that memories reside in a specific area of the brain.

_____

_____

– PART V. MULTIPLE-CHOICE QUESTIONS –

Choose the best answer to each question. Circle your choice. Check your answers against the Answer Key. Questions marked with an asterisk (*) include annotated answers.

INFORMATION PROCESSING AND MEMORY

1. The three processes involved in memory are _____.
    a. encoding, rehearsal, and retrieval
    b. memorizing, reciting, and recalling
    c. encoding, storage, and retrieval
    d. recall, recognition, and relearning

2. Encoding involves translating incoming information into a neural code and _____.
    a. organizing the information in a meaningful way
    b. rehearsing the information
    c. retaining the information for a period of time
    d. sensation

3. The process of locating and recovering an item from one's "memory bank" is termed _____.
    a. mnemonic
    b. recall
    c. retrieval
    d. a "hit"

A MODEL OF MEMORY

4. Which memory system briefly holds a largely accurate reproduction of the original sensory input?
    a. sensory memory
    b. short-term memory
    c. medium-term memory
    d. long-term memory

5. Immediately after you are briefly exposed to 20 items in a visual display, what would you probably recall?
    a. all of the items that had been transferred to STM
    b. any of the items you were instructed to recall
    c. four of the items
    d. none of the items

6. Why do echoic memories last longer than iconic memories?
    a. Unlike light, energy sound waves produce echoes for us to refer to.
    b. We do not have a second chance to review auditory information, whereas it is usually possible to refer back to visual information.
    c. Visual information is continually being replaced but auditory information is not.
    d. It is easier to concentrate on visual information.

*7. The most effective way to keep information in STM is by _____.
   a. overlearning it
   b. using a mnemonic device
   c. rehearsing it over and over
   d. converting it into a visual image

8. The capacity of STM is about _____ pieces of information if the information has been encoded according to how it sounds.
   a. 3
   b. 7
   c. 15
   d. The capacity is unlimited.

9. Information is coded in STM most commonly in _____ form.
   a. acoustic
   b. semantic
   c. procedural
   d. visual

10. If you were asked to recall the letters Q, E, T, 10 seconds after viewing the letters, the error you would most likely make would be to recall _____ instead of _____.
   a. 0 / Q
   b. F / E
   c. C / T
   d. S / T

11. The memories you have of your first day of psychology class this semester are in your _____.
   a. chronological memory
   b. LTM
   c. sensory memory
   d. STM

12. Which statement is *true* of long-term memory?
   a. Old information is "displaced" by new information.
   b. It is limited to several hundred items.
   c. Information is stored by rote only.
   d. There is no evidence for any limit to the amount of information that can be stored in long-term memory.

13. Which of the following memory sets are both included in declarative memory?
   a. short term and long term
   b. semantic and procedural
   c. semantic and episodic
   d. procedural and episodic

14. The _____ memory contains general, nonpersonal knowledge concerning the meaning of facts and concepts.
   a. episodic
   b. semantic
   c. procedural
   d. iconic

*15. Eidetic imagery is most similar to the "typical" memory in _____ memory.
    a. iconic
    b. echoic
    c. short-term
    d. long-term

16. The mnemonic device for improving recall of information from LTM that involves a meaningful arrangement of letters (for example, Roy G. Biv) is _____.
    a. method of loci
    b. acronyms
    c. peg-word system
    d. clustering

*17. If it is necessary for you to remember a list of items in a specific order, which mnemonic device would probably be least appropriate to use?
    a. narrative story
    b. method of loci
    c. clustering
    d. peg-word

18. Simply repeating words without any attempt to find meaning in them is known as
    a. maintenance rehearsal
    b. elaborative rehearsal
    c. mnemonic strategy
    d. acrostics

19. The network of association interpretation of how information is retrieved from LTM states that we retrieve facts through the process of _____.
    a. association to higher concepts
    b. spreading activation
    c. serial position
    d. triggering nodes

20. A student who is not doing well in psychology class would most likely hope that the professor would use which of the following techniques to measure memory of the material?
    a. short answer
    b. recall
    c. relearning
    d. recognition

21. The technique Ebbinghaus used to study LTM was _____.
    a. recall
    b. recognition
    c. relearning
    d. overlearning

22. Memories that are not available to our conscious awareness are known as _____ memories.
    a. implicit
    b. false
    c. explicit
    d. iconic

SOME FACTORS THAT INFLUENCE WHAT WE REMEMBER

23. If you usually study after having a few beers, there is evidence that suggests you would probably do better if you also had a few beers before taking the exam. This phenomenon is called _____ memory.
    a. context
    b. state-dependent
    c. state-delayed
    d. dual-coded

24. What would you most likely have a flashbulb memory of?
    a. your third date with your current boyfriend/girlfriend
    b. your tenth birthday party
    c. last spring vacation
    d. events surrounding an attack or bomb threat at your school

25. Advertisers who suggest that consumers had certain pleasurable experiences as a child are trying to _____.
    a. elicit implicit memories
    b. alter our schemas
    c. elicit explicit memories
    d. plant false memories

26. What do people tend to do when they try to remember information that is not consistent with their schemas?
    a. distort facts to fit their schemas
    b. change their schemas to fit the facts
    c. exert more effort to organize their schemas
    d. focus on the inconsistencies

27. To which of the following questions would people most likely estimate the tallest response?
    a. What is the height of your psychology professor?
    b. How short is your psychology professor?
    c. How tall is your psychology professor?
    d. People would give the same response to each question.

FORGETTING

28. There is a difference of opinion among psychologists concerning whether long-term memories are forgotten because of _____.
    a. motivated forgetting
    b. decay
    c. retrieval failure
    d. interference

*29. You took two years of French in high school and then two years of German in college. What would account for the observation that you have more difficulty remembering French vocabulary words than German words?
    a. anterograde interference
    b. retrograde interference
    c. retroactive interference
    d. proactive interference

30. Which explanation of forgetting states that a "forgotten" memory is not really forgotten, but only inaccessible at the current time?
    a. anterograde amnesia
    b. decay
    c. interference
    d. retrieval failure

THE BIOLOGY OF MEMORY

31. The coding of LTM by physical changes in the nervous system is referred to as _____.
    a. encoding
    b. consolidation
    c. an engram
    d. cell assemblies

32. What would the brains of rats reared in enriched environments would show when compared to rats in a regular laboratory environment?
    a. more terminal buttons
    b. more dendritic spines and synapses
    c. fewer but larger synapses
    d. larger cerebrums

33. From the case of HM (discussed in the text), it seems likely that the hippocampus and amygdala are _____.
    a. where LTMs are stored
    b. only involved in the functioning of sensory memory
    c. involved in the transferring of information from STM to LTM
    d. involved in procedural memories

IMPROVING ACADEMIC MEMORY

34. What should you do when studying for an exam?
    a. Study two hours for every hour you spend in class.
    b. Continue to study after you have mastered the material.
    c. Study until you can accurately "recite before the fact."
    d. Study until you can accurately "recite after the fact."

35. What should do after you finish studying for an exam?
    a. Reward yourself with a study break.
    b. Relax by watching TV or visiting with friends.
    c. Read assignments for other classes.
    d. Go to sleep.

Answer Key

1. c	2. a	3. c	4. a	5. b	6. b	*7. c	8. b	9. a	10. c	11. b	12. d
13. c	14. b	*15. a	16. d	*17. c	18. a	19. b	20. d	21. c	22. a	23. b	24. d
25. d	26. a	27. c	28. b	*29. c	30. d	31. b	32. b	33. c	34. d	35. d	

7. The correct choice is **c**. Unless rehearsed, information fades from STM within about 20 seconds.
    a. Overlearning is a useful technique to increase retention of LTM.
    b. Mnemonic devices are techniques to improve encoding and storage of information in LTM.
    d. Encoding the information in visual form would not be helpful because the capacity of acoustically coded STMs is seven items and STM's capacity is only three items for visually coded information.

15. The correct choice is **a**. Both eidetic imagery and iconic memory consist of vivid (and accurate) visual memories. Although these two memories differ greatly in duration, they are qualitatively similar.
    b. Echoic memories are sensory memories for auditory information.
    c. STMs typically are acoustically coded and last only about 20 seconds, whereas eidetic imagery is visual and the image lasts for several minutes.
    d. Eidetic imagery is a form of coding in LTM, but it is not the typical way LTM would be encoded by the majority of people.

17. The correct choice is **c**. Clustering involves grouping the items to be remembered into appropriate categories. In a typical example, the categories formed might not be consistent with the order in which the items need to be recalled.
    a. Narrative story would be an appropriate device as long as the items to be remembered are incorporated into the narrative story in the proper sequence.
    b. Method of loci would be appropriate if the items to be remembered are "placed" in locations along the path in the proper sequence.
    d. The peg-word system could well be the best method (of those listed) to remember the items in a specific order. This mnemonic device pegs items to words that have previously been associated with or linked to numbers.

29. The correct choice is **c**. Retroactive interference occurs when later learning (i.e., German) interferes with the recall of earlier learned information (i.e., French).
    a. Anterograde refers to a type of amnesia and not a type of interference.
    b. Retrograde refers to a type of amnesia and not a type of interference.
    d. Proactive interference would account for this situation if it was reversed, with you showing more difficulty in remembering German words than French words. Proactive interference occurs when earlier learning interferes with the memory of later learning.

– PART VI. SUMMARY TABLE –

To test your understanding of the material discussed in this chapter, complete the following table. Check your answers with those supplied in Part IX.

A MODEL OF MEMORY

Memory	Amount Stored	Duration	How Stored	How Forgotten
Sensory memory				
Short-term memory				
Long-term memory				

– PART VII. THOUGHT QUESTIONS/CRITICAL THIN KING –

Prepare answers to the following discussion questions.

1. Imagine that one week ago you moved into a new apartment and got a new phone number. If someone asks for your phone number you will probably have a hard time remembering it. Six months from now, on the other hand, you might have difficulty remembering your old phone number. Name and describe in detail the processes responsible for your failure to recall both the old and new phone numbers.

2. Eidetic imagery (or photographic memory) is more common in children than in adults. Many individuals who have eidetic imagery in childhood lose the ability as they grow older. The text states that the greater prevalence of eidetic imagery in childhood "may reflect the fact that children's memory storehouses are less cluttered with extraneous facts, thus allowing for clearer, less encumbered images." Referring to the dual-code model of memory, propose an alternative explanation for the frequency of eidetic imagery declining with age. (Hint: If children have an advantage in sensory coding, do adults have an advantage in the use of verbal coding?)

3. Explain the relationship between retrograde amnesia and consolidation.

4. In Chapter 6 the phenomenon of spontaneous recovery was described to illustrate that following extinction, all memory of a previously learned conditioned response is not eliminated. Could any of the techniques described in this chapter concerning the testing of long-term memory be useful in the Pavlovian conditioning procedure? If yes, which technique? Describe how this technique would be utilized to measure how much original learning is retained after extinction.

5. Discuss how police interviews of eyewitnesses to a crime should be structured and when they should take place in order to minimize the possibility that witnesses would recall inaccurate information.

– PART VIII. APPLICATIONS –

1. Take a few minutes to make each of the following lists. Write down in order:
   a. All the phone numbers you have had in your life
   b. The names of all your teachers from first grade through high school (When you get to the grade in which you first started changing classes and having a number of different teachers, you can either list just the homeroom teacher or all your teachers.)
   c. The names of all the presidents of the United States (Hint: Bill Clinton is the 42nd president.) Serial position effect curves (see Figure 7.15 in the text) are compiled from the results of a large number of people. Keeping in mind that the lists you wrote were from only one person, do you see evidence to support the serial position effect?

2. Take two minutes to write down the names of as many states as you can remember. Start now, before you read further.
   a. You were not given any specific instructions or strategy to help you with this recall task. There are a variety of strategies to use to approach this task (recall the states alphabetically, or geographically). The geographical strategy could take a number of approaches: start with the east coast (similar to clustering), west coast, the state you are in, the states you have lived in, tracing the states you used to drive through during family vacations (similar to the method of loci). Examine the order in which you listed the states. Did you use a strategy (or a succession of strategies)?
   b. You probably did not list all 50 states within the two-minute time limit. Obtain a map of the United States and look at it to see if you omitted groups or geographic clusters of states, or isolated states. Is there a simple explanation for why you failed to remember certain states? For example, if you've spent your whole life on the east coast, it would make sense that with a limited time frame you would recall more eastern states than western states.
   c. If your friends at college come from different states, ask a few of them to do the same task—but remember to give them the same instructions you were given: "Take two minutes to write down the names of as many states as you can remember." Examine your friends' lists to see if people from different parts of the country approach this task from different perspectives.

– PART IX. SUMMARY TABLE SOLUTION –

A MODEL OF MEMORY

Memory	Amount Stored	Duration	How Stored	How Forgotten
Sensory memory	All sensory messages being received at any time	0.3 sec. (visual) 2 sec. (auditory)	Accurate reproduction of sensory input	Decay
Short-term memory	Approximately 7 items if acoustically coded Approximately 3 items if visually or semantically coded	Up to 20 seconds longer if actively rehearsed	Usually acoustically (by sound)	Forget if not coded or rehearsed Decay, interference
Long-term memory	Unlimited	Up to a lifetime	Typically verbally	Interference, retrieval failure, motivated forgetting, and possibly decay

CHAPTER 8
MOTIVATION

– PART I. LEARNING OBJECTIVES –

When you finish studying this chapter, you should be able to do the following:

THE NATURE OF MOTIVATION

1. Define motivation and discuss the general features of motivated behavior.

MOTIVATIONAL EXPLANATIONS OF BEHAVIOR

2. Describe the instinct theory, and explain its basic flaw.

3. Describe the drive-reduction theory, and discuss three problems this theory has in attempting to explain motivation.

4. Describe how cognitive expectancies may influence motivated behavior.

5. Define and discuss the need for achievement (nACH).

6. Describe how the way children are raised may influence their nACH.

7. Define cognitive dissonance, and discuss how cognitive dissonance motivates behavior.

8. Describe the role of the stomach with regard to feelings of hunger and satiety.

9. Discuss the hypothalamic control theory of hunger, and identify the two hypothalamic areas associated with hunger and satiety.

10. Discuss the glucostatic theory of hunger.

11. Define obesity, and discuss four factors that are believed to be associated with obesity.

12. Discuss why it is difficult to lose weight and "keep it off" through dieting.

13. Describe two serious eating disorders (anorexia nervosa and bulimia), and describe the "typical" person who suffers from each disorder.

SENSATION-SEEKING MOTIVATION

14. Define arousal, and discuss the Yerkes-Dodson law concerning optimum levels of arousal for performing different types of tasks.

SEXUAL MOTIVATION AND BEHAVIOR

15. Describe the influence of hormones on male sexual motivation, and discuss research that links androgens with sexual activity.

16. Discuss research findings concerning the influence of hormones on female sexual motivation.

17. Describe the influence of psychosocial factors on human sexual motivation, and summarize cross-cultural evidence concerning the effect of cultural mores on sexual expression.

18. Define homosexuality, and describe the incidence of, and attitudes toward, homosexuality.

19. Summarize the psychosocial and biological theories concerning the development of homosexuality.

– PART II. OVERVIEW –

Motivation is defined as any condition that tends to energize and direct behavior. A number of theories have been proposed to explain motivation. The instinct theory postulated that motivated behaviors were under the control of innate behavior patterns or instincts. The instinct theory was largely unsuccessful in explaining behavior. The drive-reduction theory proposes that we are motivated into action in order to reduce unpleasant internal conditions associated with needs. Drive-reduction theory can fairly well account for some motivated behaviors related to biological needs, but has difficulty in explaining other examples of motivated behavior. The cognitive perspective of motivation emphasizes the role of mental processes, such as cognitive expectancies, in directing behavior. The cognitive expectancy is that a specific behavior will lead to a specific goal or outcome and this expectancy motivates our behavior. The need for achievement (nACH) varies from person to person. Individuals with different levels of nACH approach tasks in different ways. Additionally, cognitive dissonance theory states that individuals are motivated to minimize inconsistencies between their attitudes and behavior.

Although hunger is a very basic motive, the control of eating behavior is very complex and not entirely understood. The stomach, hypothalamus, liver, and duodenum are all involved in the control of eating. The control of eating involves the bodily monitoring of the level of sugar in the blood (glucostatic theory). A number of theories of obesity and problems associated with dieting to control weight are discussed.

The concept of arousal is introduced to explain sensation-seeking motives. There is an optimum level of arousal (which may vary from time to time and/or task to task) that results in most efficient performance.

Sexual motivation and behavior is discussed in detail. There is well-documented evidence indicating the role of hormones on male sexual interest and activity. The relationship of hormones and female sexual expression is still unclear. While biological factors exert an influence on human sexual expression, psychological and cultural conditions play a larger role in human behavior. Two types of theories related to the development of homosexuality (psychosocial and biological) are described, and it is concluded that there is no simple, universal explanation of homosexuality. Sexual orientation (heterosexual, homosexual, or bisexual) is influenced by a variety of psychosocial and biological factors unique to each individual.

– PART III. KEY TERMS/MATCHING EXERCISES –

Match the following concepts with the appropriate descriptions. Check your answers against the Answer Key.

MOTIVATIONAL EXPLANATIONS OF BEHAVIOR

Concepts	*Descriptions*
_____ 1. motivation	a. Motivation theory that is flawed because it does not explain behavior but simply relabels it
_____ 2. drive	b. Any condition that energizes and directs an organism's actions
_____ 3. incentive	c. Propose(s) that expectations are important motivators
_____ 4. instincts	d. Propose(s) that organisms engage in behavior to reduce aversive conditions
_____ 5. cognitive perspective	e. Varies in different individuals, and can be tested using TAT
_____ 6. drive reduction theory	f. External stimuli that can energize and direct behavior even when no internal drive state exists
_____ 7. instinct theory	g. Proposes that individuals behave in a manner to minimize inconsistencies in their beliefs, attitudes, opinions, and behavior
_____ 8. cognitive dissonance theory	h. Unpleasant internal conditions that motivate an organism to engage in behaviors that reduce this unpleasant state
_____ 9. need for achievement (nACH)	i. Innate patterns of behavior that occur under a certain set of conditions

Answer Key

1. b   2. h   3. f   4. i   5. c   6. d   7. a   8. g   9. e

BIOLOGICAL BASES OF MOTIVATION

Concepts	*Descriptions*
_____ 1. set point	a. Suggests that hunger is triggered when glucose is not available for use by cells
_____ 2. obese	b. Physiologically preferred level of body weight for an individual
_____ 3. glucostatic theory	c. Characterized by episodes of binge- and purge-eating behavior
_____ 4. lateral hypothalamus (LH)	d. "Satiety center"
_____ 5. anorexia nervosa	e. Suggests that eating behavior is controlled by the electrical activity of the satiety and feeding centers
_____ 6. ventromedial hypothalamus (VMH)	f. Characterized by a prolonged refusal to eat adequate amounts of food
_____ 7. hypothalamic control theory	g. Describes an individual weighing at least 20 percent more than their desirable weight
_____ 8. bulimia	h. "Feeding center"

Answer Key

1. b   2. g   3. a   4. h   5. f   6. d   7. e   8. c

SEXUAL MOTIVATION BEHAVIOR

Concepts	Descriptions
_____ 1. estrogens	a. Refers to the sex to which an individual is attracted
_____ 2. homosexual	b. Role of these in sexual motivation is far from clear.
_____ 3. androgens	c. Produced by the testes and adrenal glands
_____ 4. sexual orientation	d. Individual whose primary erotic, psychological, and social interest is in a member of the same sex

Answer Key
   1. b   2. d   3. c   4. a

– PART IV. TRUE-FALSE STATEMENTS –

Fill in the blank before each statement with either a T (true) or an F (false). Check your answers against the Answer Key. Then go back to the items that are false and make the necessary change(s) to the statements to convert the items into true statements.

DEFINING MOTIVATION

_____   1. The concept of motivation incorporates both physiological factors and cognitive conditions that influence behavior.

_____

_____

MOTIVATIONAL EXPLANATIONS OF BEHAVIOR

_____   2. Drive-reduction theory proposes that we engage in activities to obtain incentives.

_____

_____

_____   3. The idea that your likelihood of being motivated to take an advanced course in math is determined in part by your success with difficult math courses in the past is known as cognitive advantage.

_____

_____

_____   4. The Cannon-Washburn hypothesis that the hunger motive is caused by stomach contractions has been well supported by a variety of research methods.

_____

_____

_____   5. Research suggests that both the liver and duodenum contain glucoreceptors.

_____

_____

_____ 6. Once established, an organism's set point does not change.

_____

_____

_____ 7. Obese individuals have the same number of fat cells as normal-weight individuals, but these obese individuals' fat cells are 50–100 percent larger.

_____

_____

SENSATION-SEEKING MOTIVATION

_____ 8. Sensation-seeking motivations are based on our strong inclination to explore and manipulate the environment as soon as we are able.

_____

_____

_____ 9. The Yerkes-Dodson law states that, for most tasks, as arousal increases to moderate levels so does performance.

_____

_____

SEXUAL MOTIVATION AND BEHAVIOR

_____ 10. There is evidence to link androgens with sexual activity and motivation in both males and females.

_____

_____

_____ 11. Almost all human societies view homosexuality negatively.

_____

_____

Answer Key
1. T   2. F   3. F   4. F   5. T   6. F   7. T   8. F   9. F   10. T   11. F

– PART V. MULTIPLE-CHOICE QUESTIONS –

Choose the best answer to each question. Circle your choice. Check your answers against the Answer Key. Questions marked with an asterisk (*) include annotated answers.

DEFINING MOTIVATION

1. Which of the following is *not* an effect motivation has on our actions?
   a. It directs or defines the direction of the resulting behavior.
   b. It has an impact on how vigorous or intense a behavior is.
   c. It controls instinctive behaviors.
   d. It energizes or activates one to behave in a certain way.

MOTIVATIONAL EXPLANATIONS OF BEHAVIOR

2. The instinct theory of motivation _____.
   a. explains the observation that there appears to be more than one optimal level of arousal
   b. shows the influence of Darwin's theory of evolution
   c. shows the influence of behaviorism
   d. explains the observation that organisms learn to perform specific behaviors

*3. Which of the following behaviors can be most easily explained by the drive-reduction theory of motivation?
   a. Some people like to climb mountains and ride roller-coasters.
   b. A mother animal takes care of her babies.
   c. Hungry rats in a Skinner box will press a bar in order to get food.
   d. Hungry rats in a Skinner box will press a bar in order to get saccharin.

4. An external stimulus that can motivate behavior even when no internal drive state exists is a(n) _____.
   a. instinct
   b. need
   c. motive
   d. incentive

5. Which of the following statements is *not* true about need for achievement (nACH)?
   a. People with a high level tend to be optimistic about chances of success.
   b. It can be measured using TAT.
   c. Studies have found that people with high levels of nACH tend to have stronger egos.
   d. Levels of nACH vary from individual to individual.

6. According to cognitive dissonance theory, which individual would most likely undergo a change in attitude concerning the death penalty (to which they were originally opposed)? An advertising/public relations expert who wrote what?
   a. wrote a brief anti-death penalty piece as a favor to a friend
   b. wrote a brief anti-death penalty piece for a client and was paid to do so
   c. wrote a brief pro-death penalty piece as a favor to a friend
   d. wrote a brief pro-death penalty piece for a client and was paid to do so

7. There is evidence that the stomach contains
   a. caloric receptors
   b. glucoreceptors
   c. liporeceptors
   d. pressure detectors

8. If, after brain damage in an auto accident, a person gained 100 pounds in two months, you would suspect damage to the _____.
   a. ventromedial hypothalamus
   b. dorsal hypothalamus
   c. lateral hypothalamus
   d. thyroid gland

9. A potent hormone that stimulates hunger and eating is _____.
   a. leptin
   b. neuropeptide Y
   c. cholecystokinin
   d. pancreatic hormone

10. The _____ theory states that hunger results when special receptors detect a lack of availability of blood sugar.
    a. homeostatic
    b. lipostatic
    c. hypogonadic
    d. glucostatic

*11. Which one of the following does *not* stimulate hunger and eating behavior?
    a. increased levels of the hormone neuropeptide Y
    b. reduced blood-sugar levels
    c. increased levels of glycerol in the bloodstream
    d. stimulation of the lateral hypothalamus

12. Which of the following statements is true?
    a. Not all obese people eat more than people of average weight.
    b. Average-weight people have more, but smaller, fat cells than obese individuals.
    c. Obese people have lower set points than average-weight people.
    d. Obese children are no more likely than average-weight children to have weight problems as adults.

13. Following dramatic weight loss as a result of a very low calorie diet (a starvation diet), why do people frequently regain much of the "lost" weight?
    a. They "fall off the wagon" and engage in binge eating.
    b. Their bodies need to restock stored fat.
    c. Their resting metabolic rate had increased during the diet and following the diet it is reduced.
    d. Their resting metabolic rate was reduced during the diet and stays at the lower level following the diet.

14. _____ is characterized by a refusal to eat adequate amounts of food. _____ is associated with episodes of binge-eating followed by purging.
    a. anorexia nervosa / bulimia
    b. bulimia / anorexia nervosa
    c. starvation diets / apnea
    d. bulimia / obesity

SENSATION-SEEKING MOTIVATION

15. If you could operantly condition a rat to turn on a TV set in order to watch Mickey Mouse cartoons, it would illustrate that rats have _____ motives.
    a. love and belongingness
    b. acquired drive
    c. sensation-seeking
    d. biologically based

*16. According to the Yerkes-Dodson law, when should a college basketball player complete a higher percentage of free throws?
    a. in a regular season conference game
    b. in a team scrimmage
    c. when practicing alone.
    d. He should make the same percentage of free throws in all situations.

SEXUAL MOTIVATION AND BEHAVIOR

*17. Which of the following statements is true?
   a. Androgen-blocking drugs such as Depo Provera may be effective in reducing sexual interest and activity in human males.
   b. Following castration (removal of the testes), human males always report a dramatic decrease in sexual desire and behavior.
   c. Estrogens play a significant role in the sexual interest and activity of human females.
   d. There is no systematic relationship between blood-androgen levels and strength of sexual motivation in young men.

18. What is, perhaps, the strongest evidence for the importance of psychosocial factors in human sexual motivation and expression?
   a. People engage in sexual behaviors that are not related to procreation.
   b. Following menopause, most women do not experience a change in their level of sexual arousal.
   c. The cultural mores of most societies do not regulate sexuality.
   d. The only species to have highly localized patterns of sexual behavior is man.

19. Which society most actively encourages (encouraged) sexual activity?
   a. Colonial American
   b. Mangia (in the Polynesian Islands)
   c. Dani (of New Guinea)
   d. Inis Beag (on an Irish island)

20. Jane's attraction to other women is referred to as _____.
   a. heterosexuality
   b. her sexual orientation
   c. fantasy
   d. erotic attraction

21. According to the text's definition of homosexuality, which of the following is true?
   a. Only men can be homosexual; women with a "homosexual orientation" are lesbians.
   b. Homosexuals have a gender identity disorder.
   c. A homosexual cannot engage in heterosexual activities.
   d. It is not necessary to overtly express homosexual behavior to be a homosexual.

22. Which of the following statements is true?
   a. Most homosexuals report that when they were young they were seduced by older homosexuals.
   b. Homosexual and heterosexual people had dated (heterosexually) about equally in high school.
   c. Most research studies, which have examined androgen levels in heterosexual and homosexual males, have found homosexuals to have lower androgen levels.
   d. An overly seductive mother is associated with the development of homosexuality in male children.

Answer Key
   1. c   2. b   3. d   4. c   5. c   6. c   7. d   8. a   9. b   10. d   *11. c   12. a
   13. d   14. a   15. c   *16. a   *17. a   18. d   19. b   20. b   21. d   22. b

3. The correct choice is **c**. Drive-reduction theory is best suited for primary drives that are induced by internal biological needs. Hunger is an unpleasant state of tension that is reduced by eating. A hungry rat would bar-press in order to receive food.

    a. Drive-reduction theory would have difficulty explaining mountain climbing and roller-coaster riding because it seems unreasonable to postulate a need or drive associated with those behaviors. Those behaviors would best be explained by the arousal theory.

    b. The first theory to come to mind to explain maternal behavior would be instinct theory (which, as you have learned, would not provide a very insightful explanation). Although an argument could be made for maternal behavior reducing a drive associated with the hormonal state of the mother, alternative **c** is a better choice.

    d. Because saccharin, unlike food, does not satisfy hunger (or any other biological need), the drive-reduction theory has difficulty in explaining this behavior.

11. The correct choice is **c**. Increased levels of glycerol have the effect of reducing consumption of food.

    a. Studies show that injections of neuropeptide Y in animals results in voracious eating.

    b. According to the glucostatic theory, reduced levels of blood-sugar (detected by glucoreceptors) stimulate the feeding center of the lateral hypothalamus.

    d. Stimulation of the lateral hypothalamus (the feeding center) causes feeding behavior to occur.

16. The correct choice is **a**. We will assume that making free throws is a relatively easy task for a college basketball player, therefore the correct choice is **a**. A regular-season basketball game would result in the player experiencing a higher level of arousal than in the other situations described. Because the Yerkes-Dodson law states that performance is better for simple tasks with a relatively high level of arousal, performance should be better in this situation.

    b. The situations in **b** would result in lower levels of arousal and performance should be reduced.

    c. The situation in **c** would result in lower levels of arousal and performance should be reduced.

    d. The Yerkes-Dodson law states that the situation strongly affects performance; therefore this choice is incorrect.

17. The correct choice is **a**. While not guaranteed, a number of studies have shown that androgen-blocking drugs may be effective in reducing sexual interest and activity.

    b. Castration often significantly reduces sexual interest and activity, but it does not always do so. This indicates that sexual behavior is not entirely under the control of hormones.

    c. Studies with postmenopausal women, examining the effect of estrogens on female sexual interest and activity, have contradictory findings. Some studies suggest that estrogen increases sexual interest and activity while other studies do not indicate such a result.

    d. Research has shown a strong positive correlation between blood-androgen levels and strength of sexual motivation, as reflected by frequency of orgasm in young men.

– PART VI. SUMMARY TABLES –

To test your understanding of the material discussed in the chapter, complete the following tables. Check your answers with those supplied in Part IX.

THEORIES OF HUNGER, EATING, AND WEIGHT MAINTENANCE

Theory	Description	Supporting Evidence	Weaknesses
The stomach			
Hypothalamic control			
Glucostatic			

THEORIES OF MOTIVATION AND AROUSAL

Theory	Individual	Description	Strengths	Weaknesses
Instinct				
Drive reduction				
Arousal				

– PART VII. THOUGHT QUESTIONS/CRITICAL THINKING –

Prepare answers to the following discussion questions.

1. Which theory of motivation (instinct, drive-reduction, cognitive perspective) and/or arousal would best explain why a male rat in a Skinner box would bar-press in each of the following situations?
   a. To turn off an electric shock
   b. To turn on a colorful slide show
   c. To turn off a colorful slide show
   d. To get access to a sexually receptive female rat
   e. To get access to food
   f. To get access to a rat "playground"
   g. To receive intracranial self-stimulation (described in Chapter 3)
   h. To get access to saccharin

   Explain your choices.

– PART VIII. APPLICATIONS –

1. Hunger is a biological motive. However, at least for humans, eating behavior can be considered a multifactor motive partially controlled by biological, psychological, and cultural factors. We eat at specific times for a variety of reasons: we're hungry, it's mealtime, our friends invite us out for pizza, and perhaps at times when we're bored. Our choice of food is not always tied solely to our biological state of hunger. sometimes we eat a standard American meat-and-potatoes meal, at other times we might prefer a spicy Mexican or Chinese meal, or we might just want a candy bar.

   Keep a food diary for one week, recording everything you eat. Record the time you eat, what you eat, what if anything you did while eating, whether or not you felt hungry before you ate, and whether or not you felt hungry when you stopped eating. Also, record the physical activities you had each day. At the conclusion of the week, examine your food diary and try to explain your eating behavior by referring to the theories of motivation discussed in this chapter. Next, examine your food diary to determine how the different hypotheses concerning the mechanisms that control eating and weight maintenance explain your eating behavior. For example, did you typically wait until you experienced stomach pangs before stopping your activities in order to eat? Did you experience symptoms of low blood-sugar (irritable, fatigued, anxious) before stopping to eat?

2. The text described the sexual behavior and customs of three societies (Mangaian, Inis Beag, and Dani) from an anthropological perspective. The three societies widely differed in their sexual expression. Because our American society consists of a number of varied subcultures, it would be difficult to conduct a definitive study concerning the sexual behaviors and customs that would apply to all subgroups and regions of the United States. Your knowledge of the sexual behavior and attitudes of Americans is limited primarily to your personal experience and environment (family, community, and information from the media). Imagine that you are an anthropologist studying the patterns of sexual expression in the community in which you were raised. Describe the sexual behaviors and customs of the culture. Compare and contrast your culture to those described in the text. Which society described is most similar to the culture in which you were raised? Which society is most different?

– PART IX. SUMMARY TABLES SOLUTIONS –

THEORIES OF HUNGER, EATING, AND WEIGHT MAINTENANCE

Theory	Description	Supporting Evidence	Weaknesses
The stomach	Proposed by Cannon and Washburn: the stomach plays a major role in triggering hunger	Relationship between stomach contractions and reports of hunger Also, stomach apparently contains pressure detectors that signal satiety.	People without stomachs experience normal hunger. If nerves from stomach to brain are severed, hunger is still experienced
Hypothalamic control	The combined actions of the ventromedial hypothalamus (VMH) or satiety center and lateral hypothalamus (LH) or feeding center control feeding behavior	Stimulation of LH and/or destruction of VMH encourages feeding. Stimulation of VMH and/or destruction of LH discourages feeding.	Needs to explain what turns VMH and LH on and off
Glucostatic	Proposed by Mayer and Russek Glucoreceptors monitor availability of glucose in bloodstream. When unavailable, triggers hunger and eating by influencing hypothalamus	Liver and duodenum apparently contain glucoreceptors.	Needs to be combined with dual hypothalamic control therapy

THEORIES OF MOTIVATION AND AROUSAL

Theory	Individual	Description	Strengths	Weaknesses
Instinct	William James	Influenced by Darwin's theory of evolution Proposed that instincts (innate patterns of behavior that occur under certain conditions) control behavior	Today, see only remnants of theory with the study of inborn or genetic influences on behavior	Contains basic flaw of merely supply-ing another name to a behavior and not explaining it (e.g., maternal behavior accounted for by maternal instinct)
Drive reduction	Clark Hull	Influenced by behaviorism Motivated behavior results in the re-duction of an aversive condition associated with a need (e.g., food reduces hunger).	Explains primary drives (related to internal biological needs) more effectively than secondary or acquired drives	Doesn't explain why many events influence behavior that are not associated with a drive, and not all behaviors decrease after they occur as would be expected if the behavior reduced a drive
Arousal	Hebb	A minimal level of arousal (a mental and physical state) is necessary in order to engage in goal-directed or motivated behavior. An optimum level of arousal results in most efficient performance.	Yerkes-Dodson law describing relation-ship between arousal and performance is generally supported. Subsequently, has been proposed that two optimal levels of arousal can explain why we sometimes seek and other times avoid sensation	More related to sensation-seeking motives as opposed to biological motives

CHAPTER 9
EMOTION AND STRESS

– PART I. LEARNING OBJECTIVES –

When you finish studying this chapter, you should be able to do the following:

THE COMPONENTS OF EMOTIONS

1. Define emotion, and describe its four components.

THE RANGE OF HUMAN EMOTIONS

2. Describe Plutchik's conceptualization of the range of emotions (the emotion wheel).

THEORIES OF EMOTION

3. Describe and evaluate the James-Lange theory of emotion.

4. Describe and evaluate the Cannon-Bard theory of emotion.

5. Describe and evaluate the Schachter-Singer theory of emotions.

6. Describe Solomon and Corbit's opponent-process theory of emotion, and discuss what the theory proposes happens with repeated exposure to an intense emotion-arousing stimulus.

7. Define stress and describe its physiological and psychological components.

8. Discuss Selye's general adaptation syndrome (GAS) regarding the body's physiological response to stress, and describe its three phases.

9. Discuss emotional responses to stress.

10. Discuss behavioral responses to stress, and describe three types of behavioral responses to stress.

11. Define stressor and discuss three factors that contribute to an event or situation being perceived as stressful.

12. Describe and evaluate the Social Readjustment Rating Scale (SRRS).

13. Discuss the relationship between stress and coronary heart disease (CHD), and describe Type A and Type B personalities.

14. Discuss the relationship between stress and hypertension (high blood pressure).

15. Discuss the relationship between stress and cancer.

16. Discuss the research related to a possible cancer-prone personality.

17. Discuss the relationship between stress and the functioning of the immune system.

– PART II. OVERVIEW –

Emotions are closely connected with motivation. Emotion refers to a pattern of physiological activity that is preceived as subjective feelings and moods. The major components of emotion include cognitive processes, physiological arousal, and behavioral processes. A number of conflicting theories for explaining emotion have been proposed. The James-Lange theory states that in an emotion-arousing situation, one first experiences physiological and muscular responses; only after these occur is an emotion experienced. Recent studies are providing new evidence for this theory. The Cannon-Bard theory states that emotional experiences and physiological changes occur simultaneously. The Schachter-Singer theory proposes that although physiological changes occur first, the key to what emotion is experienced involves how people cognitively assesses both their physical response and the situation. Finally, Solomon and Corbit's opponent-process theory proposes that emotions exist in pairs. When one emotion is strongly aroused, eventually the opponent (or opposite) emotion will be activated to restore emotional equilibrium.

Stress is often a by-product of disruptive, unpleasant situations. A number of factors that are related to a situation being perceived as stressful are lack of control, suddenness, and ambiguity. Selye's general adaptation syndrome (GAS) describes the physiological response to stress as consisting of three phases. Initially the alarm phase occurs, and the sympathetic nervous system is activated to confront the stress. If the stress continues, in the second phase (resistance) the parasympathetic nervous system is activated to limit the body's energy expenditures while continuing to deal with the stress. If the stress continues, the exhaustion phase is eventually reached, in which the body shows wear and tear and the individual becomes more susceptible to illness. In addition to physiological responses, there are also distinct psychological responses to stress. Cognitive responses include reduced concentration, impaired performance on cognitive tasks, and disruptive thoughts. Emotional responses include anxiety, anger, and depression. Behavioral responses include confronting (fight), avoiding (flight), or adapting to the situation.

Stress is a factor in many illnesses. Certain personality characteristics are related to the tendency to develop specific illnesses. Individuals who show Type A behaviors (ambitious, competitive, easily angered) are prone to develop coronary heart disease (CHD). Type A individuals and people who suppress anger are prone to develop high blood pressure. Some evidence exists linking stress and personality characteristics to cancer. The proposed cancer-prone personality is an individual who is inhibited, conforming, inclined to depression, and tends to suppress his or her emotions. Because increased levels of stress tend to decrease the functioning of the immune system, individuals who are under stress are more likely to contract a variety of infectious illnesses and possibly cancer.

– PART III. KEY TERMS/ MATCHING EXERCISES –

Match the following concepts with the appropriate descriptions. Check your answers against the Answer Key.

EMOTION

Concepts	Descriptions
_____ 1. Canon-Bard theory	a. Proposes that cognitive processes of interpreting both the emotion-causing event and bodily changes are central to the emotion experienced
_____ 2. Plutchik's emotion wheel	b. Describes primary human emotions as consisting of four pairs of opposites (e.g., sadness and joy)
_____ 3. Schachter-Singer theory	c. Proposes that following an emotional response the opposite emotional response occurs to restore emotional equilibrium
_____ 4. emotion	d. Proposes that bodily changes and behavioral reactions precede emotions
_____ 5. James-Lange theory	e. Subjective feelings and moods that often motivate actions
_____ 6. Solomon and Corbit's opponent-process theory	f. Proposes that bodily changes, behavioral responses, and emotions occur simultaneously

STRESS

Concepts	Descriptions
_____ 1. cancer-prone personality	a. Process of appraising events (as harmful, threatening, or challenging), of assessing potential responses, and of responding to those events
_____ 2. stressors	b. Describes inhibited, compliant, conforming individuals who tend to suppress their emotions
_____ 3. general adaptation syndrome (GAS)	c. Situations or events that produce stress
_____ 4. stress	d. Describes ambitious, demanding, and easily angered individuals who are prone to heart disease
_____ 5. exhaustion	e. Second phase of the body's reaction to a stressful event that involves activation of the parasympathetic nervous system
_____ 6. Type A personality	f. Physiological response to stress originally proposed by Selye
_____ 7. resistance	g. Describes relaxed, easy-going individuals who are not easily angered
_____ 8. Type B personality	h. Third phase of the body's reaction to a stressful event that results in increased susceptibility to disease
_____ 9. alarm	i. Body's initial reaction to a stressful event that involves activation of the sympathetic nervous system
_____ 10. Social Readjustment Rating Scale (SRRS)	j. Assesses the amount of stress a person has experienced in the past year

Answer Key
  1. b   2. c   3. f   4. a   5. h   6. d   7. e   8. g   9. i   10. j

– PART IV. TRUE-FALSE STATEMENTS –

Fill in the blank before each statement with either a T (true) or an F (false). Check your answers against the Answer Key. Then go back to the items that are false and make the necessary change(s) to the statements to convert the items into true statements.

EMOTIONS

_____ 1. Subjective feelings of emotions include both a general state and a specific feeling tone.

_____

_____

_____ 2. According to Plutchik's emotion wheel, there are only eight human emotions.

_____

_____

_____ 3. According to the Cannon-Bard theory of emotion, one first experiences physiological and muscular changes, then experiences an emotion.

_____

_____

_____ 4. Schachter and Singer's theory of emotion agrees with the James-Lange theory in that emotions follow physiological and behavioral changes.

_____

_____

STRESS

_____ 5. Selye's general adaptation syndrome (GAS) emphasizes psychological factors associated with an individual's response to a stressful situation.

_____

_____

_____ 6. Psychological responses to stress include cognitive, emotional, and behavioral responses.

_____

_____

_____ 7. By definition, stress is always associated with negative events or situations.

_____

_____

_____ 8. Situations that an individual does not have control over and are sudden and ambiguous are likely to be perceived as stressful.

_____

_____

_____ 9. In the original long-term study of personality type and coronary heart disease, Type A men were three times as likely as Type B men to suffer heart attacks.

_____

_____

_____ 10. Stressful events decrease the functioning of the body's immune system.

_____

_____

Answer Key
1. T   2. F   3. F   4. T   5. F   6. T   7. F   8. T   9. F   10. T

– PART V. MULTIPLE-CHOICE QUESTIONS –

Choose the best answer to each question. Circle your choice. Check your answers against the Answer Key. Questions marked with an asterisk (*) include annotated answers.

THE COMPONENTS OF EMOTION

1. The four integral components of human emotions are _____.
   a. cognitive processes, subjective feelings, behavioral reactions, and facial expressions
   b. primary appraisal, secondary appraisal, behavioral reactions, and physiological arousal
   c. cognitive processes, subjective feelings, physiological arousal, and behavioral reactions
   d. cognitive processes, stressors, physiological arousal, and subjective feelings

2. With what is the physiological component of emotion closely associated?
   a. autonomic nervous system.
   b. central nervous system.
   c. skeletal or somatic nervous system.
   d. brain stem functions.

3. During an emotional state, which of the following would indicate physiological arousal?
   a. a sense of fear
   b. perception of the event as dangerous
   c. screaming
   d. an increase in blood pressure

THE RANGE OF HUMAN EMOTION

4. According to Plutchik's emotion wheel, emotions that are directly across from each other _____.
   a. are opponent processes
   b. have the most in common
   c. are opposites
   d. are secondary emotions

THEORIES OF EMOTION

*5. Imagine you are driving and a small child runs out in front of your car. You slam on the brakes to avoid hitting the child. It is only as you drive away and notice your heart pounding that you say to yourself, "Boy, that was scary!" For which theory of emotion does this situation give support?
   a. James-Lange only
   b. Cannon-Bard only
   c. Schachter-Singer only
   d. both James-Lange and Schachter-Singer

6. The James-Lange theory is supported by evidence that indicates which of the following?
   a. The hypothalamus is involved in emotional expression.
   b. People report less-intense emotional feelings after suffering a spinal cord injury.
   c. Following a fear response, people experience elation.
   d. Individuals tend to cognitively look for an appropriate emotional label for physiological changes.

7. What does the Cannon-Bard theory state?
   a. Emotional experiences and physical changes occur simultaneously.
   b. Physical changes are necessary for emotional experiences.
   c. Emotional experiences precede physical changes.
   d. Emotional experiences follow physical changes.

8. The Schachter-Singer theory agrees with the _____ theory in that emotions follow physical and behavioral changes, and agrees with the _____ theory in that cognitive processes are central to emotional experiences.
   a. James-Lange / opponent-process (Solomon and Corbit)
   b. James-Lange / Cannon-Bard
   c. opponent-process (Solomon and Corbit) / Cannon-Bard
   d. Cannon-Bard / James-Lange

*9. In Schachter and Singer's experiment, what did subjects who were uninformed or misinformed concerning the side effects of "Suproxin" and waited with a confederate who acted happy or euphoric, tend to do?
   a. provide no emotional label to their arousal
   b. label their arousal as happy also
   c. label their arousal as anger directed at the "silly" confederate
   d. report no changes in their physical state

10. Solomon and Corbit's opponent-process theory proposes that, with repeated exposure to a situation that produces an intense emotion, the initial emotional reaction will _____ while the opponent emotional reaction will _____.
    a. weaken / remain constant
    b. remain constant / grow stronger
    c. weaken / grow stronger
    d. grow stronger / weaken

11. Evidence that Botox injections (to reducy facial wrinkles) actually diminish the intensity of an emotion is accounted for by which theory?
    a. James-Lange
    b. Cannon Bard
    c. facial feedback
    d. Schacter-Singer

12. Which theory (theories) of emotion fail(s) to adequately recognize that emotions are more than automatic reactions to stimuli?
    a. both the James-Lange and the Cannon-Bard theories
    b. the Schachter-Singer theory
    c. the James-Lange theory
    d. Solomon and Corbit's opponent-process theory

13. The process of appraising events (as harmful, threatening, or challenging), of assessing potential responses, and of responding to those events defines _____.
    a. the general adaptation syndrome
    b. stressors
    c. adaptation
    d. feedback theory

*14. The headline in *The National Busybody* reads "97 Pound Mom Lifts Minivan Off Toddler." Which phase of the general adaptation syndrome was "Mom" in at the time?
    a. exhaustion
    b. resistance
    c. peak
    d. alarm

15. The correct order of the phases of Selye's general adaptation syndrome (GAS) is
    a. alarm, exhaustion, and resistance.
    b. peak, exhaustion, and resistance.
    c. alarm, resistance, and exhaustion.
    d. resistance, alarm, and exhaustion.

16. At which stage of GAS does the body begin to show signs of wear and tear and exhibit increased susceptibility to disease?
    a. final
    b. exhaustion
    c. resistance
    d. immunocompetence

*17. Which of the following is *not* a common cognitive response to a stressful situation?
    a. disruptive thoughts
    b. higher than normal levels of distraction
    c. feelings of anxiety
    d. impaired performance on cognitive tasks

18. The term "fight or flight" suggests which of the following psychological responses to stress?
    a. behavioral
    b. physiological
    c. emotional
    d. cognitive

*19. Which of the following events should be least stressful?
    a. having your parents tell you they are divorcing
    b. having your roommate tell you to move out
    c. having your partner initiate the break up of a long-term relationship
    d. initiating the break up of a long-term relationship

20. Which of the following characteristics is *not* associated with increasing the likelihood that an event will be perceived as stressful?
    a. ambiguity
    b. context
    c. suddenness
    d. lack of control

21. What is the main reason why ambiguous situations may cause stress?
    a. One may not be able to determine an appropriate course of action.
    b. One needs time to mobilize a defense.
    c. One may feel out of control.
    d. One may not be able to plan ahead.

22. What is one of the primary problems with the Social Readjustment Rating Scale (SRRS)?
    a. It is difficult to test the predications associated with the scale.
    b. Total life-change units can vary widely from person to person.

c. Positive events may also be stressful.

d. It does not take into consideration the fact that people experiencing the same life-change event may react very differently.

23. The evidence linking stress to _____ is less conclusive and more controversial than for the other illnesses listed.

a. malfunctioning of the immune system

b. coronary heart disease

c. cancer

d. hypertension

24. Which of the following has *not* been explored as a possible explanation for the link between Type A behavior and coronary heart disease?

a. Type A behavior may be a coping response to a naturally more reactive nervous system

b. Type A behavior decreases the functioning of the immune system

c. Type A individuals are more physiologically reactive to stress than Type B individuals

d. Type A individuals engage in more high-risk behaviors for developing coronary heart disease

25. Stress affects the immune system by _____.

a. reducing immunocompetence

c. activating the immune system

b. enhancing immunocompetence

d. destroying the immune system

26. There are some indications of the existence of a cancer-prone personality characterized by the tendency to be _____.

a. hard driving, ambitious, and competitive

b. angry, combative, and driven to achieve perfection

c. inhibited, compliant, and depressed

d. anxious, irritable, and easily embarrassed

27. What is one probable variable linking stress and cancer?

a. absence of stressful life changes

b. a Type B personality

c. hypertension

d. an impaired immune system

Answer Key

1. c   2. a   3. d   4. c   *5. d   6. b   7. b   8. b   *9 b   10. c   11. c   2. c   13. c
*14. d   15. c   16. b   *17. c   18. a   *19. d   20. b   21. a   22. d   23. c   24. b   5. a   26. c
27.d

Annotated Answers

5. The correct choice is **d**. First, the James-Lange theory proposes that physiological and muscular responses precede emotional states (I'm scared because my heart is pounding). Second, the Schachter-Singer theory proposes that emotions arise after one cognitively evaluates both the emotion-causing event and the body's physiological state.

a. This choice is incorrect because it does not include the Schachter-Singer theory.

b. The Cannon-Bard theory proposes that one would feel scared at the same time as the heart rate increased.

c. This choice is incorrect because it does not include the James-Lange theory.

9. The correct choice is **b**. Subjects who were uninformed and misinformed tended to use the confederate's behavior as a relevant cue for identifying and labeling their unexplained arousal.
    a. The informed subjects who correctly anticipated the side effects of the injection tended not to supply an emotional label to their arousal.
    c. The uninformed and misinformed subjects "adopted" the emotion of the confederate and did not respond to or evaluate it.
    d. All subjects except for the control group experienced physiological changes and would have reported so.

13. The correct choice is **d**. During the initial alarm phase, the sympathetic nervous system is activated and the body's resources are mobilized. During the alarm phase people can perform seemingly "superhuman" feats.
    a. The exhaustion phase only occurs after prolonged or repeated stress.
    b. During the resistance phase the parasympathetic nervous system is active and the person would not have the extra energy available to perform a superhuman feat.
    c. There is no peak phase in GAS.

16. The correct choice is **c**. Even though anxiety contains a cognitive element, feelings of anxiety (or any other feeling) are emotional and not cognitive responses. The choices in **a**, **b**, and **d** are common cognitive responses to stress.

18. The correct choice is **d**. First, because you are initiating the break up you have control over the situation. Second, you would probably not experience the situation as sudden because you most likely would have been thinking about breaking up for a period of time.
    a. Your parents telling you of their impending divorce is something you would lack control over, increasing the situation's stressfulness. The news of the divorce might also have been sudden, which would also increase its stressfulness.
    b. Your roommate telling you to move out could be sudden and you would not have control. It would also have a high measure of ambiguity (Where will I live?), which would further increase the stress of the situation.
    c. Unlike the situation in which you initiated the break up, in this case you have less control and would probably perceive the situation as sudden.

– PART VI. SUMMARY TABLE –

To test your understanding of the material discussed in this chapter, complete the following table. Check your answers with those supplied in Part IX.

THEORIES OF EMOTION

Theory	Description	Supporting Evidence	Weaknesses
James-Lange theory			
Cannon-Bard theory			
Schachter-Singer theory			
Solomon and Corbit's opponent-process theory			

– PART VII. THOUGHT QUESTIONS/CRITICAL THINKING –

Prepare answers to the following discussion questions:

1. Imagine that over Christmas vacation you've been separated from your boyfriend/girlfriend for three weeks. You've just arrived at the airport to meet your friend's plane. The plane is due to land any minute, and you are hurrying to get to the waiting area before the plane lands. While passing through the mandatory metal detector, you set off the alarm. The guard looks at you suspiciously and sternly

Figure 9.1

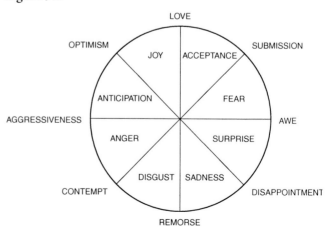

demands that you empty your pockets. You are offended and annoyed but empty your pockets until the problem is resolved and you are no longer suspected of being a terrorist. Your friend gets off the plane just as you arrive. When you see your friend's face, which instead of the warm smile you expect has a completely foreign expression (due to a very rough landing), you become concerned that your reunion may not be as happy as you expected. When your friend reaches you, he or she says, "What's wrong? You look upset?" What emotions would the different theories of emotion predict that you would be experiencing? How would these theories explain the reason for your experiencing a particular emotion?

2. In Chapter 8, you learned that there may be two optimum levels of arousal (one high and one low) that may switch back and forth. Which theory of emotion (James-Lange, Cannon-Bard, Schachter-Singer, Tomkins' facial feedback, or Solomon and Corbit's opponent process) is most consistent with this view of arousal? Explain your answer.

3. The link between stress and some illnesses (coronary heart disease, hypertension, malfunctioning of the immune system, and, perhaps, cancer) is becoming well established. It also appears that people who possess certain personality characteristics are more likely to develop specific illnesses. The Health Psychology section sidebar in this chapter suggests a number of stress-management strategies. Choose two or three of the strategies that would be most beneficial for an individual with Type A personality to use, and explain why use of these strategies would be important. Choose two or three of the strategies that would be most beneficial for an individual with a cancer-prone personality to use, and explain why use of these strategies would be important.

– PART VIII. APPLICATIONS –

1. Tomkins' facial feedback theory proposes that different facial expressions are associated with different emotional states. Cross-cultural research by Ekman found that people had 80 percent accuracy in identifying the correct emotion when viewing photographs illustrating happiness, sadness, surprise, anger, fear, and disgust. The figure (right) illustrates Plutchik's emotion wheel with the eight primary human emotions and the adjacent emotions listed.

   Do you think it would be possible to link these two conceptualizations? (Do not as yet refer to Figure 9.4 in the text, which depicts the six emotional expressions.) Do you think that emotions close to each other on the emotion wheel would be represented by similar facial expressions? Do you think that emotions opposite each other on the emotion wheel would be represented by dissimilar facial expressions? According to the emotion wheel, does it make sense that in the Ekman study fear and surprise were most commonly confused?

   Now examine Figure 9.4 to see if it provides evidence to support your answers to the questions in the preceding paragraph.

2. Holmes and Rahe's Social Readjustment Rating Scale for measuring the amount of stress a person has experienced in the last year contains questions that are relevant to people of all ages. However, as a college student, many of the typical stressors you experience (term papers, final exams, dorm living, etc.) are not listed. Develop a stress scale for college students. Identify at least 15–20 stressors commonly encountered by college students and decide on a life-*change* unit score for each stressor. What do you think would be a typical number of stress points (life-change units) for a college student to receive in a semester? What do you think would be a value associated with a high (and low) level of stress? Add up your points for the past semester and determine if your point total level (low, average, high) corresponds to the amount of stress you intuitively felt over the semester. If you have friends in psychology class who also did this application, compare your stress scales and look for similarities and differences in both the items included on the scale and the number of life-change units assigned to the stressors.

– PART IX. SUMMARY TABLE SOLUTION –

THEORIES OF EMOTION

Theory	Description	Supporting Evidence	Weaknesses
James-Lange theory	Environmental stimuli trigger physiological and muscular responses, which then activate emotional states. Different physiological responses result in different emotions.	After spinal cord injuries, people report less intense emotions. Negative emotions show specific physiological "fingerprints." Recent evidence from individuals with brain damage supports this theory.	General physiological reactions associated with a variety of emotions are similar (for example, increased heart rate).
Cannon-Bard theory	Subjective experiences and physiological and muscular responses occur simultaneously and are triggered by the thalamus	—	Perceives emotions as automatic reactions and does not discuss the role of cognition in evaluating emotions
Schachter-Singer theory	Physiological and behavioral responses occur first, and then one cognitively evaluates the situation and messages from the body to interpret or label the emotion.	Results of study with subjects who received epinephrine injections and were informed, uninformed, and misinformed	Some sudden emotional experiences seem to happen faster than would be predicted if it is necessary to evaluate the situation and physiological response.
Solomon and Corbit's opponent-process theory	Emotions exist in opponent-process fashion. After one strong emotion is experienced, the opposite emotion is activated to restore emotional balance. With repeated activation of one emotion, the intensity or the original emotion weakens and the intensity of the opponent emotion grows stronger.	Accounts for "addictive" behaviors such as mountain climbing, and also accounts for additions to drugs such as heroin	—

CHAPTER 10
COGNITION: THINKING AND LANGUAGE

– PART I. LEARNING OBJECTIVES –

When you finish studying this chapter, you should be able to do the following:

THINKING

1. Define thought, and discuss four types of activities thinking allows us to do.

2. Describe Watson's concept of subvocal speech and Skinner's concept of covert behavior.

3. Describe the two main components of thought (mental images and concepts).

4. Describe concept hierarchies, and discuss what is meant by the basic level for each concept.

5. Describe two theories (association and exemplar) that attempt to explain how we form concepts.

PROBLEM SOLVING

6. Define problem, and list the three components of a problem.

7. Discuss the three stages involved in solving a problem.

8. Describe the four different strategies for solving a problem.

9. Describe the two common heuristic strategies of means-ends analysis and working backward.

10. Discuss two characteristics of some problems that make them difficult to solve.

11. Discuss three obstacles to problem solving that result from cognitive influences.

REASONING AND DECISION MAKING

12. Explain inductive and deductive reasoning, and differentiate between the two.

13. Define a syllogism, and explain how syllogisms are used to study deductive reasoning.

14. Describe two common causes of reasoning errors.

15. Describe and explain how the representativeness heuristic may be used in decision making.

16. Describe and explain how the availability heuristic may be used in decision making.

17. Discuss how the manner in which a problem is formulated influences subjective probabilities in decision making.

LANGUAGE

18. Describe the four levels of rules of language: phonemes, morphemes, syntax, and semantics.

19. Describe two major theories of language acquisition (learning perspective, genetic perspective), and discuss the strengths and weaknesses of each.

20. Describe and give examples to illustrate the five stages in the universal sequence of language acquisition.

21. Discuss the major brain structures that are involved in language.

22. List five primary criteria of all human languages, and use these criteria to describe and evaluate research designed to teach language to chimpanzees.

23. Describe and evaluate two different perspectives concerning the interrelationship of thinking and language.

– PART II. OVERVIEW –

Thinking (or thought) refers to internal processes intended to solve problems and make decisions. Two components of thought are mental images and concepts. Concepts allow us to simplify our understanding of objects and events by grouping items into general cognitive categories. Two theories concerning how concepts are learned are discussed. The association theory states that concepts develop as a result of acquiring stimulus-response associations. The exemplar theory proposes that we structure natural concepts that we learn in everyday life around typical examples or prototypes.

A problem exists when there is a discrepancy between one's present state and goal state. Problem solving involves developing a strategy to bring about the goal state. There are a number of problem-solving strategies: trial and error, testing hypotheses, algorithms, and heuristics. Algorithms systematically try every possible solution and are commonly used in computer programming. Heuristics are rule-of-thumb strategies designed to result in quick solutions. Problems that are not well defined or are complex are difficult to solve. Mental sets, functional fixedness, and confirmation bias are all obstacles an individual brings to a situation that makes a problem difficult to solve.

There are two types of logical reasoning. Inductive reasoning involves generalizing from specific instances to reach a general conclusion. Deductive reasoning describes a situation that begins with general observations or assumptions and leads to a conclusion being drawn concerning specific instances. Deductive reasoning is often studied by using syllogisms.

Decision-making occurs when one alternative is selected while other alternatives are rejected. People frequently resort to short-cut or heuristic approaches to make many decisions. The representativeness heuristic involves making decisions based on preconceived ideas concerning characteristics that represent a category. The availability heuristic involves making decisions based on how easily relevant information is recalled and available to use.

There are four levels of analysis used to describe language. The most basic element is the individual sounds—or phonemes—that are used. The smallest unit in a language that has meaning is the morpheme. Syntax describes the rules (or grammar) that state how words are combined into meaningful phrases or sentences. The final level of analysis concerns semantics, or the rules that determine the meaning of sentences and words.

Two theories concerning language acquisition are discussed. The learning perspective proposes that children learn language in a way similar to how they learn many other tasks—through selective reinforcement and imitation. The genetic perspective, which proposes that language acquisition is controlled by an innate mechanism (the Language Acquisition Device), offers a more thorough accounting of the sequence of language acquisition. All over the world children progress from crying, cooing and babbling, holophrases, and condensed speech to more complex sentences. Certainly language acquisition involves both innate structures and experiences to develop normally.

Two language areas of the brain are described. Damage to Broca's area results in an inability to speak fluently. Damage to Wernicke's area results in difficulties comprehending speech.

The interrelationship of thinking and language is discussed. Whorf's hypothesis that language rigidly structures or determines thought is not generally accepted. However, it is well accepted that some thoughts are easier to express in certain languages. There is also some evidence that thoughts influence the structure of an individual's language.

– PART III. KEY TERMS/MATCHING EXERCISES –

Match the following concepts with the appropriate descriptions. Check your answers against the Answer Key.

THOUGHT

Concepts	Descriptions
_____ 1. association theory	a. Represents general cognitive categories
_____ 2. basic level of a concept	b. Proposes that concepts are structured around prototypes
_____ 3. concepts	c. Proposes that concepts are acquired through the learning of stimulus-response associations
_____ 4. exemplar theory	d. Collection of internal processes directed toward solving a problem
_____ 5. thought	e. Optimal level of a concept hierarchy that is naturally used when one thinks about an object or event

Answer Key
   1. c   2. e   3. a   4. b   5. d

PROBLEM SOLVING

Concepts	Descriptions
_____ 1. trial and error	a. Problem-solving strategy often employed by computers to systematically test every possible solution
_____ 2. testing hypotheses	b. Problem-solving strategy that uses rule-of-thumb strategies leading to a quick solution
_____ 3. problem	c. Problem-solving strategy that starts with a goal and progresses in steps toward the original state or problem
_____ 4. heuristics	d. Exists when there is a discrepancy between present status and desired goal
_____ 5. working backwards	e. Tendency to avoid looking for evidence that would disprove the hypothesis
_____ 6. algorithm	f. Problem-solving strategy that involves trying possible solutions, one at a time, to see which is correct
_____ 7. confirmation bias	g. Problem-solving strategy that utilizes hypotheses to more efficiently and systematically search for the correct solution to a problem
_____ 8. mental set	h. Tendency to approach a problem in a predetermined way regardless of the requirements of the specific problem

Answer Key
   1. f   2. g   3. d   4. b   5. c   6. a   7. e   8. h

REASONING AND DECISION MAKING

Concepts	Descriptions
_____ 1. syllogism	a. Form of reasoning that begins with general assumptions that serve as a basis for drawing conclusions
_____ 2. representativeness heuristic	b. Form of reasoning in which a conclusion is reached by generalizing from specific instances
_____ 3. availability heuristic	c. Consists of two premises and a conclusion
_____ 4. inductive reasoning	d. Tendency to accept or reject a specific conclusion regardless of how logical that conclusion is
_____ 5. belief-bias effect	e. Process that occurs whenever one is faced with an array of alternative choices and one option is chosen while rejecting others
_____ 6. deductive reasoning	f. Strategy in which the likelihood of something is judged by intuitively comparing it to preconceived notions about a few characteristics of a category
_____ 7. decision making	g. Strategy that bases decisions primarily on the degree to which information can be accessed from memory

Answer Key

1. c   2. f   3. g   4. b   5. d   6. a   7. e

LANGUAGE

Concepts	Descriptions
_____ 1. linguistic-relativity hypothesis	a. First-sentence form used by children
_____ 2. language-acquisition device (LAD)	b. Proposed "prewiring" of an infant's brain to learn language
_____ 3. syntax	c. Rules of grammar that govern how words can be combined to form meaningful phrases and sentences
_____ 4. morpheme	d. Associated with the ability to speak
_____ 5. semantics	e. Individual or basic sounds that comprise a language
_____ 6. phonemes	f. Associated with the ability to comprehend speech
_____ 7. condensed speech	g. Smallest unit of meaning in a language
_____ 8. Broca's area	h. Study of meaning in language
_____ 9. Wernicke's area	i. Whorf's view that language determines thought

Answer Key

1. i   2. b   3. c   4. g   5. h   6. e   7. a   8. d   9. f

– PART IV. TRUE/FALSE STATEMENTS –

Fill in the blank before each statement with either a T (true) or an F (false). Check your answers against the Answer Key. Then go back to the items that are false and make the necessary change(s) to the statements to convert the items into true statements.

THOUGHT

_____ 1. Watson's idea that thought involves subvocal or implicit speech is now well accepted.

_____

_____

_____ 2. One component of thought is manipulation of concepts in a systematic or logical manner.

_____

_____

_____ 3. Exemplar theory suggests that everyday concepts are usually structured around prototypes.

_____

_____

PROBLEM SOLVING

_____ 4. The first step in problem-solving behavior involves generating possible solutions.

_____

_____

_____ 5. A main difference between the problem-solving strategies of algorithms and trial and error is that algorithms are more systematic.

_____

_____

_____ 6. When an individual incorrectly approaches a problem by applying strategies that have previously been successful with similar problems, that person is showing confirmation bias.

_____

_____

REASONING AND DECISION MAKING

_____ 7. The first step in deciding if a syllogism is valid is to determine if each of the two premises are true statements.

_____

_____

_____ 8. The belief bias effect would cause an individual to accept believable but logically invalid conclusions.

_____

_____

_____ 9. When decision alternatives are framed in terms of gains, people tend to avoid risks.

_____

_____

LANGUAGE

_____ 10. The specific language a child is exposed to greatly affects the form (syntax and semantics) of the child's first sentences.

_____

_____

_____ 11. Careful evaluation of the research designed to teach language to chimpanzees leads to the unequivocal conclusion that only humans possess language.

_____

_____

_____ 12. There is very little support for Whorf's linguistic-relativity hypothesis that language determines or structures thought.

_____

_____

Answer Key
1. F   2. F   3. T   4. F   5. T   6. F   7. F   8. T   9. T   10. F   11. F   12. T

– PART V. MULTIPLE-CHOICE QUESTIONS –

Choose the best answer to each question. Circle your choice. Check your answers against the Answer Key. Questions marked with an asterisk (*) include annotated answers.

THOUGHT

1. What do you do when you mentally group objects or events into general cognitive categories?
    a. solve a problem
    b. form a mental image
    c. form a concept
    d. make a decision

*2. You would most likely have the shortest reaction time to answer which of the following questions?
    a. Is a grandmother a person?
    b. Is a newborn infant a person?
    c. Is a child a person?
    d. Is a college student a person?

3. The concept _____ is subordinate to the concept _____.
    a. dog / bulldog
    b. animal / dog
    c. teacher / person
    d. animal / bird

4. Which of the following is a prototype?
   a. Siamese cat
   b. house cat
   c. tomcat
   d. Persian cat

5. When we encounter a novel instance of a concept, such as an exotic bird we have never seen before, we correctly label it bird on the basis of stimulus generalization. What theory of concept formation supports this view?
   a. association theory
   b. hypothesis-testing theory
   c. exemplar theory
   d. prototype theory

PROBLEM SOLVING

6. Problems consist of three components. Which of the following is *not* a component of a problem?
   a. the goal state
   b. generating possible solutions
   c. the rules or restrictions that govern possible strategies
   d. the original state of the situation

7. When is trial-and-error problem solving most effective?
   a. There is a wide range of solutions.
   b. There is a narrow range of solutions.
   c. Strategies are needed.
   d. There must be a "quick-fix."

8. When one systematically moves through a series of subgoals coming closer to a final solution, one is using the problem-solving strategy of _____.
   a. working backward
   b. testing hypotheses
   c. algorithm
   d. means–ends analysis

*9. If the number of possible solutions to a problem is large and there is a limited amount of time available to solve the problem, which two problem-solving strategies would *least* likely be used?
   a. algorithm and testing hypotheses
   b. trial and error and algorithm
   c. heuristics and algorithm
   d. heuristics and trial and error

10. _____ in contrast to _____ do (does) not guarantee a correct solution to a problem, but when they work they tend to allow for more rapid solutions.
    a. incubation / heuristics
    b. heuristics / incubation
    c. algorithms / heuristics
    d. heuristics / algorithms

11. Which of the following makes it more difficult to solve a problem?
    a. the problem contains a syllogism
    b. the problem is deceptively simple
    c. the problem involves basic concepts
    d. the problem is ill-defined

12. When we are unable to think of a novel use for a given object that would aid in solving a problem, we experience _____.
    a. functional fixedness
    b. mental set
    c. dead-end thinking
    d. confirmation bias

13. As a result of confirmation bias, why might people might jump to a conclusion incorrectly in attempting to solve a problem?
    a. They tend to approach a problem in a predetermined way if the approach has been successful in the past.
    b. They stop an algorithm prematurely.
    c. They have a prototype of the correct solution.
    d. They do not look for evidence that will disprove their hypothesis.

REASONING AND DECISION MAKING

14. If you decide to vote for a candidate you know little about solely because he or she is a Republican (or a Democrat) and you are too, you would be using _____ to guide your decision.
    a. deductive reasoning
    b. inductive reasoning
    c. productive reasoning
    d. confirmation bias

15. Reasoning in which we reach a general conclusion by beginning with specific instances is called _____.
    a. deductive reasoning
    b. inductive reasoning
    c. syllogistic reasoning
    d. functional fixedness

16. With _____ you can never be absolutely certain that you have reached a correct conclusion.
    a. algorithms
    b. syllogisms
    c. deductive reasoning
    d. inductive reasoning

17. The discipline of formal logic uses _____ to study reasoning.
    a. syllogisms
    b. formal concepts
    c. representative heuristics
    d. belief bias

*18. When is syllogism judged to be true?
    a. Both premises are true.
    b. The logically obtained conclusion is also consistent with everyday beliefs.
    c. The conclusion applies to every conceivable combination of all possible meanings of the premises.
    d. The converse of each premise is also true (for example, if "all As are Bs" is the premise and "all Bs are As" is a true statement).

19. The process that occurs whenever one is faced with an array of alternative choices, and one option is chosen while others are rejected, describes _____.
    a. decision making
    b. formal logic

   c.   problem solving

   d.   functional fixedness

20. Many everyday decisions are made through the use of _____.
   a.   syllogisms
   b.   algorithms
   c.   heuristics
   d.   artificial intelligence

21. When making a decision, how easily you can recall a piece of information is an important component of _____.
   a.   the framing heuristic
   b.   the availability heuristic
   c.   the representativeness heuristic
   d.   means-end analysis

LANGUAGE

22. The smallest unit of language that has meaning in a given language is the _____.
   a.   word
   b.   morpheme
   c.   syllable
   d.   phoneme

23. A course in grammar would be primarily concerned with _____; a literature course would more likely be concerned with _____.
   a.   syntax / semantics
   b.   semantics / syntax
   c.   syntax / morphemes
   d.   morphemes / semantics

*24. Which language-acquisition perspective could best account for a young child (whose parents speak English grammatically) saying, "I goed to the zoo yesterday"?
   a.   syntactical
   b.   Whorfian
   c.   genetic
   d.   learning

25. In genetic theory, what is the "prewiring" of the brain, presumed to facilitate the child's learning of grammar, known as?
   a.   programmed-language generator
   b.   language-acquisition device
   c.   programmed-linguistic achiever
   d.   surface/deep structure

26. Which of the following observations does *not* offer strong support for the genetic or "prewired" perspective of language acquisition?
   a.   Babies whose parents reinforce their early attempts at meaningful sounds vocalize more than institutionalized babies who receive less attention.
   b.   Under highly variable conditions, language acquisition follows an invariable sequence among children all over the world.
   c.   When infants begin babbling, they babble sounds that are both phonemes and not phonemes of their future language.
   d.   The telegraphic speech in young children is similar all over the world.

27. By the age of _____ most children have learned the majority of the basic grammatical rules for combining nouns, adjectives, and verbs into meaningful sentences.
    a. two or three
    b. three or four
    c. four or five
    d. five or six

*28. Which of the following is a basic question that chimpanzee research has *not* conclusively answered?
    a. Can chimps talk?
    b. Can chimps convey meaning through the use of symbols?
    c. Can chimps communicate?
    d. Can chimps learn language?

29. The chimpanzee Washoe was taught _____.
    a. to speak
    b. American Sign Language
    c. Yerkish
    d. to manipulate plastic symbols and combine them in an apparently meaningful fashion

30. Whorf's hypothesis that people think differently in different languages is called the _____ hypothesis.
    a. linguistic-relativity
    b. genetic
    c. exemplar
    d. linguistic-acquisition-device

31. What did the experiment comparing memory for colors between American and Dani individuals find?
    a. Americans are more successful in selecting the correct hue
    b. The Dani are more successful in selecting the correct hue
    c. Both Americans and Dani found the task very easy and made few mistakes.
    d. The performance of the Americans and Dani did not significantly differ.

32. Which of the following statements is *false*?
    a. It is often easier to express a particular concept or idea in one language as opposed to another.
    b. Thoughts and/or perceptions are largely determined or structured by our language.
    c. Expanding language through education and reading enhances our thinking processes.
    d. It is often easier to make a distinction about certain features of the environment in one language as opposed to another.

33. Which of the following positions is supported by the observation that young children do not talk about objects that are not present in their immediate environment until they have mastered object permanence?
    a. Mental images are necessary for thought to occur.
    b. Children have a limited vocabulary.
    c. Thought has an impact on the structure of language.
    d. Language determines thought.

Answer Key
  1. c   *2. c   3. c   4. b   5. a   6. b   7. b   8. d   *9. d   10. a   11. d   12. a
  13. b   14. d   15. a   16. c   17. a   *18. c   19. b   20. b   21. a   22. b   23. a   *24. c
  25. b   26. a   27. c   *28. d   29. b   30. a   31. d   32. b   33. c

2. The correct choice is **c**. Child is the most general of the choices presented and is more typical of the concept person than grandmother (**a**), newborn infant (**b**), and college student (**d**). Research has shown that reaction times are faster when questions such as these contain typical examples.

9. The correct choice is **b**. Algorithms will guarantee a correct solution, but they are time consuming. The trial-and-error strategy is most effective when there is a small number of possible solutions.
   a. Testing hypotheses would be an effective strategy to narrow the number of solutions to try.
   c. Heuristics would be an effective strategy to use because a quick solution is desired.
   d. See the note for **c** above.

18. The correct choice is **c**. This statement is one of the three requirements for judging a syllogism to be true.
   a. In a syllogism both premises are presumed to be true.
   b. This relates to the belief-bias effect. It is not necessary for a valid syllogism to be consistent with everyday beliefs.
   d. The converse of a premise does not need to be true.

24. The correct choice is **c**. The genetic perspective states that when children learn the basic rules of grammar, they tend to make mistakes of overgeneralization.
   a. The syntactical perspective does not exist.
   b. The Whorfian or linguistic-relativity hypothesis is not concerned with how language is acquired.
   d. The learning perspective would have difficulty explaining why the child said "goed" if he or she had never heard the word before and thus could not be imitating another's speech.

28. The correct choice is **d**. Depending on the interpretation of the results of the research and the definition of language utilized, different answers to the question "Can chimps learn language?" are possible.
   a. Talk refers to verbal language. Chimps do not have the vocal apparatus to communicate verbally.
   b. The behavior of Sarah and Lana indicate that chimps are capable of conveying meaning through the use of symbols.
   c. Chimps, like many species, can communicate.

– PART VI. SUMMARY TABLES –

To test your understanding of the material discussed in this chapter, complete the following tables. Check your answers with those supplied in Part IX.

THEORIES OF CONCEPT FORMATION

Theory	Individual	Assumption	Strengths	Weaknesses
Association				
Exemplar				

PROBLEM-SOLVING STRATEGIES

Strategy	Description	Advantages	Limitations
Trial and error			
Testing Hypotheses			
Algorithms			
Heuristics			

THEORIES OF LANGUAGE ACQUISITION

Theory	Individual	Description	Supporting Evidence	Weaknesses
Learning				
Genetic				

– PART VII. THOUGHT QUESTIONS/CRITICAL THINKING –

Prepare answers to the following discussion questions.

1. Discuss the relationship between problem solving and decision making.

2. Discuss how a police detective might use deductive reasoning to try to solve a crime. How might the detective use inductive reasoning to try to solve the same crime?

3. Heuristic problem-solving strategies are frequently considered helpful and use a repertoire of "quick-fix" methods for dealing with problems, based on both experience with strategies that have worked in the past and our own personal storehouse of accumulated knowledge. Mental sets frequently cause problems to be more difficult to solve and are described as "a tendency to approach a problem in a set or predetermined way regardless of the requirements of the specific problem." Could a heuristic also be a mental set? Could a mental set also be a heuristic? Explain your answers.

4. Whorf's idea that language determines thought is not generally accepted and was not supported by the color-memory experiment with American college students and Dani individuals. Do you think the results of the experiment might have been different if American and Dani children, first becoming aware of the concept of color (perhaps 3- or 4-year-olds), were the subjects in this experiment? Explain your answer. (You might want to consider both the ideas that language determines thought and that thought structures language.)

– PART VIII. APPLICATIONS –

1. If you're like many college students, you might like to watch game shows on TV. If so, this application should not be objectionable to you. If you don't normally watch game shows, this application might turn you into a "couch potato." Choose a game show in which contestants compete against each other (e.g., "Wheel of Fortune," "Hollywood Squares," "The Price Is Right"). Watch the show carefully for two or three days and record the "choices" of each contestant. Do your records suggest that contestants used some sort of strategies? If so, which strategies were most common? Were some strategies more successful than others? If you were the contestant on the show, what strategy would you have used? Did contestants fall victim to some of the obstacles to problem solving such as mental sets or confirmation bias?

2. It's one thing to read about the early language of young children, and it's another thing to actually hear and observe it. Try to observe and record the language of at least three young children ($1^{1/2}$–5 years old). Ideally the children will be different ages. If you know families with young children, use them. If you don't, you will have to be more creative. For example, ask at a day care center or Sunday school if you may observe. (It is not a good idea to just "hang out" at a playground and follow children around. Your interest in the children might be misinterpreted.) Note the age of each child and record about 25 statements from each child. Write down exactly what the child says. When you are finished, examine your records for evidence of holophrases, condensed speech, and overgeneralization. How well do your observations compare to the information in the text?

– PART IX. SUMMARY TABLES SOLUTIONS –

THEORIES OF CONCEPT FORMATION

Theory	Individual	Assumption	Strengths	Weaknesses
Association	Hull	Learn stimulus–response associations between common elements (S)-concepts (R)	Explains how to generalize concepts	—
Exemplar	Rosch	Natural concepts are structured around typical examples or prototypes. The better the match between the prototype and object, the more readily the object is included in the concept.	In experimental situations, people have faster reaction times to "Is ___ a ___?" questions when using examples of concepts that are more typical than when using less typical examples.	—

PROBLEM-SOLVING STRATEGIES

Strategy	Description	Advantages	Limitations
Trial and error	Try different solutions one at a time in random order until correct solution is found.	Works satisfactorily if limited number of possible solutions	May not be the most efficient strategy if there is a large number of possible solutions
Testing Hypotheses	Develops hypothesis to narrow the number of possible solutions and then tries those selected solutions	More efficient than trial and error if large number of possible solutions	May need to come up with additional hypothesis if first does not lead to correct solution
Algorithms	The systematic exploration of every possible solution (used by computers)	Guarantees a correct solution if one is aware of all possible solutions	Requires a lot of time and effort For real-life problems one may not be aware of all possible solutions.
Heuristics	Rule-of-thumb strategies that are based on both experience with strategies that have worked in the past and personal knowledge Two common heuristic strategies are means-ends analysis and working backward.	May lead to quick solutions	Are not guaranteed to produce a correct solution

THEORIES OF LANGUAGE ACQUISITION

Theory	Individual	Description	Supporting Evidence	Weaknesses
Learning	Skinner Bandura	Learn to shape sounds into words and words into sentences through selective reinforcement and imitation	Babies whose parents reinforce their early attempts at meaningful sounds vocalize more than institutionalized children who receive less attention.	Many words a child says are not words they have heard and could not be imitating. Children show the same sequence of language acquisition even though their experience varies widely.
Genetic	Chomsky	People are "prewired" by the innate language-acquisition device to recognize phonemes, morphemes, syntax, and semantics.	Universal sequence of language acquisition Infants recognize virtually all consonant sounds.	Needs to be combined with the learning perspec-tive to account for the specific language and grammar acquired

CHAPTER 11

DEVELOPMENT 1: CONCEPTION THROUGH CHILDHOOD

– PART I. LEARNING OBJECTIVES –

When you finish studying this chapter, you should be able to do the following:

DEVELOPMENTAL ISSUES

1. Describe the two sides of the nature-nurture controversy, and discuss the current perspective psychologists have concerning the controversy.

2. Discuss the opposing views regarding whether development is characterized by continuity (with quantitative changes) or discontinuity (with qualitative changes).

3. Define and give an example of a critical period, and summarize research on whether there are critical periods in human development.

DEVELOPMENTAL RESEARCH

4. Describe three different research designs used to study development, and explain the strengths and weaknesses of each.

THE BEGINNING OF LIFE

5. Define chromosomes, genes, and DNA, discussing how the three terms are interrelated.

6. Explain how monozygotic and dizygotic twins differ, and explain why psychologists are interested in studying these two types of twins.

7. Discriminate between genotypes and phenotypes; explain how dominant, recessive, and sex-linked genes influence the phenotype.

8. Describe the symptoms of a number of genetic disorders, and discuss the genetic causes of each.

PRENATAL DEVELOPMENT

9. Name and describe the three stages of prenatal development

PHYSICAL DEVELOPMENT

10. Describe the development of the brain from birth to the end of childhood, and discuss how early experiences influence brain development.

11. Describe physical growth from birth to the end of childhood, and explain the cephalocaudal and proximodistal patterns of growth.

12. Describe motor development from birth to the end of childhood, and discuss hereditary and environmental influences on motor development.

COGNITIVE DEVELOPMENT

13. Define Piaget's basic concepts: schemas, assimilation, and accommodation; discuss how these are interrelated.

14. Give the ages associated with Piaget's sensorimotor stage of cognitive development, and summarize the major changes that take place in this stage.

15. Give the ages associated with Piaget's preoperational stage of cognitive development, and summarize the major changes that take place in this stage.

16. Give the ages associated with Piaget's concrete-operations stage of cognitive development, and summarize the major changes that take place in this stage.

17. Give the ages associated with Piaget's formal-operations stage of cognitive development, and summarize the major changes that take place in this stage.

18. Describe any gender differences in cognitive abilities.

PSYCHOSOCIAL DEVELOPMENT

19. Define attachment, and describe the three stages of child–caretaker attachment.

20. Describe the effects of attachment deprivation in monkeys and humans, and summarize research concerning whether these effects can be reversed.

21. Describe infants who show secure and insecure attachment, and discuss factors that influence the type of attachment an infant will display.

22. Describe father–child attachment.

23. Describe three styles of parenting, and indicate the influence that each may have on the personality of a child.

24. List the ages associated with Erikson's eight stages of psychosocial development, and explain the crisis faced in each stage.

GENDER IDENTITY

25. Define gender identity, and outline six levels of biological factors that influence gender identity.

26. Describe three conditions resulting in abnormal prenatal sexual differentiation, and discuss how these conditions relate to gender identity.

27. Discuss social-learning factors in gender identity, and explain why the interactional model is commonly used to account for gender identity.

28. Define gender roles, and describe four important agents that influence the socialization of gender roles.

– PART II. OVERVIEW–

This chapter begins with a discussion of a number of historical issues related to the study of development. The central issue is the nature-nurture controversy. Individuals who emphasize the role of learning and experience in controlling development support the nurture view and visualize development as exhibiting continuity and being characterized by quantitative changes. Individuals who support the nature view emphasize the role of maturation and genetics in development and view development as a process that unfolds in a predetermined fashion characterized by discontinuity and qualitative changes. Another issue concerns critical periods. Although critical periods (a specific time frame during which an aspect of behavior is easily acquired) exist in some animals, most contemporary psychologists do not support the idea of critical periods with regard to many aspects of human development.

The basic mechanisms of heredity and genetics are described. A number of genetic disorders (Huntington's disease, PKU, and Down syndrome) are described, and the mechanisms of transmission of the disorders are explained.

Prenatal development is composed of three stages. The first two weeks are the germinal (or zygote) stage. The embryonic stage (third to eighth week) is a period of rapid growth and differentiation of a number of body systems. During the fetal stage (third month to birth) bone and muscle tissue form, and organs and body systems continue to develop. At birth, the infant's brain contains most—if not all—of the neurons he or she will ever have. For the first several years of life neural networks continue to develop and may be influenced by environmental stimulation. Physical and motor development of the child follows two distinct patterns: cephalocaudal (from head to foot) and proximodistal (from inner to outer) patterns.

Piaget's stage theory proposes that cognitive development is governed by the processes of assimilation and accommodation, which serve to maintain (assimilation) and revise (accommodation) our schemas or mental structures for understanding the world around us. Piaget's theory contains four stages of cognitive development, each having qualitatively different types of thinking and limitations. The sensorimotor infant learns through sensing and doing and acquires object permanence or the realization that objects continue to exist even when they are not within view. Preoperational children (age 2–7) are capable of symbolic thought or language, but their thought process is severely limited by intuitive thought and the immediate appearance of objects. Children in the concrete-operations stage (age 7–12) are capable of logical thought and can apply rules (mental operations) to situations that are concrete but not to abstract or hypothetical situations. Children in the formal-operations stage (age 12+) are capable of abstract thought and are more systematic in their problem-solving approach.

How the attachment is formed between an infant and the primary caretaker is described. Harlow's research with monkeys that experienced early social deprivation is discussed and related to human experiences. Erikson's stage theory of psychosocial development divides the life cycle into eight stages of development. At each stage, the individual is concerned with a specific issue or crisis that must be resolved in order for development to proceed in a healthy fashion.

This chapter concludes with a discussion of gender identity (one's subjective sense of being male or female) and gender roles (societal standards of behavior appropriate for each sex). A number of biological factors combine to influence the development of a male or female body type—and thus a male or female gender identity. In general, psychosocial factors also influence gender identity, and socialization greatly influences the development of gender roles.

– PART III. KEY TERMS/MATCHING EXERCISES –

Match the following concepts with the appropriate descriptions. Check your answers against the Answer Key.

DEVELOPMENTAL ISSUES AND DEVELOPMENTAL RESEARCH

Concepts	Descriptions
_____ 1. nurture	a. Simultaneously evaluates subjects of different ages in order to study development
_____ 2. critical periods	b. View that development unfolds in a genetically determined fashion
_____ 3. nature	c. Time interval during which proper experience greatly facilitates an aspect of development
_____ 4. longitudinal design	d. Evaluates a group of subjects at several different times in order to study development
_____ 5. cross-sequential design	e. View that development is determined by experiences
_____ 6. cross-sectional design	f. Evaluates subjects of different ages at more than one time in order to study development

Answer Key
  1. e   2. c   3. b   4. d   5. f   6. a

THE BEGINNING OF LIFE

Concepts	Descriptions
_____ 1. concordant	a. Identical twins that develop from a single egg and therefore have the same genetic material
_____ 2. heterozygous	b. When an individual has two similar genes for a specific trait and the same genotype and phenotype
_____ 3. homozygous	c. Gene that is only expressed in the phenotype when an individual has two similar or only one gene for the trait
_____ 4. genes	d. Fraternal twins that develop from separate eggs and thereby do not have the same genetic material
_____ 5. dizygotic twins	e. When an individual has two dissimilar genes for a specific trait and does not have the same genotype as phenotype
_____ 6. monozygotic twins	f. Composed of DNA and determines or influences physical and behavioral traits
_____ 7. dominant gene	g. Explains why males are more likely than females to exhibit a number of recessive genetic traits
_____ 8. sex-linked inheritance	h. Describes the degree to which twins share a particular trait
_____ 9. recessive gene	i. Gene that is always expressed in the phenotype
_____ 10. phenylketonuria (PKU)	j. Along with chorionic villi sampling, provides two methods to detect birth defects *in utero*
_____ 11. amniocentesis	k. Results from an extra 21st chromosome and is characterized by distinctive appearance and mental retardation
_____ 12. recessive gene	l. Incurable disorder caused by a dominant gene that is not apparent until age 35–40
_____ 13. Down syndrome	m. Genetic condition that, if undiagnosed and treated, can cause mental retardation

Answer Key
  1. h   2. e   3. b   4. f   5. d   6. a   7. i   8. g   9. c   10. m   11. j   2. l   13. k

PRENATAL DEVELOPMENT AND PHYSICAL DEVELOPMENT

Concepts	Descriptions
_____ 1. proximodistal	a. Lasts from the third through the eighth week of prenatal development when the embryo is extremely vulnerable to negative environmental events
_____ 2. cephalocaudal	b. Pattern of development that proceeds from head to foot
_____ 3. embryonic stage	c. Pattern of development that proceeds from inner (or close to the body) to outer (or farther away from the body)
_____ 4. fetal stage	d. Extends from the third month of development until birth
_____ 5. germinal (zygote) stage	e. Refers to the first two weeks of development during which time the amniotic sac, umbilical cord, and placenta are established

Answer Key
   1. c   2. b   3. a   4. d   5. e

COGNITIVE DEVELOPMENT

Concepts	Descriptions
_____ 1. concrete-operations stage	a. Involves restructuring existing knowledge to account for new information
_____ 2. sensorimotor stage	b. Stage of cognitive development in which object permanence is developed
_____ 3. formal-operations stage	c. Mental structures for organizing information
_____ 4. preoperational stage	d. Stage of cognitive development in which the child is first capable of decentration and can use mental operations
_____ 5. accommodation	e. Involves interpreting new information in accordance with one's existing knowledge
_____ 6. assimilation	f. Stage of cognitive development characterized by abstract thought and the systematic testing of hypothetical solutions
_____ 7. schemas	g. Stage of cognitive development characterized by centration and egocentrism

Answer Key
   1. d   2. b   3. f   4. g   5. a   6. e   7. c

PSYCHOSOCIAL DEVELOPMENT

Concepts	Descriptions
_____ 1. attachment	a. An intense emotional tie that develops between two individuals
_____ 2. permissive	b. Parental style characterized by strictly enforced rules where, typically, minimal warmth is expressed
_____ 3. authoritative	c. Parental style characterized by open discussion and rule-making in an atmosphere of warmth
_____ 4. authoritarian	d. Parental style characterized by few demands; reluctance to punish inappropriate behavior
_____ 5. indiscriminate attachment	e. Develops at about 6–7 months, when infants respond more positively to regular caregivers
_____ 6. separate attachment	f. Develops around 12–18 months, when infants take an active social interest in a variety of people
_____ 7. specific attachment	g. Describes up to 6 months of age, when infants respond equally to anyone

Answer Key

1. a   2. d   3. c   4. b   5. g   6. f   7. e

GENDER IDENTITY

Concepts	Descriptions
_____ 1. gender identity	a. Process by which male and/or female structures develop
_____ 2. gender roles	b. Process whereby society conveys behavioral expectations to the individual
_____ 3. socialization	c. Individual's subjective sense of being male or female that is influenced by biological and social-learning factors
_____ 4. sexual differentiation	d. Individuals with ambiguous or contradictory sex characteristics
_____ 5. hermaphrodite	e. Societal standards of behavior that are considered normal and appropriate for each sex

Answer Key

1. c   2. e   3. b   4. a   5. d

– PART IV. TRUE/FALSE STATEMENTS –

Fill in the blank before each statement with either a T (true) or an F (false). Check your answers against the Answer Key. Then go back to the items that are false and make the necessary change(s) to the statements to convert the items into true statements.

DEVELOPMENTAL ISSUES AND DEVELOPMENTAL RESEARCH

_____ 1. Developmental psychologists who emphasize maturation view development as occurring in stages that are qualitatively different.

_____

_____

_____ 2. A major drawback of the cross-sectional design is that it takes an extended period of time to collect all the necessary information.

_____

_____

THE BEGINNING OF LIFE

_____ 3. The terms "chromosome," "gene," and "DNA molecules" are arranged from largest to smallest independent unit.

_____

_____

_____ 4. Huntington's disease is a genetic condition that newborn infants are routinely screened for; if the condition is present, dietary changes can prevent the symptoms of the disease.

_____

_____

PRENATAL DEVELOPMENT

_____ 5. By the end of the eighth week of prenatal development, almost all of an embryo's organs are formed and the heart is already functioning.

_____

_____

_____ 6. Results of experiments with rats suggest that early experience effects the anatomy and biochemistry of the brain.

_____

_____

COGNITIVE DEVELOPMENT

_____ 7. The process of assimilation allows one to adapt and change schemas as new information is gained.

_____

_____

_____ 8. Children are first able to understand the principle of conservation in the preoperational stage of cognitive development.

_____

_____

PSYCHOSOCIAL DEVELOPMENT

_____ 9. Harlow's research with infant monkeys raised in isolation with artificial mothers demonstrated the high level of importance the feeding situation has in establishing an attachment to the "mother."

_____

_____

_____ 10. According to Erikson's theory of psychosocial development, the major conflict of adolescence is identity versus role confusion.

_____

_____

GENDER IDENTITY

_____ 11. Chromosomal makeup (XX or XY) determines gender identity.

_____

_____

_____ 12. Assimilation refers to the process whereby society conveys behavioral expectations to the individual.

_____

_____

Answer Key
1. T   2. F   3. T   4. F   5. T   6. T   7. F   8. F   9. F   10. T   11. F   12. F

– PART V. MULTIPLE-CHOICE QUESTIONS –

Choose the best answer to each question. Circle your choice. Check your answers against the Answer Key. Questions marked with an asterisk (*) include annotated answers.

DEVELOPMENTAL ISSUES

1. Which of the following is true foor individuals who believe that learning and experience largely determine development?
   a. They view maturation as an important process.
   b. They support the nurture side of the nature-nurture controversy.
   c. They support the nature side of the nature-nurture controversy.
   d. They see development as being comprised of qualitatively distinct stages.

2. In the nature-nurture controversy, the majority of contemporary psychologists _____.
   a. tend to support the nurture side
   b. tend to support the nature side
   c. are interested in how nature and nurture interact to influence development
   d. are interested in identifying specific behaviors that can be explained by referring only to nature or only to nurture

3. Unlike psychologists who emphasize the role of learning, psychologists who emphasize maturation view development as a _____ process that results in _____ changes.
   a. continuous / qualitative
   b. continuous / quantitative
   c. discontinuous / qualitative
   d. discontinuous / quantitative

4. If you believe that certain experiences must occur during a specific window of time in our lives in order for development to proceed normally, which of the following views would you support?
   a. Critical periods exist.
   b. Critical periods can be indefinitely extended.
   c. Imprinting is responsible for much of human development and behavior.
   d. Critical periods do not exist.

DEVELOPMENTAL RESEARCH

*5. A parent who measures his or her child each year by putting a mark on the wall to note how tall that child is would basically be using a _____ design.
   a. correlational
   b. cross-sequential
   c. cross-sectional
   d. longitudinal

6. Lewis Terman's classic long-term study of gifted children is of which research design?
   a. cross-sectional design
   b. longitudinal design
   c. cross-sequential design
   d. double-blind design

7. The research design used in developmental research that attempts to overcome some of the drawbacks associated with the other two designs is the _____ design.
   a. cross-longitudinal
   b. cross-sequential
   c. cross-sectional
   d. longitudinal

THE BEGINNING OF LIFE

*8. If a woman gives birth to twins, and one of the twins is a boy and the other a girl, it can be concluded that the twins are _____ twins.
   a. monozygotic
   b. dizygotic
   c. identical
   d. You require more information before you can reach a conclusion.

9. If a woman gives birth to twins who are both boys, it can be concluded that the twins are _____ twins.
   a. monozygotic
   b. dizygotic
   c. identical
   d. You require more information before you can reach a conclusion.

10. If an individual is homozygous for a specific trait, his or her genotype and phenotype will _____.
    a. be consistent
    b. not be consistent
    c. only be consistent if that person has at least one dominant gene
    d. only be consistent if that person has at least one recessive gene

*11. Which of the following is true of a person who is heterozygous for a sex-linked recessive trait (e.g., red-green color blindness)?
    a. The person will not exhibit the recessive trait in his/her phenotype.
    b. The person is female.
    c. The person may have offspring who exhibit the recessive trait regardless of the genetic makeup of the other parent.
    d. All of the above are correct.

12. Which of the following genetic abnormalities does not result from a defective gene?
    a. sickle-cell anemia
    b. phenylketonuria (PKU)
    c. Down syndrome
    d. Huntington's disease

PRENATAL DEVELOPMENT

13. In order, the three stages of prenatal development are _____, _____, and _____.
    a. embryonic, fetal, prenatal
    b. germinal, nonviable, viable
    c. germinal, embryonic, fetal
    d. embryonic, germinal, fetal

14. The period from the third through the eighth week of prenatal development that is characterized by very fast growth and differentiation of many organs is called the _____ stage.
    a. embryonic
    b. fetal
    c. germinal
    d. zygote

15. Which of the following is true of a newborn's brain?
    a. It has only 25 percent of the neurons of an adult.
    b. It has 75 percent of all the neurons it will ever have.
    c. It has 50 percent of all the neurons it will ever have.
    d. It has most—if not all—of the neurons it will ever have.

PHYSICAL DEVELOPMENT

16. The physical growth of children is more rapid during the first _____ year(s) of life, after which growth stabilizes at about two or three inches a year until the adolescent growth spurt.
    a. one
    b. two
    c. three
    d. four

17. That babies have proportionally larger heads than adults illustrates the _____ pattern of development.
    a. proximocaudal
    b. proximodistal

    c. cephalocaudal

    d. cephalodistal

18. Early experience or training _____ the rate at which children acquire motor skills such as standing, walking, and bladder control.

    a. does not significantly accelerate

    b. significantly accelerates

    c. significantly slows down

    d. This effects children in an unpredictable fashion.

COGNITIVE DEVELOPMENT

19. A mental structure that guides future behavior while providing a framework for making sense out of new information is called _____.

    a. an operation

    b. a schema

    c. accommodation

    d. assimilation

20. A child sees a cow and says, " Look, Mommy, at the big doggie." According to Piaget he or she is using a mental process known as _____.

    a. conservation

    b. centration

    c. assimilation

    d. accommodation

21. The process of _____ is used when it is necessary to modify or revise a schema to account for new information.

    a. restructuring

    b. accommodation

    c. assimilation

    d. either assimilation or accommodation

22. The correct order of Piaget's stages of cognitive development is _____, _____, _____ and _____.

    a. sensorimotor, concrete operations, preoperational, formal operations

    b. preoperational, sensorimotor, concrete operations, formal operations

    c. concrete operations, preoperational, sensorimotor, formal operations

    d. sensorimotor, preoperational, concrete operations, formal operations

23. When is a child first capable of imitating the facial expression of another?

    a. within a few days of birth

    b. at about six months of age

    c. in the latter part of the sensorimotor stage

    d. in the early preoperational stage

*24. If a child believes that a nickel is more desirable to have than a dime, that child is probably in the _____ stage of cognitive development.

    a. concrete operations

    b. preoperational

    c. formal operations

    d. sensorimotor

25. A child begins to use logic to solve problems during the _____ stage of cognitive development, and can first think abstractly in the _____ stage of cognitive development.
    a. formal operations / concrete operations
    b. preoperational / concrete operation
    c. concrete operations / formal operations
    d. preoperational / formal operations

26. Regarding gender differences in cognitive abilities, males surpass females in _____.
    a. spatial
    b. logical
    c. mathematical
    d. verbal

PSYCHOSOCIAL DEVELOPMENT

27. Harlow's study revealed that _____ was more important in attachment than being fed.
    a. the odor of the feeding mother
    b. the type of food being given
    c. contact comfort
    d. the taste of the milk

28. The effects of emotional and social deprivation in infancy _____.
    a. have devastating and irreversible effects
    b. can be overcome if the child later receives plenty of loving nurturance
    c. can be overcome in humans but not in monkeys
    d. can be overcome in monkeys but not in humans

29. What is the "strange situation" used to evaluate?
    a. a child's stage of cognitive development
    b. infant–mother attachment
    c. mother–infant attachment
    d. a child's stage of psychosocial development

30. Infants in the process of forming a secure attachment to their primary caretaker would be in the _____ stage of Erikson's theory of psychosocial development.
    a. security versus insecurity
    b. trust versus mistrust
    c. belongingness versus rejection
    d. intimacy versus isolation

31. While in an unfamiliar environment, an infant who shows apprehension and tends not to leave his or her mother's side to explore would be said to be _____ attached.
    a. overly
    b. securely
    c. insecurely
    d. permissively

32. The parent who establishes reasonable rules in an atmosphere of warmth and open dialogue would be a(n) _____ parent.
    a. authoritarian
    b. authoritative

c. permissive

d. autocratic

33. The stage of Erikson's theory of psychosocial development that is characterized by an extensive reflection concerning past accomplishments and failures concerns the _____ crisis.

a. ego integrity versus despair

b. initiative versus guilt

c. generativity versus stagnation

d. industry versus inferiority

GENDER IDENTITY

*34. For every developing individual, during the first few weeks of prenatal development what do the gonads have the capacity to become?

a. either testes or ovaries

b. either a penis or a clitoris

c. Both of the above

d. Neither of the above

35. Which of the following is not a biological factor that influences gender identity?

a. gonadal sex

b. sex of the internal reproductive structures

c. sex differentiation of the brain

d. androgyny

36. Which of the following is true of pseudohermaphrodites?

a. They possess sexually ambiguous external reproductive structures.

b. They have gonads that match their chromosomal sex.

c. They have both ovaries and testes.

d. Both a and b are correct.

37. If your daughter developed breasts but even after several years did not begin menstruation, and all other causes had been ruled out, a medical doctor would most likely diagnose _____.

a. the presence of two Y chromosomes

b. androgen insensitivity syndrome

c. DHT deficient male syndrome

d. fetally androgenized female syndrome

38. Concerning gender identity, most researchers support the _____.

a. perceptual model

b. overwhelming importance of psychosocial factors over biological factors

c. overwhelming importance of biological factors over psychosocial factors

d. interactional model

39. Socialization is most directly associated with _____.

a. gender roles

b. gender reality

c. the timing of puberty

d. gender identity

   1. b   2. c   3. c   4. a   *5. d   6. b   7. b   *8. b   9. d   10. a   *11. d   12. c
   13. c   14. a   15. d   16. c   17. c   18. a   19. b   20. c   21. b   22. d   23. a   *24. b
   25. c   26. a   27. c   28. b   29. b   30. b   31. c   32. b   33. a   *34. a   35. d   36. d
   37. b   38. d   39. a

Annotated Answers

5. The correct choice is **d**. The longitudinal design would require measuring the height of a child (or more accurately a number of children) at several different times.
    a. A correlational design would require measuring a number of children on two variables (e.g., height and age) to determine the relationship between the variables.
    b. A cross-sequential design would require measuring a number of children of different ages at more than one time.
    c. The cross-sectional design would require measuring a number of children of different ages (e.g., 6, 8, 10) at one specific time.

8. The correct choice is **b**. Dizygotic or fraternal twins do not have the same genetic makeup. Because one twin is a girl having two X chromosomes, and the other twin a boy having one X and one Y chromosome, these twins must be dizygotic.
    a. Monozygotic twins have exactly the same genetic makeup and are the same sex.
    c. Identical twins is another term for monozygotic twins.
    d. The fact that the sex of the twins differ is sufficient to allow you to draw a conclusion.

11. The correct choice is **d**. All of the alternatives are correct.
    a. Because an individual who is heterozygous for the trait has at least one dominant gene, he or she would not show the recessive trait.
    b. Because males only have one gene for sex-linked traits (their Y chromosome does not contain the gene), a heterozygous individual must be female.
    c. If a heterozygous female were to conceive a child with a male who did not have the recessive gene, there is a 50 percent probability that any sons they would have would receive the recessive gene from the mother and exhibit the recessive trait.

24. The correct choice is **b**. A preoperational child (for example, a 4-year-old) whose thinking is governed by appearances would interpret the larger nickel as bigger and more desirable than the smaller dime.
    a. A child in the concrete-operations stage, who is capable of decentration, would logically evaluate the nickel and dime according to their monetary worth and ignore the physical size of the coins.
    c. A child in the formal-operations stage would be able to approach the problem in the same manner as the concrete-operational child, and additionally might approach the problem from an abstract perspective.
    d. It would be unrealistic to view a sensorimotor child as thinking of either the nickel or dime as particularly desirable.

34. The correct choice is **a**. The term gonads relates to either the male testes or female ovaries. If H-Y antigen is prenatally present during the first few weeks, the gonadal tissue differentiates into testes. If H-Y antigen is not present, the gonadal tissue differentiates into ovaries.
    b. The penis and/or clitoris do not develop from the gonads. The development of both is determined after the gonads develop. If the gonadal tissue becomes testes, the testes normally secrete sufficient levels of androgens to influence the development of the penis.
    c. This choice is incorrect because **b** is incorrect.
    d. This choice is incorrect because **a** is correct.

– PART VI. SUMMARY TABLES –

To test your understanding of the material discussed in this chapter, complete the following tables. Check your answers with those supplied in Part IX.

PIAGET'S THEORY OF COGNITIVE DEVELOPMENT

Stage	Ages	Characteristics	Limitations
Sensorimotor			
Preoperational			
Concrete operations			
Formalo perations			

BIOLOGICAL FACTORS INFLUENCING GENDER IDENTITY

Factor	Influence
Chromosomal sex	
Gondal sex	
Hormonal sex	
Sex on internal organ	
Sex of external organ	
Sex differentiation of the brain	

– PART VII. THOUGHT QUESTIONS/CRITICAL THINKING –

Prepare answers to the following discussion questions.

1. Describe what Piaget's position would be regarding the nature-nurture controversy.

2. Genetic counseling allows couples to estimate the probability of conceiving a child with a specific genetic disorder. Imagine that you are a genetic counselor helping the following couples decide on whether or not to conceive. In each of the following examples, determine the probability of conceiving a child who would exhibit the genetic disorder in their phenotype.
   a. For a trait in which the disorder is associated with a recessive gene (for example, PKU):
       (1) Both parents are homozygous for the dominant gene.
       (2) Both parents are homozygous for the recessive gene.
       (3) One parent is homozygous for the dominant gene and the other parent is heterozygous.
       (4) One parent is homozygous for the recessive gene and the other parent is heterozygous.
       (5) Both parents are heterozygous
       (6) One parent is homozygous for the dominant gene and the other parent is homozygous for the recessive gene.
   b. For a trait in which the disorder is associated with a dominant gene (for example, Huntington's disease):
       (1) Both parents are homozygous for the dominant gene.
       (2) Both parents are homozygous for the recessive gene.
       (3) One parent is homozygous for the dominant gene and the other parent is heterozygous.
       (4) One parent is homozygous for the recessive gene and the other parent is heterozygous.
       (5) Both parents are heterozygous.

3. What would you tell your brother and sister-in-law who are concerned about their four-year-old child who had previously grown at a steady and fairly rapid rate but has only grown two inches in the past year?

4. For each of the following examples, determine at which stage of cognitive development the child is. Explain your reasoning.
   a. I have a vivid memory of sitting at the kitchen table while my two children were standing and twirling themselves around in circles. After spinning for a while they asked, "Are you dizzy yet, Mom?"
   b. You place five toy dogs and three toy cats on a table and ask a child, "Are there more dogs or more animals?" Child #1 replies, "More dogs." Child #2 replies, "More animals."

5. A couple is considering adopting an eight-month-old infant who was recently placed in foster care after a history of abuse and neglect in the biological family. The couple is concerned whether or not adopting this child is a good idea or if they would be "asking for trouble" in the future. Based on the information in the text concerning the effects of early social deprivation and attachment, what advice would you give the couple?

6. Imagine that you and your spouse just had a baby who was born with sexually ambiguous external reproductive structures. In order to help you decide whether it would be best to raise your child as your son or as your daughter, what questions would you ask the doctor?

– PART VIII. APPLICATIONS –

1. Imagine that you are a developmental psychologist interested in studying how children of different ages respond and adjust to changing schools in the middle of a school year. Design three studies to evaluate the topic: a cross-sectional design, a longitudinal design, and a cross-sequential design. For each of the three designs: What age(s) of children would you study? When or how long after the school change would you evaluate the children? Discuss possible weaknesses or limitations associated with each design. Which design would give you the most complete information?

2. Problem: You are given six different-colored plastic tokens (red, orange, yellow, green, blue, and purple). List all the possible pairs of colors that can be made from these six colors. Write down your solution to the problem.

   For the following three solutions to the problem, decide at what stage of cognitive development an individual would be who would give each solution.
   a. It's easy, you could have R&O, Y&G, B&P.
   b. R&O, Y&G, B&P, R&G, B&G, Y&P, B&R, Y&R, B&O, G&P, R&B.
   c. R&O, R&Y, R&G, R&B, R&P, O&Y, O&G, O&B, O&P, Y&G, Y&B, Y&P, G&B, G&P, B&P.

   Refer back to your own solution. What stage of cognitive development does your solution suggest?

– PART IX. SUMMARY TABLES SOLUTIONS –

PIAGET'S THEORY OF COGNITIVE DEVELOPMENT

Stage	Ages	Characteristics	Limitations
Sensorimotor	0–2	Learns through sensing and doing Acquires object permanence Can perform goal-directed behavior	Does not think, per se, just senses and does
Preoperational	2–7	Can think symbolically (language) Thoughts dependent on appearance or are intuitive Exhibits egocentrism	Incapable of conservation because shows centration
Concrete operations	7–12	Uses logical mental operations Masters conservation because shows decentration	Cannot yet think abstractly and hypothetically
Formal operations	12+	Abstract thought Systematically tests hypotheses to solve problems	Unlike other stages, a variety of situations may postpone or prevent individuals from entering this stage.

BIOLOGICAL FACTORS INFLUENCING GENDER IDENTITY

Factor	Influence
Chromosomal sex	Y chromosome is necessary for complete development of internal and external male sex organs (normal male XY) If there is no Y chromosome, female external sex organs develop Two X chromosomes are necessary for complete development of internal and external female sex organs (normal female XX).
Gondal sex	During first few weeks of development, presence of Y chromosome causes gonads to become testes. Without Y chromosome, gonads become ovaries.
Hormonal sex	Male gonads (testes) secrete androgens that cause development of external male sex organs. Without androgens (or too low a level of androgen), female structures develop.
Sex on internal organ	Follows from gonadal sex (above)
Sex of external organ	Follows from hormonal sex (above)
Sex differentiation of the brain	During prenatal development, level of testosterone results in sex differences in the hypothalamus and cerebral hemispheres.

CHAPTER 12

DEVELOPMENT 2: ADOLESCENCE TO THE END OF LIFE

– PART I. LEARNING OBJECTIVES –

When you finish studying this chapter, you should be able to do the following:

ADOLESCENCE

1. Define adolescence, and discuss how adolescence differs in different societies.

2. Summarize the physical changes of puberty, and describe secular growth trends.

3. Compare the effects of early and late maturation on boys and girls.

4. Describe the formal-operational thinking of the adolescent, and discuss factors that facilitate or hinder the development of formal-operational thought.

5. Define morality, and summarize and evaluate Kohlberg's theory of moral development.

6. Describe the adolescent's search for identity, and discuss the role parents and the peer group play in the process of establishing an identity.

7. Discuss a number of factors that influence adolescent sexual behavior.

ADULTHOOD

8. List the ages commonly associated with the three periods of adulthood, and discuss why use of these categories may not always be appropriate.

9. Summarize the changes in physical capacities in early and middle adulthood.

10. Discuss hormonal changes for men and women during early and middle adulthood, and describe the double standard of aging.

11. Discuss the evidence as to whether or not intelligence changes during adulthood. Evaluate crystallized and fluid intelligence separately.

12. Discuss how Erikson's developmental task of early adulthood—intimacy versus isolation—is related to the single, cohabitation, and married lifestyles.

13. Discuss how Erikson's developmental task of middle adulthood—generativity versus stagnation—is related to commitments to parenting and work.

14. Compare younger and middle-aged adults in terms of job satisfaction.

15. Describe recent changes concerning the number of women in the work force and discuss advantages and disadvantages for dual-career families.

THE OLDER YEARS

16. Describe changes in life expectancy since 1900, and discuss the phrase "the graying of America."

17. Summarize the physical changes that occur in the older years, and discuss how some of these changes may be reduced or compensated for.

18. Describe the genetic clock (or programmed) and accumulating damages theories concerning the physical process of aging, and discuss the implications of each.

19. Describe the cognitive abilities of older adults, and discuss the symptoms and probable causes of senile dementia and Alzheimer's disease.

20. Discuss factors related to "successful aging," and compare two theories concerning the psychosocial adjustment to aging.

21. Discuss the role of close relationships and social support on health in the older years.

– PART II. OVERVIEW –

Adolescence (approximately ages 12–20), or the transition from childhood to adulthood, is characterized by a number of dramatic changes. The adolescent growth spurt results in a rapid physical growth that is markedly different from the slow and steady growth characteristic of middle and late childhood. Sexual maturity is reached shortly after completion of the adolescent growth spurt (typically two years in duration). Cognitively, the adolescent may enter Piaget's stage of formal operations and become capable of abstract and hypothetical thought—able to approach problems in a more systematic manner than younger children. The psychosocial development of adolescence is exemplified by the tendency of adolescents to be strongly influenced by the peer group and a striving for independence from the parents. The adolescent is concerned with establishing a sense of identity and may experiment with many identities or roles before establishing a firm sense of identity.

Kohlberg's theory of moral development has three levels of moral reasoning. It proposes that individuals progress in their moral reasoning from a self-serving approach to morality, to an approach to morality governed by a desire to gain approval and maintain social order. In Kohlberg's fifth level of moral development (which is attained by only 25 percent of adults), the individual's moral reasoning affirms individual rights and ethical principles.

During adulthood (prior to age 65) an individual reaches his or her physical and reproductive peak and then begins to decline. Depending on what aspect of cognitive or intellectual functioning is being referred to, cognitive abilities may increase (crystallized intelligence) or reach a peak in early adulthood and then decline (fluid intelligence).

According to Erikson's theory of psychosocial development, during early adulthood the individual is concerned with establishing intimacy. Most commonly, marriage is viewed as the way to establish intimacy, but cohabitation and remaining single (if the individual has an appropriate network of friends) can alternatively fulfill intimacy needs. According to Erikson, middle adulthood is characterized by a desire to achieve continual productivity or generativity, which is associated with a commitment to raising children and/or employment (career).

There are many negative stereotypes associated with the older years (after age 65). However, most older adults continue to function very well. Many of the physical changes associated with the older years may be compensated for (e.g., hearing aids) or postponed if the individual regularly exercises. Although a small but significant number of elderly individuals do suffer from senile dementia, 90 percent or more of older adults show little cognitive deterioration. Alzheimer's disease is the most common form of senile dementia and is currently being extensively studied. Evidence suggests that Alzheimer's disease may result from the abnormal processing and accumulation of an extra cellular protein called beta-amyloid protein. Older individuals who have relatively good health, close ties to family and friends, and are financially secure tend to have the best psychosocial adjustment to aging. Older individuals frequently conduct life reviews examining their past successes and failures. Life reviews are consistent with Erikson's view that the main task of the older years is to achieve a sense of integrity that is associated with one's successes in earlier stages of psychosocial development.

– PART III. KEY TERMS/MATCHING EXERCISES –

Match the following concepts with the appropriate descriptions. Check your answers against the Answer Key.

ADOLESCENCE

Concepts	Descriptions
_____ 1. secular growth trends	a. Period of rapid physical growth that precedes sexual maturity
_____ 2. puberty	b. Characterized by the capacity to mentally manipulate objects and use deductive reasoning
_____ 3. secondary sex characteristics	c. Characterized by a desire to gain the approval of others or maintain social order
_____ 4. adolescence	d. Period of development that lasts for several years; the transition between childhood and adulthood
_____ 5. formal-operational thinking	e. Describe(s) difference(s) in the physical growth and age of sexual maturity that exist between generations or societies
_____ 6. adolescent growth spurt	f. Characterized by a desire to avoid punishment or to obtain rewards
_____ 7. conventional morality	g. Characterized by a desire to affirm the values of society or to uphold universal ethical principles
_____ 8. postconventional morality	h. Approximately two-year period of rapid physical change that culminates in sexual maturity
_____ 9. preconventional morality	i. Result(s) from the release of increased levels of gonadotropins during puberty

Answer Key
1. e   2. h   3. i   4. d   5. b   6. a   7. c   8. g   9. f

ADULTHOOD

Concepts	Descriptions
_____ 1. crystallized intelligence	a. According to Erikson's psychosocial theory, the primary developmental task of middle adulthood
_____ 2. menopause	b. Includes language skills and knowledge of how to reason, and tends to improve during one's lifetime
_____ 3. generativity	c. Describe(s) the physiological changes associated with women's transition from fertility to infertility
_____ 4. cohabitation	d. Living together in a sexual relationship without being married
_____ 5. climacteric	e. Includes(s) the ability to conceptualize abstract information and draw inferences; tends to decline steadily after age 30
_____ 6. intimacy	f. According to Erikson's psychosocial theory, the primary developmental task of early adulthood
_____ 7. fluid intelligence morality	g. Cessation of menstruation that commonly occurs between age 45–50)
_____ 8. andropause	h. Gradual hormonal changes experienced by men

Answer Key
1. b   2. g   3. a   4. d   5. c   6. f   7. e   8. h

THE OLDER YEARS

Concepts	Descriptions
_____ 1. activity theory	a. Ability of the heart, lungs, and so forth to perform at levels above normal range that declines with age
_____ 2. accumulating damages theory	b. Proposes that physical aging and duration of life is basically the result of the body wearing out
_____ 3. genetic clock (programmed) theory	c. Proposes that older people tend to reminisce about past accomplishments and failures
_____ 4. disengagement theory	d. Proposes that the duration of life is limited by the inability of cells to divide more than a predetermined number of times
_____ 5. organ reserve	e. Condition that affects cognitive abilities and may be caused by an accumulation of beta-amyloid
_____ 6. senile dementia	f. Proposes that older individuals are more likely to be happy if they reduce their level of activity by reducing social obligations and taking time to relax
_____ 7. integrity	g. Proposes that older individuals are more likely to be happy if they maintain a high level of involvement in activities
_____ 8. Alzheimer's disease	h. Describes a variety of conditions characterized by cognitive symptoms, altered personalities, and interpersonal difficulties
_____ 9. life review	i. According to Erikson's psychosocial theory, the primary developmental task of the older years

Answer Key
   1. g   2. b   3. d   4. f   5. a   6. h   7. i   8. e   9. c

– PART IV. TRUE/FALSE STATEMENTS –

Fill in the blank before each statement with either a T (true) or an F (false). Check your answers against the Answer Key. Then go back to the items that are false and make the necessary change(s) to the statements to convert the items into true statements.

ADOLESCENCE

_____ 1. Adolescence refers to the approximately two-year period of rapid physical change that culminates in sexual maturity.

_____

_____

_____ 2. Secular growth trend refers to the observation that in recent times industrial societies' adolescents reach sexual maturity at a later age than previous generations.

_____

_____

_____ 3. Typically by late childhood or early adolescence, an individual would be functioning at the level of conventional morality.

_____

_____

_____ 4. An important part of an adolescent's establishing an identity is gaining independence from parents.

_____

_____

ADULTHOOD

_____ 5. The term climacteric refers to physiological changes associated with the transition from fertility to infertility for both men and women.

_____

_____

_____ 6. The results of longitudinal studies suggest that people retain their intellect well into middle age.

_____

_____

_____ 7. Fluid intelligence allows us to draw inferences about relationships among patterns of stimuli and to solve problems and is linked closely to education.

_____

_____

_____ 8. Single life has become more popular than ever; according to statistical projections, it is expected that only half of the 20-year-olds in the year 2000 will eventually marry.

_____

_____

THE OLDER YEARS

_____ 9. The brain begins to decrease in size as a result of neuron loss by about age 40.

_____

_____

_____ 10. Alzheimer's disease is the most common form of senile dementia.

_____

_____

_____ 11. The activity theory proposes that the aging process is a consequence of wear and tear on one's body.

_____

_____

_____ 12. Individuals who make the best psychosocial adjustment to the older years tend to be in good health, to be financially secure, and to have close ties with family and friends.

_____

_____

– PART V. MULTIPLE-CHOICE QUESTIONS –

Choose the best answer to each question. Circle your choice. Check your answers against the Answer Key. Questions marked with an asterisk (*) include annotated answers.

ADOLESCENCE

1. Which of the following would *not* be included in a definition of adolescence concerning youth in the United States today?
    a. It typically spans age 12–20.
    b. It is marked by a specific rite of passage.
    c. It is a time of social role development.
    d. It is a time of dramatic physiological change.

2. It would be appropriate for parents to be concerned if their _____ started to undergo the beginning of puberty.
    a. 8-year-old girl
    b. 8-year-old boy
    c. 14-year-old girl
    d. 16-year-old boy

*3. Which of the following is true about the adolescent growth spurt
    a. It occurs at a younger age in boys than in girls.
    b. It refers to a four-year time span of rapid physical growth in early adolescence.
    c. It is completed before a child reaches sexual maturity.
    d. It occurs after a child reaches sexual maturity.

*4. Which of the following is a secondary sex characteristic?
    a. pubic hair
    b. a penis or vagina
    c. adult height
    d. none of the above

5. Advantages such as being poised, popular, and academically successful are associated with _____.
    a. early-maturing girls
    b. late-maturing girls
    c. early-maturing boys
    d. late-maturing boys

6. When people have cognitively matured to the point at which they can explore hypothetical or "what if" possibilities, Piaget would say that they are in the _____ stage.
    a. sensorimotor
    b. preoperational
    c. concrete-operations
    d. formal-operations

7. Approximately _____ of American college students would be considered to be in the formal-operations stage of cognitive development.
   a. 15 percent
   b. 50 percent
   c. 80 percent
   d. 95 percent

*8. Kohlberg was more interested in a person's _____ rather than in his or her _____.
   a. moral behavior / moral reasoning
   b. yes or no answer to a moral dilemma / moral behavior
   c. yes or no answer to a moral dilemma / moral reasoning
   d. moral reasoning / yes or no answer to a moral dilemma

9. According to Kohlberg, a period in which moral judgments are derived from moral or ethical principles and personal values, and not from authority figures, is the _____ stage.
   a. concrete-conventional
   b. postconventional
   c. preconventional
   d. conventional

10. In response to Kohlberg's moral dilemma concerning Heinz, a person answers, "He shouldn't have stolen the drug because it's against the law to steal." That person would be classified at the _____ stage of moral development.
   a. second
   b. third
   c. fourth
   d. fifth

11. The popular image of the teenage years as a time of rebellion, storm, and stress is _____.
   a. substantiated by studies
   b. applicable only to early adolescent years
   c. more myth than fact
   d. true only in America

12. An adolescent is most influenced by the peer group in matters concerning _____.
   a. dress and hair styles
   b. moral values
   c. career choice
   d. politics

ADULTHOOD

13. Most people reach the peak of their reproductive capacities and enjoy the best health of any time in their lives during _____.
   a. middle adulthood
   b. early adulthood
   c. later adulthood
   d. late adolescence

14. When does physical strength tend to peak?
    a. late adolescence
    b. the mid- to late twenties
    c. the early thirties
    d. the mid- to late thirties

15. What is one problem with cross-sectional studies on intelligence?
    a. The older group experienced less formal education.
    b. The older group has less experience with standardized tests.
    c. Groups have experienced varied cultural conditions.
    d. All of the above reasons are valid.

16. _____ intelligence results from accumulated knowledge and is closely linked to education and experience. _____ intelligence allows a person to conceptualize abstract information and is relatively independent of education.
    a. Crystallized / fluid
    b. Fluid / crystallized
    c. Problem-finding / dialectic-operation
    d. Dialectic-operation / problem-solving

17. What does research indicate about crystallized intelligence?
    a. It peaks in early adulthood and remains at that level.
    b. It peaks in early adulthood and then steadily declines.
    c. It peaks in middle adulthood and then slowly declines.
    d. It increases with age.

18. To what did one study link satisfaction with single life?
    a. avoiding the fear of divorce
    b. the number and types of friendships
    c. not needing sexual relations
    d. having more money to spend

*19. The text does *not* include research findings indicating that cohabitation _____.
    a. is not a factor in subsequent marital adjustment
    b. results in fewer subsequent divorces
    c. results in more subsequent divorces
    d. has no effect on a subsequent marriage

20. Approximately _____ out of 10 American adults marry at least once.
    a. 6
    b. 7
    c. 8
    d. 9

21. The nurturing of children is _____.
    a. incompatible with a successful career
    b. helpful in the expression of generativity
    c. helpful in the expression of intimacy
    d. helpful in the discovery of an identity

22. Over the past few decades, what is true about the proportion of Americans 65 and over?
    a. It has stabilized after an increase in the early 1900s.
    b. It has grown at twice the rate of the rest of the population.
    c. It has grown at three times the rate of the rest of the population.
    d. It has slightly decreased.

23. Which of the following vision problems is *not* increasingly common in the older years?
    a. night vision problems
    b. perceiving color
    c. farsightedness
    d. nearsightedness

24. People over age 65 are *less likely* than younger people to suffer from _____.
    a. hypertension
    b. hearing loss
    c. digestive problems
    d. arthritis

25. The _____ theory of aging is supported by the observation that identical twins have very similar life spans.
    a. genetic clock or programmed
    b. climacteric
    c. accumulating damages
    d. activity

26. What is a possible explanation of why fluid intelligence declines in older years and crystallized intelligence remains the same?
    a. Fluid intelligence is genetic.
    b. Fluid intelligence is learned.
    c. Older people are not challenged to use their fluid intelligence.
    d. Older people do not need fluid intelligence.

27. To what does current evidence link the cause of Alzheimer's disease?
    a. an excess of the beta-amyloid protein
    b. a defective gene on chromosome 21
    c. environmental factors
    d. gene mutations on several chromosomes

28. Of the population that is over 65, _____ show little or no cognitive deterioration.
    a. 10 percent
    b. 25 percent
    c. 60 percent
    d. 90 percent

29. Satisfaction with life in general, feelings of well-being, and marital satisfaction _____ among the aged than among younger adults.
    a. are more similar
    b. tend to be higher
    c. tend to be slightly lower
    d. tend to be dramatically lower

*30. The _____ theory suggests that people will more likely experience happiness in their "golden years" if they cut back on the stresses associated with an active life.
   a. disassociation
   b. activity
   c. inactivity
   d. disengagement

31. Erikson's developmental task of the older years—ego integrity versus despair—is consistent with the idea that older people _____.
   a. select a lifestyle that reflects their personality
   b. are concerned with problem finding
   c. conduct a life review
   d. demonstrate postconventional thought

32. A number of studies have demonstrated the health benefits of _____ in reducing risks of disease and prolonging life in the older years.
   a. an early retirement
   b. postponing retirement until the mid-seventies
   c. social support
   d. financial security

Answer Key

1. b	2. b	*3. c	*4. a	5. c	6. d	7. b	*8. d	9. b	10. c	11. c	12. a
13. b	14. b	15. d	16. a	17. d	18. b	*19. b	20. d	21. b	22. b	23. d	24. c
25. a	26. c	27. a	28. d	29. b	*30. d	31. c	32. c				

Annotated Answers

3. The correct choice is **c**. Sexual maturity is typically attained soon after the adolescent growth spurt is completed.
   a. Because girls typically enter and complete puberty two years before boys do, the adolescent growth spurt occurs at a younger age for girls than for boys.
   b. The adolescent growth spurt is two years in duration and not four years.
   d. The adolescent growth spurt occurs before sexual maturity is attained.

4. The correct choice is **a**. Secondary sex characteristics refer to physical changes of the body that occur during puberty and are controlled by gonadotropins and testosterone (in males) and estrogens (in females). Pubic hair is present in mature males and females and is not present in either sex prior to puberty.
   b. The penis and vagina are primary sex characteristics present from birth.
   c. Adult height is reached during puberty, but it is not a secondary sex characteristic. Secondary sex characteristics are related to gonadotropins and sex hormones, whereas adult height is controlled by other growth hormones.
   d. This choice is incorrect because choice **a** is correct.

8. The correct choice is **d**. Kohlberg was interested in the thought process (moral reasoning) and not in the yes or no answer a person gave in response to a moral dilemma. People at very different stages of development could give the same yes or no answer. For example, "Yes, he should steal it because if he let his wife die he would get in trouble" (stage 1); and "Yes, if he had failed to act in this fashion to save his wife, he would not have lived up to his own standards of conscience" (stage 6).
   a. Kohlberg's theory is not concerned with an individual's actual actions (moral behavior). In fact, moral behavior and moral reasoning often do not go hand in hand.
   b. The person's yes or no answer was not what Kohlberg was most interested in. He was interested in the person's moral reasoning.

c. This choice has the two correct components of Kohlberg's approach to studying moral development, but here the components are reversed.

19. The correct choice is **b**. The text does not mention any studies to indicate that cohabitation leads to fewer subsequent divorces.
    a. The text reports that no differences in subsequent marital adjustment were found based on whether couples had cohabitated or had had traditional courtships.
    c. The text reports, for example, that one study found more marriages fail within 10 years if the couple lived together before marriage than if the couple did not cohabitate.
    d. The text reports, for example, that another study found that cohabitation did not have any influence on subsequent marital happiness.

30. The correct choice is **d**. This theory proposes that if older individuals cut back or disengaged themselves from stressors and took time to relax, more likely they would be happy or content.
    a. There is no disassociation theory related to successful aging.
    b. Unlike the disengagement theory, the activity theory proposes that the key to successful aging is to remain active and involved in activities.
    c. There is no inactivity theory related to successful aging.

– PART VI. SUMMARY TABLE –

To test your understanding of the material discussed in this chapter, complete the following tables. Check your answers with those supplied in Part IX.

ADOLESCENCE, ADULTHOOD, AND THE OLDER VIEWS

Type of Development	Adolescence	Adulthood	Older Years
Physical			
Cognitive			
Psychosocial			

– PART VII. THOUGHT QUESTIONS/CRITICAL THINKING –

Prepare answers to the following discussion questions.

1. In many families in which both father and son are athletically inclined, it is a memorable occasion when the son first beats the father in a game of one-on-one basketball (or some other similar event). Assume that the father was 25 years old when the son was born. Predict how old each would be when the son first beats his father.

2. Discuss possible reasons why there are more advantages associated with being an early-maturing boy than an early-maturing girl.

3. The influence of Piaget's theory of cognitive development is apparent in many aspects of development. Discuss each of the following examples from a Piagetian perspective.
   a. Erikson states that the primary developmental task of adolescence is establishing an identity. Why doesn't this crisis develop at a younger age?
   b. Kohlberg's theory of moral development is in many ways an outgrowth of Piaget's theory. At which level of cognitive development would an individual most likely be at each of Kohlberg's levels of moral development? Explain.

4. Explain why you believe or disbelieve that it is reasonable for women to go through a definite transition from fertility to infertility (menopause and the climacteric) usually between age 45–50, whereas men remain fertile for a much longer period of time and only gradually become infertile.

– PART VIII. APPLICATIONS –

1. The text describes Kohlberg's theory of moral development, and Table 12.1 provides sample answers to the Heinz dilemma illustrating the six levels of moral development. This application involves evaluating the stage of moral reasoning of three or four individuals. Ideally, the individuals should range in age from junior high age through college or adulthood. However, if you do not have access to young individuals, using only college students is acceptable. Read the Heinz dilemma to each individual and ask them the following questions. Record their responses to each question.
   a. Should Heinz have stolen the drug? Why or why not?
   b. What's to be said for obeying the law in this situation? In general?
   c. If the husband doesn't love his wife, is he obligated to steal the drug for her? Why or why not?
   d. Would it be as moral to steal the drug for a stranger as for his wife? Why or why not?
   e. If Heinz steals the drug and is arrested, should the judge sentence him or let him go free? Explain.

   Decide at which stage of moral development you believe each individual is functioning. Because an individual's answers may not be completely consistent, this may be a difficult task. Did you find that older individuals gave answers that were characteristic of higher levels of moral development?

2. This chapter discusses Erikson's last four stages of development: adolescence (identity vs. role confusion), early adulthood (intimacy vs. isolation), middle adulthood (generativity vs. stagnation), and late adulthood (ego integrity vs. despair). Prepare a brief list of questions that relate to the various stages. Select one individual from each stage of life to interview. (You may use yourself to represent one stage; your relatives may be a good source to represent the other stages.) Briefly interview each individual to see if his or her experiences are consistent with Erikson's theory. Do the results of your interviews support Erikson's theory?

– PART IX. SUMMARY TABLE SOLUTIONS –

ADOLESCENCE, ADULTHOOD, AND THE OLDER VIEWS

Type of Development	Adolescence	Adulthood	Older Years
Physical	Period of rapid growth (adolescent growth spurt) Sexual maturity (puberty) is attained.	Physical abilities peak during early adulthood and then begin gradually to decline. Reproductive abilities also peak in early adulthood and slowly decline in men, while women show a marked transition from fertility to infertility (the climacteric).	Although many bodily systems decline, most individuals maintain relatively good health.
Cognitive	Formal-operations stage of cognitive development emerges; capable of abstract thought, deductive reasoning, and able to use strategies to approach problem solving	Crystallized intelligence (accumulated knowledge) continues to increase with age, while fluid intelligence (conceptualizing abstract information) peaks in early adulthood and then steadily declines.	For most individuals, crystallized intelligence continues to improve or remain stable, while fluid intelligence continues to decline. Small percentage of individuals experience severe reduction in mental functioning, or senile dementia.
Psychosocial	Concerned with identity formation or dealing with questions such as "Who am I?" and "Where am I headed?" Strives to gain independence from parents and is strongly influenced by the peer group	In early adulthood, concerned with finding intimacy In middle adulthood, concerned with generativity, which is associated with raising a family and employment (career)	Concerned with evaluating life and hopefully achieving a sense of integrity Feelings of satisfaction with life tend to be higher in older individuals than in young adults.

CHAPTER 13

INTELLIGENCE

– PART I. LEARNING OBJECTIVES –

When you finish studying this chapter, you should be able to do the following:

DEFINING AND MEASURING INTELLIGENCE

1. List and discuss two categories of behavior both psychologists and laypeople believe are characteristics of intelligent individuals, and describe a third category of behavior often included by laypeople.

2. Summarize a variety of ways in which intelligence has been defined, and discuss the operational definition of intelligence that is generally used.

3. Describe the approach Binet used to develop an intelligence test.

4. Define intelligence quotient (IQ), and describe how it is determined.

5. Discuss how Terman adapted Binet's test for American children and developed the Stanford-Binet test.

6. Explain why Wechsler developed the Wechsler Adult Intelligence Scale (WAIS), and describe its basic design.

7. Describe a number of group intelligence tests, and compare the advantages and disadvantages of group and individual intelligence tests.

EVALUATING INTELLIGENCE TESTS

8. List and describe the four steps in developing a standardized test.

9. Define reliability and validity, and describe several ways each is measured.

10. Define aptitude test and achievement test, and discuss why the differences between these two types of tests are not as clear-cut as these definitions imply.

THEORIES OF INTELLIGENCE

11. Compare and contrast the factorial theories of intelligence proposed by Spearman, Thurstone, and Guilford.

12. Discuss Sternberg's information-processing approach to problem solving, and describe how good problem solvers differ from other individuals when solving a problem.

13. Describe Sternberg's triarchic theory of successful intelligence.

14. Discuss Gardner's theory of multiple intelligences.

BIAS IN INTELLIGENCE TESTING

15. Define cultural bias, and describe the influence cultural bias may have on the intelligence test scores of individuals.

HEREDITARY AND ENVIRONMENTAL INFLUENCES ON INTELLIGENCE

16. Differentiate between the hereditarian and environmentalist views on intelligence.

17. Discuss the procedures involved in and results of twin studies concerning intelligence.

18. Summarize the evidence concerning the relative effects of nature and nurture on intelligence, and discuss the heritability of intelligence.

RACIAL DIFFERENCES IN INTELLIGENCE

19. Describe the difference in average IQ scores between whites and blacks, and discuss factors that contribute to this average difference.

– PART II. OVERVIEW –

Intelligence is a concept that all are familiar with, but because it refers to an abstract quality it is difficult to precisely define. It is therefore difficult to determine how to measure intelligence. Perhaps the best operational definition of intelligence is that it is what is measured by intelligence tests.

In 1905, the first practical intelligence test was developed in France by Binet in order to predict children's future success in school (specifically, the test was designed to predict those children who would have difficulty in a regular classroom). The average IQ (100) is calculated by the following formula: mental age/chronological age x 100. An American version of Binet's test (the Stanford-Binet test) was developed by Terman. The Wechsler Adult Intelligence Scale (WAIS) was developed to determine the IQ of older adolescents and adults and provides more detailed information than the Stanford-Binet test.

There are four primary steps involved in developing a test (either an intelligence test or other type of psychological test): (1) developing a pool of test items, (2) evaluating the test items, (3) standardizing the test, and (4) establishing norms. Additionally, for a test to be worthwhile and allow a psychologist to trust its results, it must have reliability (give consistent results for an individual) and validity (accurately measure what it is intended to measure).

Three factorial theories of intelligence that attempted to describe the factors or abilities that contribute to intelligence are discussed. Spearman believed that intelligence consisted of a general intelligence (g-factor) and also a number of specific abilities (s-factors). A person with a higher level of g-factor would tend to perform better on many tasks than a person with a lower level of g-factor. Thurstone believed that intelligence consisted of seven independent primary mental abilities. Guilford believed that intellectual tasks could be described as involving a number of operations (how we think) and contents (what we think about) that produce a number of different products. By calculating all the possible combinations of the above, he proposed that there were 150 kinds of intelligence. More recently, two theorists have attempted to describe the process of intelligence or how people effectively solve problems and interact with their environment. Sternberg's triarchic theory proposed that intelligence is composed of three separate abilities (componential, experiential, and contextual). An individual need not have similar intellectual levels concerning these three abilities. Gardner provided a view of intelligence that is much broader than the other approaches and describes intelligence as being composed of seven multiple intelligences that include musical, body, and interpersonal and intrapersonal intelligence.

A number of studies involving twins have been conducted to help determine the relative influence of heredity and environment on intelligence. Both factors exert an influence on an individual's IQ, but most psychologists believe that heredity plays the more prominent role. Environmental factors exert a more obvious effect in situations in which a disadvantaged environment tends to result in lower IQs than would develop in a more appropriate environment. Animal studies are also used to determine the influences of heredity versus environment.

Racial differences in average IQ exist, with American blacks scoring, on average, about 15 points lower than American whites. This result may be due to blacks being more likely to come from disadvantaged environments than whites, and to a cultural bias in the IQ test items. As differences in economic conditions diminish, we have witnessed a decrease in this IQ difference.

– PART III.   KEY TERMS/MATCHING EXERCISES –

Match the following concepts and/or individuals with the appropriate descriptions. Check your answers against the Answer Key.

INTELLIGENCE

Concepts	Descriptions
_____ 1. achievement test	a. Terman's American version of Binet's intelligence test
_____ 2. intelligence quotient (IQ)	b. Designed to predict an individual's ability to learn new information or new skill
_____ 3. Army Alpha and Army Beta tests	c. Mental age/chronological age **x** 100
_____ 4. Stanford-Binet test	d. Two of the first group-administered intelligence tests
_____ 5. reliability	e. Two group-intelligence tests commonly used today
_____ 6. standardization procedures	f. Actual or calendar age of an individual
_____ 7. validity	g. Designed to measure what an individual has already learned
_____ 8. Wechsler Adult Intelligence Scale (WAIS)	h. Refer(s) to whether a test measures with dependable consistency
_____ 9. aptitude tests	i. Reflect(s) the average test performance of a particular group of people
_____ 10. mental age	j. Provide(s) an estimate of the amount of variation in a trait that is due to genetic factors
_____ 11. chronological age	k. Refer(s) to whether a test accurately measures what it is intended to measure
_____ 12. intelligence	l. Refer(s) to uniform and consistent procedures for administering and scoring a test
_____ 13. heritability	m. Corresponds to the age of an average child who receives a similar test score on an IQ test
_____ 14. norm	n. Provides an overall IQ as well as a verbal and performance IQ
_____ 15. Otis-Lennon School Ability Test and Cognitive Abilities Test	o. Operationally defined as that which intelligence tests measure

Answer Key
  1. g   2. c   3. d   4. a   5. h   6. l   7. k   8. n   9. b   10. m   11. f   12. o
13. j   14. i   15. e

Individuals	Descriptions
_____ 1. Spearman	a. Proposed that there are 150 kinds of intelligence
_____ 2. Wechsler	b. Developed an intelligence test for late adolescents and adults that calculates verbal and performance IQs as well as overall IQ
_____ 3. Galton	c. Proposed that intelligence is composed of general intelligence and specific intellectual abilities
_____ 4. Binet	d. Adapted Binet's test for American children
_____ 5. Guilford	e. Proposed that intelligence includes a diversity of abilities, some of which (such as musical talent) are not typically included in definitions of intelligence
_____ 6. Thurstone	f. Developed an information-processing approach to problem solving and the triarchic theory of successful intelligence
_____ 7. Terman	g. Developed the first intelligence test, but it was not successful in measuring intelligence
_____ 8. Sternberg	h. Developed the first modern intelligence test
_____ 9. Gardner	i. Proposed that intelligence is a composite of seven primary mental abilities

Answer Key

1. c   2. b   3. g   4. h   5. a   6. i   7. d   8. f   9. e

– PART IV. TRUE-FALSE STATEMENTS –

Fill in the blank before each statement with either a T (true) or an F (false). Check your answers against the Answer Key. Then go back to the items that are false and make the necessary change(s) to the statements to convert the items into true statements.

DEFINING AND MEASURING INTELLIGENCE AND EVALUATING INTELLIGENCE TESTS

_____   1. Both laypeople and psychologists tend to view intelligence as being composed of verbal ability, practical problem-solving ability, and social competence.

_____

_____

_____   2. A good operational definition of intelligence is "the ability to think abstractly."

_____

_____

_____   3. Stanford adapted Binet's test for American children and developed the Stanford-Binet test.

_____

_____

_____   4. The Stanford-Binet test allows for the calculation of overall IQ and also of the verbal and performance IQ.

_____

_____

_____ 5. The first step in developing a test is to standardize the test.

_____

_____

_____ 6. If a person took the same IQ test three times and received a similar score each time, it could be said that this test is reliable.

_____

_____

THEORIES OF INTELLIGENCE

_____ 7. Spearman believed that a person high in s-factor intelligence would score relatively high on most tests.

_____

_____

_____ 8. Sternberg and Gardner's models of intelligence seek to understand intelligence as a process.

_____

_____

HEREDITARY AND ENVIRONMENTAL INFLUENCES ON INTELLIGENCE

_____ 9. Twin studies have not yielded conclusive evidence in the nature-nurture controversy, but they tend to lend support to the importance of heredity in determining intelligence.

_____

_____

_____ 10. Genetic factors account for 60 percent of one's intelligence.

_____

_____

RACIAL DIFFERENCES IN INTELLIGENCE

_____ 11. Most psychologists believe that differences in intelligence between racial groups are largely—if not exclusively—the result of environmental factors.

_____

_____

Answer Key
1. F   2. F   3. F   4. F   5. F   6. T   7. F   8. T   9. T   10. F   11. T

– PART V. MULTIPLE-CHOICE QUESTIONS –

Choose the best answer to each question. Circle your choice. Check your answers against the Answer Key. Questions marked with an asterisk (*) include annotated answers.

DEFINING AND MEASURING INTELLIGENCE

1. To evaluate what hypothesis did Sir Francis Galton design his intelligence test?
    a.   accuracy of the equation MA/CA x 100 =IQ
    b.   inferiority of men
    c.   superiority of the upper class
    d.   negative effect of a disadvantaged background

2. "The ability to think abstractly" is a definition of intelligence proposed by _____.
    a.   Sternberg
    b.   Binet
    c.   Wechsler
    d.   Terman

*3. In developing his intelligence test, Binet reasoned that a child with high intelligence would perform on the intelligence test similar to a(n) _____.
    a.   child of the same chronological age
    b.   older child of average intelligence
    c.   older child of below-average intelligence
    d.   child of the same age and of average intelligence

*4. Who of the following would have the highest IQ?
    a.   mental age of 5, and chronological age of 5
    b.   mental age of 10, and chronological age of 8
    c.   mental age of 5, and chronological age of 6
    d.   mental age of 10, and chronological age of 10

5. A college student would most likely take which intelligence test?
    a.   WAIS
    b.   CAT
    c.   Stanford-Binet
    d.   Army Alpha

6. Which of the following is *not* an advantage of group-administered intelligence tests compared to individual intelligence tests?
    a.   can be given to a number of people at the same time
    b.   are quicker to administer
    c.   encourage the best possible performance from individuals
    d.   are more easily scored

EVALUATING INTELLIGENCE TESTS

7. Which of the following is *not* a step involved in developing an intelligence test?
    a.   calculating a child's IQ
    b.   establishing test norms
    c.   evaluating the test items
    d.   standardizing the test

*8. While developing his intelligence test, Binet asked many French children of varying ages the test items to determine how these children performed on the test. Why did Binet do this?
    a.   to develop standardization procedures
    b.   to determine the numerical value of the average IQ

c. to verify the reliability of the test

d. to develop test norms

9. Because intelligence tests _____, one should receive the same IQ score regardless of who administers and scores the test.

   a. are standardized

   b. have established norms

   c. are valid

   d. are reliable

10. What percentage of people taking an IQ test achieve scores within the 85 to 115 range?

    a. 75 percent

    b. 68 percen

    c. 95 percent

    d. 50 percent

11. What would a person be doing if he/she wanted to evaluate the consistency of a test and decided to divide the test into half and score each half separately to see if the two scores were similar?

    a. assessing the concurrent reliability

    b. assessing the concurrent validity

    c. calculating the split-half reliability

    d. calculating the split-half validity

12. If a test measures what it is supposed to measure, it has _____.

    a. validity

    b. norms

    c. reliability

    d. consistency

13. To assess the _____ validity of a test, individuals' test scores are compared with their scores on other measures known to be good indicators of the skill or trait being assessed.

    a. alternate

    b. predictive

    c. concurrent

    d. standard

14. What are achievement tests designed to do?

    a. predict ability to learn new information or new skills

    b. measure what one has already learned

    c. determine one's intelligence quotient

    d. None of the above choices apply

15. Which of the following is designed to measure a type of ability that is different from the type of ability measured by the other three tests?

    a. aptitude tests

    b. Otis-Lennon School Ability Test (OLSAT)

    c. achievement tests

    d. Wechsler Adult Intelligence Scale (WAIS)

THEORIES OF INTELLIGENCE

*16. _____ is the psychologist who would believe that it may be appropriate to say of an individual, "He is highly intelligent" (or not intelligent) because there is a general or overall component of intelligence.
   a. Sternberg
   b. Gardner
   c. Thurstone
   d. Spearman

17. What did Thurstone believe about human intelligence?
   a. It consists of a g-factor and s-factors.
   b. It contains componential, experiential, and contextual components.
   c. It is composed of seven independent mental abilities.
   d. It consists of 150 different kinds of intelligence.

18. Guilford used the term content to describe _____.
   a. how we think
   b. what we think about
   c. how we apply our thinking
   d. primary ability

19. The approaches of_____ provide models to describe the structure of intelligence (factorial theories). The approaches of _____ attempt to understand the process of intelligence.
   a. Sternberg and Gardner / Spearman, Thurstone, and Guilford
   b. Spearman, Thurstone, and Guilford / Sternberg and Gardner
   c. Spearman and Guilford / Sternberg, Thurstone, and Gardner
   d. Sternberg, Thurstone, and Gardner / Spearman and Guilford

20. Which of the following theoretical models of intelligence does *not* use the factor-analysis technique?
   a. Guilford's
   b. Thurstone's
   c. Spearman's
   d. Steinberg's

21. Good problem solvers who score high on intelligence tests _____ than people who score low on intelligence tests.
   a. take a longer time to encode information
   b. take a shorter time to encode information
   c. arrive at the correct solution faster
   d. make more careless mistakes

22. _____ is the psychologist who defines intelligence to include a number of abilities (such as musical ability and interpersonal abilities) that are not typically included in definitions of intelligence.
   a. Guilford
   b. Wechsler
   c. Gardner
   d. Steinberg

BIAS IN INTELLIGENCE TESTING

23. Which statement is true?
   a. Motivation when taking the intelligence test is not a factor affecting IQ.
   b. Race is not a factor affecting IQ.

c. Truly culture-fair IQ tests are available.

d. Possibly no truly culture-fair or culture-free intelligence tests exist at this time.

HEREDITARY AND ENVIRONMENTAL INFLUENCES ON INTELLIGENCE

24. Which two people would you expect to have IQs that are most similar?
    a. a parent and child
    b. fraternal twins reared together
    c. two same-sex siblings
    d. identical twins reared apart

25. Studies of identical twins reared together and apart provide evidence to support _____.
    a. only the hereditarian view
    b. only the environmentalist view
    c. the hereditarian view and, to a lesser degree, the environmentalist view
    d. the environmentalist view and, to a lesser degree, the hereditarian view

26. What do most psychologists generally believe concerning the contributions of nature and nurture in influencing human intelligence?
    a. The relative contribution of genetic factors is greater than that of environmental factors.
    b. The relative contribution of environmental factors is greater than that of genetic factors.
    c. Genetic and environmental factors are equally important.
    d. Genetic factors account for 75% of an individual's intelligence.

27. _____ is the psychologist who proposed that the difference in average IQ scores between blacks and whites is due primarily to genetic factors.
    a. Jensen
    b. Skeels
    c. Sternberg
    d. Scarr

RACIAL DIFFERENCES IN INTELLIGENCE

28. There is _____ overlap between the IQ scores of blacks and whites.
    a. no
    b. a small
    c. a moderate
    d. a large

29. A study in Minneapolis showed that black children adopted into white, middle-class families had IQs similar to the _____.
    a. average IQ of black children
    b. average IQ of white children
    c. IQs of white children adopted into middle-class families
    d. None of the above choices are correct

Answer Key

1. c	2. d	*3. b	*4. b	5. a	6. c	7. a	*8. d	9. a	10. b	11. c	12. a
13. c	14. b	15. c	*16. d	17. c	18. b	19. b	20. d	21. a	22. c	23. d	24. d
25. c	26. a	27. a	28. d	29. c							

3. The correct choice is **b**. Binet reasoned that all children follow the same course of intellectual development, but differ on the rate at which they progress. A child of high intelligence (with a relatively rapid rate of progress) should perform similarly to an older child of average intelligence (with a slower rate of progress).

   a. A child of the same age would only show similar test performance if the other child was also highly intelligent. If the other child was of average intelligence, that child would not perform as well as the highly intelligent child.

   c. Although c is technically correct, it is not the simplest, most logical, most informative, or "best" answer to the question. A child of average intelligence would also perform similarly to an older child with below-average intelligence.

   d. The highly intelligent child would perform at a higher level than a child of the same age who has average intelligence. The highly intelligent child would have an older mental age than the child with average intelligence.

4. The correct choice is **b**. Using the formula MA/CA x 100 = IQ, this child would have an IQ of 125, and (10/8 x 100 = 125).

   a. This child would have an IQ of 100, and (5/5 x 100 = 100).

   c. This child would have an IQ of 83, and (5/6 x 100 = 83).

   d. This child would have an IQ of 100, and (10/10 x 100 = 100).

8. The correct choice is **d**. Test norms refer to the average performance of a particular group of people. Binet was determining the average performance of 6-, 7-, 8- (and so on) year-old children.

   a. Standardization procedures refer to the way a test is administered and scored.

   b. Selecting the numerical value of the average IQ is unrelated to the performance of children of varying ages. Any numerical value could have been selected to correspond to the average IQ.

   c. The reliability or consistency of the test would be evaluated at a later stage in the test's development.

16. The correct choice is **d**. Spearman proposed that intelligence is composed of a general factor and a number of specific abilities. A person with a high g-factor could appropriately be described as highly intelligent because he or she would tend to consistently perform at a high level on many types of tests of mental ability.

   a. Sternberg's triarchic theory of successful intelligence proposes that intelligence consists of three different abilities and that a high (or average or low) level of one type of ability does not necessarily correspond with high (or average or low) levels of the other abilities.

   b. Gardner proposed a theory of multiple intelligences consisting of seven different kinds of intelligence. You would have to specify which type of intelligence you were talking about in order to describe an individual as highly intelligent.

   c. Thurstone proposed that intelligence is a composite of seven primary abilities that are independent. Because it is possible for an individual to be highly intelligent on one (or some) abilities and average or below average on other abilities, it would generally be inappropriate to say that person is highly intelligent.

– PART VI. SUMMARY TABLES –

To test your understanding of the material discussed in this chapter, complete the following tables. Check your answers with those supplied in Part IX.

MODELS OF INTELLIGENCE

Psychologist/Model	Type of Model (Structural or Process)	Description
Gardner/ Multiple intelligences		
Guilford/ Structure of intellect		
Spearman/ Two-factor		
Sternberg/ Triarchic		
Thurstone		

RESEARCH SUGGESTING HEREDITARY AND ENVIRONMENTAL INFLUENCES ON IQ

Type of Research	Support for Hereditary Influences	Support for Environmental Influences
Twin		
Animal		

– PART VII. THOUGHT QUESTIONS/CRITICAL THINKING –

Prepare answers to the following discussion questions.

1. Imagine that you are the parent of two children, a 5-year-old and a 10-year-old. You have only limited financial resources and realize that you have only enough money to send one child to college. You decide to designate the college fund for the more intelligent child. Explain—in detail—how IQ tests would allow you to determine which child is more intelligent. What IQ score and how large of a

difference in IQ scores between your two children would be large enough to justify sending only the more intelligent child to college?

2. A psychology instructor teaches three sections of general psychology and is concerned that the students from classes that take their exams after other classes have already been tested are getting some overly helpful hints concerning the contents of the exam. In order to limit this information flow, the instructor decides that, for the next exam (covering three chapters) each class will receive an exam that will only contain questions from one of the chapters. Each class will be tested on a different chapter. Additionally, the instructor did not inform the students about the plan prior to administering the test. Evaluate this testing procedure by referring to the concepts of reliability and validity. Would this be an appropriate (or fair) way to test students' knowledge of the material? Why or why not?

3. Should the older twin in a set of identical twins have a higher IQ than the second-born twin? Why or why not?

4. Jensen received a lot of negative publicity for proposing that the differences in IQs between blacks and whites is genetic (with blacks being genetically "inferior"). Similarly, in recent years a number of public individuals have received negative attention (and frequently been fired) as a result of proposing that blacks have a genetic advantage in athletic endeavors (for example, professional sports). The text discusses why Jensen's logic is flawed. Explain how the athletic-superiority-of-blacks argument is similarly flawed.

– PART VIII. APPLICATIONS –

1. The text distinguishes between aptitude tests (which are designed to measure ability to learn new information or skills) and achievement tests (which are designed to measure what one has already learned). By this point in the semester, you have probably had several psychology-related achievement tests and should have a fairly good idea as to what psychology is about and what psychologists actually do. Imagine that you are the head of the Psychology Department at your college and are planning to develop a psychology aptitude test to give incoming freshmen planning on majoring in psychology. Your intent is to redirect to other majors those students who are unlikely to be successful as psychology majors. Describe the types or categories of questions you would include on this psychology aptitude test, and discuss why these would be included.

2. Imagine that, over college break, you get into a discussion with one of your parents' friends concerning IQ tests. Your parents' friend does not believe in IQ tests and has three points concerning IQ tests.
   a. He believes that the score a person gets on an IQ test depends more on luck than on anything else. He states that whether or not a person is in a good mood when taking the intelligence test is a critical variable and doubts that a person would receive the same score if he or she took the test again a week or month later.
   b. He also believes that IQ tests for children are meaningless because children are continually learning new information. For example, an IQ test taken at the beginning of the school year would not be relevant at the end of the school year because children would be able to correctly answer many more questions.
   c. Finally, his major criticism involves the types of questions that are on an IQ test. He states that IQ tests are meaningless because they do not ask questions related to what intelligence really is. He defines an intelligent person as an individual with common sense, who is creative and well-rounded, with music and athletic abilities.

Prepare a rebuttal to each of his criticisms.

– PART IX. SUMMARY TABLES SOLUTIONS –

MODELS OF INTELLIGENCE

Psychologist/Model	Type of Model (Structural or Process)	Description
Gardner/ Multiple intelligences	Process	Broadly defines intelligence to include seven kinds of abilities: linguistic, logical-mathematic, spatial, musical, bodily kinesthetic, interpersonal, and intrapersonal
Guilford/ Structure of intellect	Structural	Intelligence consists of 150 separate abilities that are composed of combinations of operations (how one thinks), contents (what one thinks about), and products of applying a particular operation to a particular content.
Spearman/ Two-factor	Structural	Intelligence is composed of an overall or general intelligence (g-factor) and specific intellectual abilities (s-factors) An individual with a high g-factor would tend to score higher on most tests than a person with a low g-factor.
Sternberg/ Triarchic	Process	Intelligence is composed of three independent, different abilities: componential (ability to master the steps involved in problem solving), experiential (ability to combine experience in novel ways to solve problems), and contextual (proficient at adapting to the environment).
Thurstone	Process	Intelligence is a composite of seven primary mental abilities: verbal comprehension, numerical ability, spatial relations, perceptual speed, word fluency, memory, and inductive reasoning.

RESEARCH SUGGESTING HEREDITARY AND ENVIRONMENTAL INFLUENCES ON IQ

Type of Research	Support for Hereditary Influences	Support for Environmental Influences
Twin	Identical twins (reared together or apart) have a higher correlation of IQ scores than all other "pairs" of individuals.	Correlation of IQs lower for identical twins reared apart than for identical twins reared together
Animal	Rats raised to be "maze-bright" or "maze-dull" differed substantially in one measure of intelligence.	Maze-bright rats were not superior in all types of learning tasks.

CHAPTER 14
PERSONALITY THEORIES AND ASSESSMENT

– PART I. LEARNING OBJECTIVES –

When you finish studying this chapter, you should be able to do the following:

DEFINING PERSONALITY

1. Define personality.

2. Briefly discuss the differing perspectives of the two broad types of personality theory.

THEORIES OF PERSONALITY: TRAIT THEORIES

3. Describe Allport's trait theory; and define cardinal, central, and secondary traits.

4. Describe Cattell's trait theory, define surface and source traits, and describe the 16 Personality Factors Questionnaire (16PF).

5. Evaluate the evidence concerning whether or not an individual's behavior is as consistent as trait theorists would predict.

PSYCHOANALYTIC THEORY OF PERSONALITY

6. Describe the historical context within which Freud developed the psychoanalytic theory of personality.

7. Define and discuss the importance of the unconscious mind to Freud's theory, and discuss what Freud believed to be man's primary drives.

8. Describe Freud's three structures of personality—the id, ego, and superego—and discuss how they are interrelated and interact.

9. Describe events that result in anxiety and how the ego shields itself from harsh aspects of reality.

10. List two characteristics all defense mechanisms share, and describe six defense mechanisms.

11. Summarize Freud's theory of psychosexual development, and describe each of its five stages.

12. Evaluate psychoanalytic theory by summarizing both criticisms of the theory and theoretical perspectives that are still utilized.

13. Discuss Jung's neo-Freudian theory of personality.

14. Discuss Adler's neo-Freudian theory of personality.

HUMANISTIC PERSONALITY THEORIES

15. Discuss the basic assumptions common to humanistic personality theories.

16. Describe Rogers' theory of personality, and discuss the importance of the relationship between our experiences and self-concept and between the ideal and real self.

17. Describe Maslow's theory of personality, and describe a number of characteristics of a self-actualized individual.

18. Discuss the contributions of humanistic personality theories to the current view of personality, and summarize criticisms of these theories.

BEHAVIORAL AND SOCIAL-LEARNING PERSONALITY THEORIES

19. Describe Skinner's behavioral approach to personality, including how he would define personality, and discuss how behavioral theory would explain consistencies and inconsistencies in a person's behavior.

20. Discuss how the social-learning approach differs from the behavioral approach, and describe Bandura's social-cognitive theory.

21. Discuss the contributions of behavioral and social-learning approaches to the field of personality research, and summarize the criticisms of the two approaches.

BIOLOGICAL DETERMINANTS OF PERSONALITY

22. Discuss the evidence regarding the influence of genetics on personality traits.

23. Describe the type of information that is gained by using behavioral observation, and discuss the limitations of this approach to personality assessment.

24. Describe the type of information that is gained by using interviews, and discuss the limitations of this approach to personality assessment.

25. Define paper-and-pencil questionnaire, and describe the Minnesota Multiphasic Personality Inventory (MMPI and MMPI-2).

26. Discuss the assumptions underlying projective tests, and describe the Rorschach inkblot test and Thematic Apperception Test (TAT).

– PART II. OVERVIEW –

Personality refers to the distinctive patterns of behavior shown by an individual. A number of personality theories are described. Trait theories attempt to describe dimensions of personality characteristics or traits. Allport proposed three categories of traits (cardinal, central, and secondary) that vary in power durability. Cattell proposed that surface traits (such as friendliness and tidiness) form clusters of 16 primary or source traits. Source traits exist in eight pairs of polar opposites. Trait theories only describe personality, whereas other personality theories attempt to explain personality and how personality develops.

Freud's psychoanalytic theory emphasizes the role of the unconscious and three structures of personality (id, ego, and superego). Freud maintained that man's primary motivations were sexual and aggressive in nature, and he viewed personality as shaped by the ongoing conflict between these urges and the demands of society. Personality is largely determined during childhood when an individual progresses through five stages of psychosexual development. At each stage the child experiences sexual gratification through a different erogenous zone. Psychoanalytic theories that accept some and reject other aspects of Freud's theory are neo-Freudian theories. Neo-Freudians believe that Freud overemphasized sexual and aggressive impulses. Jung and Adler are two prominent neo-Freudians.

Humanistic theorists believe that man's primary motivation is to develop or grow in a positive manner. Rogers emphasizes the role of the self-concept and how people subjectively respond to experiences. Maslow studied exceptionally healthy and well-adjusted individuals. He proposed that when all lesser needs are met, people are motivated to reach their fullest potential, or self-actualize.

The behavioral and social-learning personality theorists emphasize the role of external factors. Skinner's behavioral approach emphasizes external contingencies that shape our personalities. Behaviorists believes that "personality" is determined by an individual's specific reinforcement history; if the environmental determinants were to change, so would that individual's personality. Bandura and other social-learning theorists share many ideas with Skinner. However, unlike Skinner, they emphasize the interaction between cognitive factors and external events.

This chapter concludes with a discussion of a number of techniques psychologists use to describe or assess an individual's personality. Behavioral observation and interviews supply a wide variety of information of a global nature. For a more detailed view of an individual's personality, psychologists use two types of personality tests: only one type of personality test follows: paper-and-pencil questionnaires such as the MMPI. Projective tests are designed to assess the unconscious and are open-ended and ambiguous. The Rorschach inkblot test and TAT are two well-known projective tests.

– PART III. KEY TERMS/MATCHING EXERCISES –

Match the following concepts and/or individuals with the appropriate descriptions. Check your answers against the Answer Key.

PERSONALITY THEORISTS

Individuals	*Descriptions*
_____ 1. Adler	a. Developed theory by studying healthy people; emphasized positive over negative qualities
_____ 2. Allport	b. Proposed that the primary force shaping personality was an individual's striving for superiority
_____ 3. Bandura	c. Proposed that a person's personality is composed of central, surface, and for some individuals, cardinal traits
_____ 4. Cattell	d. Proposed that behavior (or personality) and cognitive factors show reciprocal determinism
_____ 5. Freud	e. Proposed that surface traits cluster into 16 primary or source traits
_____ 6. Jung	f. Proposed that personality "traits" only appear to exist because of the stability of an individual's environment and pattern of reinforcement
_____ 7. Maslow	g. Proposed that the key to adjustment and happiness is a consistency or congruence between self-concept and experience
_____ 8. Rogers	h. Developed psychoanalytic theory that depicts personality as shaped by an ongoing conflict between primary drives and societal pressures
_____ 9. Skinner	i. Distinguished between the personal and collective unconscious and introduced the concepts of introversion and extroversion

Answer Key
   1. b   2. c   3. d   4. e   5. h   6. i   7. a   8. g   9. f

PSYCHOANALYTIC THEORY

Concepts	Descriptions
_____ 1. ego	a. From age 3–5 or 6 during which children experience the Oedipus or Electra complex
_____ 2. id	b. Second component of personality to develop that operates according to the reality principle and acts as the personality's mediator
_____ 3. defense mechanism	c. First 12–18 months of life during which a child receives pleasure through sucking, chewing, and biting
_____ 4. superego	d. Involve(s) denying or distorting reality and is used by the ego to protect it from anxiety
_____ 5. unconscious mind	e. From puberty on, when sexual feelings reemerge and an individual seeks to gratify these drives through sexual relations with people outside the family
_____ 6. phallic stage	f. "Storehouse" for repressed thoughts and feelings that is central to psychoanalytic theory
_____ 7. oral stage	g. From age 5–6 until puberty, during which sexual drives remain unexpressed
_____ 8. latency stage	h. Biological component of personality that contains the libido and operates according to the pleasure principle
_____ 9. anal stage	i. From age 1 or 1 1/2–3 when the anal area is the center of pleasure feelings
_____ 10. genital stage	j. Contains the moral values and standards of parents and society and consists of the conscience and ego ideal

Answer Key
1. b   2. h   3. d   4. j   5. f   6. a   7. c   8. g   9. i   10. e

DEFENSE MECHANISMS

Concepts	Descriptions
_____ 1. reaction formation	a. Involves denying unacceptable thoughts from consciousness and involved in all other defense mechanisms
_____ 2. rationalization	b. Involves retreating to behavior associated with an earlier stage of development to gain a sense of security
_____ 3. sublimation	c. Involves substituting a self-justifying excuse or explanation for the real reasons for one's behavior
_____ 4. repression	d. Involves replacing unacceptable impulses with an acceptable opposite impulse
_____ 5. projection	e. Involves attributing one's unacceptable impulses to someone else
_____ 6. regression	f. Involves a redirection of impulses into a socially acceptable activity
_____ 7. displacement	g. Involves redirecting impulse-driven behavior from primary targets to secondary targets that arouse less anxiety

Answer Key
1. d   2. c   3. f   4. a   5. e   6. b   7. g

PERSONALITY THEORIES (NEO-FREUDIAN, HUMANISTIC, BEHAVIORAL, SOCIAL-LEARNING)

Concepts	Descriptions
_____ 1. reciprocal determinism	a. Concept that is basically similar to Freud's view of the unconscious as a reservoir for repressed thoughts
_____ 2. personal unconscious	b. Refers to one's belief that he or she can perform adequately and deal effectively with a particular situation
_____ 3. humanistic theory	c. Principle that proposes that behaviors and personalities are shaped by an interaction between cognitive and environmental factors
_____ 4. striving for superiority	d. Results when children perceive parents as indifferent, harsh, or erratic
_____ 5. self	e. Personality theories that maintain man's primary motivation is to strive to develop, change, and grow in pursuit of the full realization of human potential
_____ 6. basic anxiety	f. Personality theories that agree with Freud in some areas (such as the role of the unconscious) but disagree regarding the emphasis he placed on aggressive and sexual conflicts
_____ 7. neo-Freudian theories	g. Personality theories that emphasize the role of external events in personality formation
_____ 8. self-efficacy	h. Universal urge to achieve self-perfection through successful adaptation to life's circumstances, meeting and mastering challenges, and personal growth
_____ 9. self-actualization	i. Maslow's concept that refers to the need to reach one's own highest potential and to do the things done best in one's own unique way
_____ 10. collective unconscious	j. Basic core of one's being that glues the elements of personality together
_____ 11. behaviorist and social learning theories	k. Similar for all people; contains ancestral memories and archetypes

Answer Key

1. c   2. a   3. e   4. h   5. j   6. d   7. f   8. b   9. i   10. k   11. g

THE ASSESSMENT OF PERSONALITY

Concepts	Descriptions
_____ 1. MMPI	a. Type of objective test in which each item is referenced or associated with one of the standardized groups that were used in developing the test
_____ 2. projective tests	b. Best known and most widely used objective personality inventory that is appropriate for differentiating normal from disturbed individuals
_____ 3. paper-and-pencil tests	c. Objective self-report inventories to measure characteristics of personality
_____ 4. Rorschach inkblot test	d. Loosely structured personality assessment tests containing ambiguous stimuli designed to tap unconscious thoughts and feelings
_____ 5. criterion-keyed test	e. Involves having individuals describe what they "see" in a series of black blots
_____ 6. TAT	f. Involves having a person tell a "story" about what is going on in a series of cards depicting scenes

Answer Key
1. b   2. d   3. c   4. e   5. a   6. f

– PART IV. TRUE-FALSE STATEMENTS –

Fill in the blank before each statement with either a T (true) or and F (false). Check your answers against the Answer Key. Then go back to the items that are false and make the necessary change(s) to the statement to convert the items into true statements.

DEFINING PERSONALITY

_____ 1. Descriptive theories and theories that attempts to explain differences associated with individuals' personalities comprise the two main approaches of personality theories.

_____

_____

TRAIT THEORIES OF PERSONALITY

_____ 2. Allport developed the 16PF questionnaire in order to measure cardinal, central, and secondary traits.

_____

_____

_____ 3. One main criticism of trait theories is that people do not behave as consistently from one situation to another as trait theories would tend to predict.

_____

_____

PSYCHOANALYTIC THEORY OF PERSONALITY

_____ 4. The ego operates according to the pleasure principle and seeks immediate gratification.

_____

_____

_____ 5. To Freud, the dynamics of personality center around conflict between the impulse-driven id, the guilt-inducing superego, and the ego or mediator.

_____

_____

_____ 6. The Electra complex, like the Oedipus complex, takes place during the oral stage of psychosexual development.

_____

_____

HUMANISTIC PERSONALITY THEORIES

_____ 7. Humanistic theorists believe that man's primary motivation is to strive for superiority.

_____

_____

_____ 8. According to Maslow, self-actualized individuals tend to be conformists.

_____

_____

BEHAVIORAL AND SOCIAL-LEARNING PERSONALITY THEORIES

_____ 9. The behavioral approach emphasizes the role of environmental contingencies in shaping and maintaining specific personality chatacteristics

_____

_____ 10. The social-learning approach emphasizes the role of an individual social context in influencing personality.

_____

_____

THE ASSESSMENT OF PERSONALITY

_____ 11. Both behavioral observation and interviews might be influenced by observer bias.

_____

_____

_____ 12. Criterion-keyed tests include the MMPI and TAT.

_____

_____

– PART V. MULTIPLE-CHOICE QUESTIONS –

Choose the best answer to each question. Circle your choice. Check your answers against the Answer Key. Questions marked with an asterisk (*) include annotated answers.

DEFINING PERSONALITY

1. What is a common theme in definitions of personality?
    a. The unconscious mind plays a prominent role.
    b. The environment shapes our personalities.
    c. Personality refers to distinctive patterns of behavior.
    d. Man's primary motivations are negative in nature.

2. Personality psychology may best be described as the study of _____.
    a. how much personality an individual has
    b. individuals
    c. the development of personality traits
    d. the consistency of personality traits

TRAIT THEORIES OF PERSONALITY

3. Trait theories of personality attempt to _____ personality.
    a. predict
    b. describe
    c. explain
    d. describe and explain

4. Allport called traits that guide nearly all of a person's behavior _____ traits.
    a. cardinal
    b. central
    c. secondary
    d. surface

5. According to Allport, most people can be characterized by a relatively small number of generalized and enduring _____ traits.
    a. personality
    b. source
    c. cardinal
    d. central

6. The 16 Personality Factor Questionnaire was created by _____.
    a. Maslow
    b. Bandura

c. Cattell

d. Allport

7. According to Cattell, clusters of surface traits combine to give rise to _____ traits.

    a. source

    b. global

    c. central

    d. cardinal

8. Which of the following is *not* a common criticism of trait theories?

    a. These do not explain behavior but only label behavior as being the result of a personality trait.

    b. People's behavior is not as consistent from situation to situation as trait theories would have us believe.

    c. They do not attempt to describe behavior.

    d. They do not explain how personality develops.

PSYCHOANALYTIC THEORY OF PERSONALITY

9. Which of the following is <u>not</u> emphasized by Freud's psychoanalytic theory?

    a. the influence of early childhood experiences on personality development

    b. man's aggressive urges

    c. the influence of the unconscious mind

    d. man's striving to develop, change, and grow

10. The storehouse of largely unconscious, biologically based, instinctive drives that provide the basic energy source for the entire personality system describes the _____.

    a. superego

    b. id

    c. libido

    d. ego

11. The psychic structure that seeks to delay gratification when satisfaction might bring disapproval from others is the _____.

    a. preconscious

    b. id

    c. ego

    d. superego

*12. Which concept does *not* belong with the other three?

    a. reality principle

    b. ego-ideal

    c. superego

    d. conscience

13. A person who tends to be selfish, demanding, and disregards the rights of other people would appear to have a stronger _____ than _____.

    a. ego / superego

    b. ego-ideal / conscience

    c. superego / id

    d. id / superego

14. The _____ uses _____ to protect itself from harsh aspects of reality.

    a. ego / fixations

    b. id / offense mechanisms

c.   superego / defense mechanisms

d.   ego / defense mechanisms

15.   The most basic defense mechanism that underlies all other defense mechanisms is _____.

a.   repression

b.   distortion

c.   regression

d.   rationalization

*16.   A mother who unconsciously hates her child and says, "We have a bad relationship because the child hates me," would be using the defense mechanisms of _____.

a.   displacement

b.   reaction formation

c.   regression

d.   projection

17.   Which of the following pairs of terms do *not* belong together?

a.   anal stage / toilet training

b.   latency stage / Oedipus complex

c.   oral stage / sucking

d.   phallic stage / genital stimulation

18.   Inadequate or excessive gratification during any psychosexual stage may cause _____.

a.   the death wish

b.   a fixation

c.   repression

d.   regression

19.   With the exception of one, all of the following Freudian concepts continue to influence personality psychology today. Which is the exception?

a.   that unresolved conflicts are central to many psychological problems

b.   defense mechanisms

c.   that sex is the dominant motivating force throughout life

d.   the unconscious mind

20.   _____ suggested that all people acquire a feeling of inferiority early in childhood.

a.   Adler

b.   Rogers

c.   Jung

d.   Allport

HUMANISTIC PERSONALITY THEORIES

21.   Personality theories that believe man's primary motivation is to develop or grow and emphasize an individual's subjective view of reality are _____ theories.

a.   psychoanalytic

b.   social-learning

c.   trait

d.   humanistic

22.   According to Rogers, if your self-concept is consistent with your experiences, then you _____.

a.   will probably self-actualize

b.   have high self-efficacy

c. will be likely to show maladjustment

d. will be likely to show a healthy adjustment

23. According to Rogers, the person that you would like to become is your _____ self.

    a. goal

    b. ideal

    c. real

    d. future

24. Maslow proposed that if all lesser needs are met, a person would be motivated toward

    a. self-determination

    b. self-actualization

    c. self-esteem

    d. the third force

25. Which of the following is *not* a characteristic of a self-actualized person?

    a. has a lively sense of humor

    b. is creative

    c. tends to require the company of others

    d. is open and spontaneous

26. What is one main criticism of humanistic theories?

    a. They emphasize the unconscious id more than the conscious superego.

    b. It is difficult to conduct experiments examining the concepts of humanistic theories.

    c. They do not emphasize negative influences on personality development.

    d. They completely ignore cognitive factors.

BEHAVIORAL AND SOCIAL-LEARNING PERSONALITY THEORIES

27. How would Skinner explain why one student would respond positively to a B on a test while another student would respond negatively?

    a. One student has a stronger superego than the other.

    b. One student has more self-efficacy than the other.

    c. The students have different personality traits.

    d. The students have different histories of reinforcement.

28. About what do behavioral and social-learning theorists share similar perspectives?

    a. the importance of external events

    b. whether or not environmental factors influence personality

    c. the importance of the libido

    d. the existence of personality traits

29. What principle is involved in the following situation? You find the students at your college to be friendly because most of them smile and say "Hi" when you greet them, whereas your roommate finds the students to be unfriendly and says no one ever smiles or says "Hi" to her.

    a. rationalization

    b. self-efficacy

    c. reciprocal determinism

    d. basic anxiety

30. What would Bandura's concept of self-efficacy suggest about a boy who thinks himself a bad athlete?

    a. He would not play many sports.

    b. He would spend a great deal of time practicing alone in order to improve.

c. Either of the above may be true.

d. Neither of the above may be true.

31. The heritability of personality traits such as emotionality, sociability, and activity is approximately _____ percent.

a. 25

b. 33

c. 50

d. 75

32. Twin studies have shown that the personalities of identical twins reared apart are _____ as (than) the personalities of identical twins reared together.

a. as similar

b. less similar

c. more similar

d. more dissimilar

THE ASSESSMENT OF PERSONALITY

33. Which of the following is *not* an important method used to assess an individual's personality?

a. psychoanalysis

b. paper-and-pencil questionnaires

c. projective tests

d. behavioral observation

*34. With which type of assessment technique would you expect a number of psychologists to draw the most similar conclusions?

a. paper-and-pencil questionnaires

b. projective tests

c. behavioral observation

d. interviews

35. Which of the following is a limitation of the MMPI?

a. It can lead to improper diagnosis when used with individuals of different backgrounds than those the test was based on.

b. It is unable to be used in diagnosing.

c. It contains too few questions.

d. It was normed on normal individuals.

*36. Which type of personality theorist would be *least* likely to utilize projective personality tests?

a. neo-Freudian

b. psychoanalytic

c. behaviorist

d. All of the above would be equally likely to use projective tests.

37. If a psychologist asks you to tell a story concerning a scene on a card he or she shows you, that psychologist is giving you the _____.

a. MMPI

b. TAT

c. 16PF

d. Rorschach inkblot test

38. Personality assessment techniques designed to tap unconscious thoughts and feelings are _____.
   a. interviews
   b. subjective tests
   c. projective tests
   d. objective tests

Answer Key

1. c	2. b	3. b	4. a	5. d	6. c	7. a	8. c	9. d	10. b	11. c	*12. a
13. d	14. d	15. a	*16. d	17. b	18. b	19. c	20. a	21. d	22. d	23. b	24. b
25. c	26. b	27. d	28. a	29. c	30. a	31. c	32. a	33. a	*34. a	35. a	*36. c
37. b	38. c										

Annotated Answers

12. The correct choice is **a**. The ego is the structure of the personality that operates according to the reality principle.
   b. The ego-ideal is one subsystem of the superego.
   c. The superego has two subsystems.
   d. The conscience is the second subsystem of the superego.

16. The correct choice is **d**. Projection involves attributing your own unacceptable impulses (hating your child) to someone else (it's the child who hates me).
   a. Displacement refers to redirecting behavior from one person (your boss who reprimanded you unfairly) to another person (your child). You want to hit your boss but would instead hit your child.
   b. Reaction formation involves replacing an unacceptable impulse with its acceptable opposite impulse. If the mother in the example were to use reaction formation, she would say she loves her child and most likely would be an overly loving indulgent mother.
   c. Regression involves having your behavior revert to a less-mature stage of development and is not directly concerned with the person's impulses or thought processes. Perhaps a mother who hates her child would throw a temper tantrum and ask her child, "Why do you make me hate you?"

34. The correct choice is **a**. Because paper-and-pencil questionnaires (MMPI, CAT) are objective tests, these would be scored the same by all psychologists. In scoring a paper-and-pencil questionnaire, the psychologist simply adds up or tallies an individual's responses to the questions.
   b. Because projective tests (Rorschach inkblot test, TAT) are ambiguous to take, they are also ambiguous to score. The interpretation of these tests is subjective, and psychologists do not always agree on how to properly score responses.
   c. Psychologists might not make similar observations or reach similar conclusions with behavioral observation because even if the psychologists observed exactly the same behavior, each psychologist's observations would be subject to observer bias.
   d. As is the case with behavioral observations, interviews are subject to observer bias because the basic data of interviews is difficult to quantify and is therefore subject to the psychologist's individual or unique interpretation.

36. The correct choice is **c**. Projective tests are designed to tap unconscious thoughts and feelings. Because the behaviorists reject the influence of inner forces (both conscious and unconscious) they would not use projective tests.
   a. Neo-Freudians would utilize projective tests because they are concerned with the unconscious.

b. Psychoanalytic theorists (Freud and the neo-Freudians) would utilize projective tests. The unconscious mind is central to Freud's theory, and a Freudian would utilize projective tests to help "unlock" the unconscious.

d. This choice is incorrect because behaviorists (c) would not be at all likely to use projective tests.

– PART VI. SUMMARY TABLES –

To test your understanding of the material discussed in this chapter, complete the following tables. Check your answers with those supplied in Part IX.

SUMMARY OF PERSONALITY THEORIES

Type of Theory	Individual(s)	Basic Assumptions or Description	Strengths	Criticisms and/or Limitations
Trait				
Psychoanalytic				
Neo-Freudian				

SUMMARY OF PERSONALITY THEORIES (continued)

Type of Theory	Individual(s)	Basic Assumptions or Description	Strengths	Criticisms and/or Limitations
Behaviorist				
Social-learning				
Humanistic				

PERSONALITY TESTS

Test	Projective or Objective)	Description	Strengths	Weaknesses
MMPI				
Rorschach Inkblot Test				
TAT				

– PART VII. THOUGHT QUESTIONS/CRITICAL THINKING –

Prepare answers to the following discussion questions.

1. Describe the id, ego, and superego by using an analogy to a company in which labor and management have just called in a mediator to resolve problems with the union contract agreement that is being negotiated.

2. Defense mechanisms are the ego's method of protecting oneself from the harsh aspects of reality. Think of the ego as frequently having a choice of which defense mechanism to use in a given situation. Describe how the ego could deal with each of the following situations by using at least three of the following: repression, rationalization, projection, displacement, regression, and reaction formation.
    a. A student gets a D on a test in a subject that is required for his or her major.
    b. A young man's fiancée just broke off their engagement.
    c. Your boss tells you that you cannot take your vacation during the week you requested.

3. You know yourself better than anyone else does. Which type of personality theory described in the text best accounts for your present personality (or distinctive pattern of behavior)? Explain.

4. If you were employed in the personnel department of a company and could give one personality test to potential employees, which of the tests described in the text would you use? Why did you choose that test over the other tests?

– PART VIII. APPLICATIONS –

1. Each of the types of personality theories described in the text have some aspects of personality that they account for in an adequate-to-good manner. However, no one theory supplies a complete and thorough explanation for all aspects of and influences on personality. To account for personality as a whole it may be necessary to mix and match from among the different theories, or to take the positives or strengths and reject the negatives or weaknesses of each theory. What do you see as the components of such a mixed-and-matched personality theory?

2. Describe each of the following individual's personalities from the psychoanalytic, behaviorist, and/or social-learning and humanistic perspectives:
    a. John is a 24-year-old who has had a series of unsuccessful relationships with the opposite sex. His girlfriends typically break up with him after a couple of months. They state that he is unable to compromise and is selfish. John was the only child in an upper-middle-class family. John is planning a career in business because he believes that he should be fairly successful in that field and should make enough money to live comfortably.
    b. Diane is 35 years old; now that her youngest child is in school, she has decided to return to college and complete her teaching degree. She feels that she has a "calling" to teach young children. Her family is supportive of her plans, and her many friends feel that with her warm and caring personality she will make an excellent teacher.
    c. Tom is a 10-year-old problem child, and his parents are at a loss as to what to do about the situation. Tom has a history of being disruptive at school and is a bully. He takes no responsibility for his actions and says that the other children pick on him and start fights. Recently, some of the other children's belongings have been stolen, and Tom's teacher suspects him. Tom denies any wrongdoing. His parents have always believed Tom's side of the story in the past and do so in this situation. Tom's dad, who feels that you should "Do what you have to do" and not let other people get in your way, is considering going to the school board to have the teacher reprimanded for falsely accusing Tom.

– PART IX. SUMMARY TABLES SOLUTIONS –

SUMMARY OF PERSONALITY THEORIES

Type of Theory	Individual(s)	Basic Assumptions or Description	Strengths	Criticisms and/or Limitations
Trait	Allport Cattell	Attempt to identify specific dimensions or characteristics associated with different personalities Traits account for consistency in the behavior of an individual and also account for differences in behavior between individuals.	Provide methods (e.g., Cattell's 16PF) to assess basic characteristics	Describe, but do not explain, dynamics of personality or how personality develops An individual's behavior may not be consistent from one situation to the next.
Psychoanalytic	Freud	Personality is shaped by an ongoing conflict between primary urges (sexual and aggressive) and pressures of civilized society. In other terms, between the impulse-driven id and the guilt-inducing superego with the ego attempting to reconcile both with the demands of reality Personality is essentially formed during childhood as child progresses through five stages of psychosexual development	Perspective concerning unconscious, defense mechanisms, and unresolved conflicts being central to many psychological problems; still used today	Difficult to test experimentally because of lack of operational definitions and precise predictions Focuses on troubled individuals, therefore theory tends to emphasize negative components Too strong an emphasis on early childhood experiences determining personality
Neo-Freudian	Jung Adler	Agree with Freud regarding the role of the unconscious, importance of childhood experiences, and basic interpretation of the structure of personality Disagree with Freud regarding the emphasis on sexual conflict and aggressive impulses, and importance of biological determinants of personality	With emphasis on social influences, supply a broader framework than Freudian theory	Many of the same limitations as Freudian theory, but because some neo-Freudian theorists make more specific predictions concerning future behavior and personality, are more easily scientifically tested

SUMMARY OF PERSONALITY THEORIES *(continued)*

Type of Theory	Individual(s)	Basic Assumptions or Description	Strengths	Criticisms and/or Limitations
Behaviorist	Skinner	Emphasizes the role of external events in personality formation Personality is the sum total of individuals' overt and covert responses to the world around them. Personality "traits" are the result of stable environment and consistent patterns of reinforcement.	Emphasis on behavior change and experimental research	Completely disregards not only the role of the unconscious, but also conscious cognitive processes
Social-learning	Bandura	Adds cognitive processes to behaviorist approach Personality shaped by interaction between cognitive and environmental factors	Similar to behaviorist and more well rounded with the inclusion of cognitive factors	Tends to ignore the truly human dimensions of personality that are the focus of humanistic theories
Humanistic	Rogers Maslow	Man's primary motivation is to develop, change, and grow toward full realization of potential. Emphasizes individual's subjective view of reality	Focus on positive dimensions of personality (creativity, spontaneity, joy, love) Focus on healthy personality	Key terms are subjective and lack operational definitions, so it is difficult to test experimentally. Largely ignores the influence of environmental factors

PERSONALITY TESTS

Test	Projective or Objective	Description	Strengths	Weaknesses
MMPI	Objective	Designed for diagnosing psychological disorders Contains 566 true-false statements about individuals' behaviors, thoughts, and emotional reactions Scored on 10 clinical scales (e.g., depression, schizophrenia, paranoia) and also has four validity scales	Differentiates well between disturbed and normal individuals (between the two groups)	Does not reliably differentiate among disturbed and normal individuals (within each group) Low test-retest reliability
Rorschach Inkblot Test	Projective	Consists of 10 cards with inkblots Individual describes what inkblot looks like or brings to mind. Complex scoring system results in subjective interpretation	One of the most widely used techniques for clinical diagnosis and personality assessment	Interpretation is highly subjective, therefore is of questionable validity However, the Rorschach is typically used along with other assessment procedures.
TAT	Projective	Consists of 30 cards of vague and ambiguous scenes and one blank card Individual tells a "story" related to the scene. Psychologist typically looks for common themes in the stories.	Is a useful tool for research purposes and has adequate levels of validity	Similar to the Rorschach, interpretation is subjective It is typically used for diagnostic purposes along with other assessment techniques.

CHAPTER 15
BEHAVIORAL DISORDERS

– PART I. LEARNING OBJECTIVES –

When you finish studying this chapter, you should be able to do the following:

DEFINING ABNORMAL BEHAVIOR

1. Discuss four criteria that may be used to distinguish normal from abnormal behavior.

2. Summarize the development of the *Diagnostic and Statistical Manual (DSM)* classification system from *DSM-I* through *DSM-IV-R*.

ANXIETY DISORDERS

3. Define anxiety, and list seven types of anxiety disorders.

4. Describe panic disorder, and discuss the relationship between panic disorder and agoraphobia.

5. Define phobia, and describe two types of social phobias and two specific phobias.

6. Describe obsessive-compulsive disorder.

7. Describe posttraumatic stress disorder (PTSD), and explain how it differs from other anxiety disorders.

8. Describe generalized anxiety disorder.

9. Summarize the psychoanalytic, behavioral, and biological perspectives of anxiety disorders.

SOMATOFORM DISORDERS

10. Describe the general characteristics of somatoform disorders, and list three types of somatoform disorders.

11. Describe somatization disorder and hypochondriasis, and differentiate between the two.

12. Describe conversion disorder.

13. Summarize the psychoanalytic, behavioral, and biological perspectives of somatoform disorders.

DISSOCIATIVE DISORDERS

14. Describe the general characteristics of dissociative disorders, and list three types of dissociative disorders.

15. Describe and differentiate between dissociative amnesia and dissociative fugue disorder.

16. Describe dissociative identity disorder, and discuss what type of childhood experiences appear to be associated with this disorder.

17. Summarize the psychoanalytic, behavioral, and biological perspectives of dissociative disorders.

MOOD DISORDERS

18. Describe the general characteristic of mood disorders, and list three mood disorders.

19. Describe major depressive disorder.

20. Describe bipolar disorder (manic-depressive disorder).

21. Describe seasonal affective disorder (SAD).

22. Summarize and evaluate the psychoanalytic, cognitive-behavioral, genetic, and biochemical perspectives of mood disorders.

23. Discuss the evidence that mood disorders involve an interaction of biological predispositions and psychological factors.

SCHIZOPHRENIA

24. Describe the five primary symptoms of schizophrenia.

25. Describe the three stages of schizophrenia.

26. List the five subtypes of schizophrenia, and describe the secondary symptoms associated with each subtype.

27. Summarize and evaluate the psychoanalytic, behavioral, and biological perspectives of schizophrenia.

PERSONALITY DISORDERS

28. List the characteristics that are common to personality disorders, and describe the three clusters of personality disorders.

29. Describe antisocial personality disorder, and summarize the psychoanalytic, behavioral, and biological perspectives concerning antisocial personality disorder.

– PART II. OVERVIEW –

The term abnormal behavior relates to behavioral disorders. The four criteria for abnormality are atypicality, maladaptivity, emotional discomfort, and social unacceptability. All four criteria do not need to be present for a behavior to be considered abnormal. This chapter discusses several categories of psychological disorders and a number of specific disorders in each category.

The anxiety disorders, which are the most common disorders in the United States, all involve anxiety (feelings of dread or apprehension) typically accompanied by physiological reactions such as an increased heart rate and muscle tension. The anxiety disorders differ in the ways or the situations in which individuals experience anxiety. The anxiety disorders include panic disorder, agoraphobia, specific and social phobias, obsessive-compulsive disorder, posttraumatic stress disorder, and generalized anxiety disorder.

The primary symptoms of the somatoform disorders are physical in nature, but there is no physical basis for these symptoms. Somatization disorder involves a number of chronic physical symptoms (such as aches and pains). Hypochondriasis is characterized by an individual believing that physical symptoms are indications of serious health problems. Conversion disorders involve a person experiencing sensory or motor disturbances (such as blindness or paralysis).

The dissociative disorders are characterized by thoughts and feelings that generate anxiety being dissociated (or removed) from conscious awareness. The dissociative disorders involve memory loss or a change in identity. Dissociative amnesia, dissociative fugue disorder, and dissociative identity disorders are all dissociative disorders.

The primary symptom of the mood disorders is depression, which is characterized by feelings of sadness, dejection, and hopelessness, and physical symptoms (such as changes in activity level and eating and sleeping patterns). Major depressive disorders occur when an individual is in a deep, enduring depression. Bipolar disorder is characterized by periods of depression alternating with periods of mania or elevated mood (elation and euphoria). Recurrent episodes of depression that occur in either the winter or summer are diagnosed as seasonal affective disorders (SAD).

The schizophrenic disorders are very severe and disabling, with primary symptoms being disturbances of thought, emotion, perception, and behavior. A number of subtypes of schizophrenia exist, which are differentiated according to the primary and secondary symptoms that are present, including disorganized, catatonic, paranoid, and undifferentiated. An additional subtype—residual schizophrenia—is used to describe the schizophrenic individual who is "recovered or in remission."

Personality disorders refer to long-term, well-developed styles of behavior or personality traits that are maladaptive. Individuals with personality disorders typically do not feel they "have a problem" and tend to refuse treatment. Antisocial personality disorder is very disruptive. Individuals with this disorder show a chronic and continuous disregard for the rights of others and rules of society and do not experience guilt or remorse for their actions.

Throughout this chapter, the psychoanalytic, behavioral, and biological perspectives of psychological disorders are discussed. While the psychoanalytic perspective provides explanations for the disorders discussed in this chapter, these explanations are not supported by experimental evidence. The behavioral perspective offers explanations for a number of disorders that rely on Pavlovian and operant-conditioning. The biological perspective of psychological disorders receives strong support and has led to promising and effective treatments to be discussed in the next chapter.

– PART III. KEY TERMS/MATCHING EXERCISES –

Match the following concepts with the appropriate descriptions. Check your answers against the Answer Key.

BEHAVIORAL DISORDERS: OVERVIEW

Concepts	Descriptions
_____ 1. somatoform disorders	a. Freud's term for severe psychological disorders characterized by reduced contact with reality, disturbances of thinking, and loss of ability to function socially
_____ 2. schizophrenia	b. Disorders characterized by extreme disruptions of perceptions, thoughts, emotions, and behavior
_____ 3. abnormal behavior	c. Defined by emphasizing atypicality, maladaptivity, emotional discomfort, and social unacceptability
_____ 4. mood disorders	d. Disorders involving a separation of thoughts and feelings that causes anxiety from conscious awareness and that are characterized by memory loss or a change in identity
_____ 5. anxiety disorders	e. Disorders characterized by rigid maladaptive behavior or personality traits that tend to develop at a young age and have a poor prognosis for treatment
_____ 6. psychosis	f. Freud's term for psychological disorders that, while distressing and often debilitating, do not involve loss of contact with reality and inability to perform daily tasks
_____ 7. personality disorders	g. Disorders that have depression as the primary symptom
_____ 8. neurosis	h. Characterized by feelings of dread or apprehension that are frequently accompanied by physiological reactions
_____ 9. dissociative disorders	i. Disorders that are expressed through physical symptoms

Answer Key

1. i   2. b   3. c   4. g   5. h   6. a   7. e   8. f   9. d

ANXIETY DISORDERS

Concepts	Descriptions
_____ 1. social phobia	a. Characterized by fear and avoidance of being in open and public places
_____ 2. posttraumatic stress disorder	b. Characterized by reexperiencing and avoidance of stimuli associated with a traumatic event, or numbing of general responsiveness and increased arousal
_____ 3. agoraphobia	c. Characterized by persistent unshakable thoughts frequently associated with irresistible repetitious behaviors
_____ 4. generalized anxiety disorder	d. Characterized by sudden episodes of extreme anxiety with both psychological and physiological components that frequently occur for no apparent reason
_____ 5. phobias	e. May involve either an irrational fear of social situations or fear of performing specific behaviors (such as talking or eating publicly)
_____ 6. panic disorder	f. Characterized by persistent apprehension or anxiety in a wide range of situations
_____ 7. simple phobias	g. Relatively common irrational fears of specific objects or situations that are infrequently addressed in clinical settings because they are not very disruptive to the individual
_____ 8. obsessive-compulsive disorder	h. Characterized by inappropriate fear and avoidance of specific situations or objects

Answer Key

1. e   2. b   3. a   4. f   5. h   6. d   7. g   8. c

SOMATOFORM DISORDERS AND DISSOCIATIVE DISORDERS

Concepts	Descriptions
_____ 1. hypochondriasis	a. Involves a sudden loss of memory, usually after a particularly stressful or traumatic event
_____ 2. dissociative fugue disorder	b. Characterized by a variety of physical symptoms that the individual believes to be associated with serious illnesses
_____ 3. conversion disorder	c. Characterized by multiple and recurrent physical symptoms (such as headaches, dizziness, and different bodily pains) that do not have a physical cause
_____ 4. dissociative identity disorder	d. Characterized by an alternation between an original or primary and one or more secondary or subordinate personalities
_____ 5. somatization disorder	e. Typically of brief duration and involves a loss of memory during which the person travels from place to place
_____ 6. dissociative amnesia	f. Manifested by either a sensory disturbance (such as blindness or loss of feeling to parts of the body) or a motor disturbance (such as paralysis) that does not have a physical cause

1. b   2. e   3. f   4. d   5. c   6. a

MOOD DISORDERS, SCHIZOPHRENIA, AND PERSONALITY DISORDERS

Concepts	Descriptions
_____ 1. catatonic schizophrenia	a. Characterized by an extended period of time during which the individual experiences a variety of psychological, psychomotor, and physical manifestations of depression
_____ 2. seasonal affective disorder	b. Subtype of schizophrenia that is diagnosed if the schizophrenic individual does not manifest specific symptoms associated with other subtypes of schizophrenia
_____ 3. residual schizophrenia	c. Subtype of schizophrenia that shows the most severe personality disintegration, characterized by extreme disturbances of thought, speech, and constant mood changes
_____ 4. disorganized schizophrenia	d. Subtype of schizophrenia with the dominant secondary symptom of well-organized delusional thought
_____ 5. antisocial personality disorder	e. Subtype of schizophrenia with secondary symptoms of extreme motor disturbances, which may range from stuporous immobility to agitation
_____ 6. bipolar disorder	f. Characterized by a history of chronic and continual disregard for the rights of others and rules of society, a lack of remorse, and very self-centered behavior
_____ 7. undifferentiated schizophrenia	g. Characterized by extreme mood swings with episodes of depression alternating with euphoria
_____ 8. major depression	h. Subtype of schizophrenia applied during the third stage of schizophrenia when symptoms are markedly diminished or absent
_____ 9, paranoid schizophrenia	i. Describes recurrent patterns of depression that are triggered or associated with seasonal changes (such as the decrease in exposure to light during the winter)

Answer Key
   1. e   2. i   3. h   4. c   5. f   6. g   7. b   8. a   9. d

– PART IV. TRUE/FALSE STATEMENTS –

Fill in the blank before each statement with either a T (true) or an F (false). Check your answers against the Answer Key. Then go back to the items that are false and make the necessary change(s) to the statements to convert the items into true statements.

DEFINING AND CLASSIFYING BEHAVIORAL DISORDERS

_____ 1. If a behavior is unusual or atypical, it is sufficient to determine that the behavior is abnormal or disordered.

_____

_____

_____ 2. Unlike *DSM-I* and *II*, *DSM-IV-R*'s two main diagnostic categories are the neuroses and psychoses.

_____

_____

ANXIETY DISORDERS

_____ 3. In the United States the most common psychological disorders are anxiety disorders.

_____

_____

_____ 4. A person who does not leave his or her house because of fear associated with being in public places suffers from social phobia.

_____

_____

_____ 5. Panic attacks have been linked to use of nicotine (smoking).

_____

_____

DISSOCIATIVE DISORDERS

_____ 6. Dissociative disorders include dissociative amnesia, conversion disorders, and dissociative identity disorder.

_____

_____

SOMATOFORM DISORDERS

_____ 7. Freud believed that somatoform disorders were the result of an individual dealing with anxiety by converting it into physical symptoms.

_____

_____

MOOD DISORDERS

_____ 8. Major depressive disorder is much more common than bipolar disorder.

_____

_____

_____ 9. In most cases, major depression lifts over a period of months, even if the individual does not receive treatment.

_____

_____

_____ 10. Considerable evidence supports the psychoanalytic perspective of mood disorders.

_____

_____

SCHIZOPHRENIA

_____ 11. Undifferentiated schizophrenics show more severe personality disintegration than individuals with the other subtypes of schizophrenia.

_____

_____

_____ 12. Of the subtypes of schizophrenia, paranoid schizophrenics show the least impairment in ability to carry out daily functions.

_____

_____

PERSONALITY DISORDERS

_____ 13. Personality disorders typically develop in middle adulthood.

_____

_____

_____ 14. Disregard for the rights of others and impulsivity are two characteristics associated with antisocial personality disorder.

_____

_____

Answer Key
  1. F   2. F   3. T   4. F   5. T   6. F   7. T   8. T   9. T   10. F   11. F   12. T
  13. F   14. T

– PART V. MULTIPLE-CHOICE QUESTIONS –

Choose the best answer to each question. Circle your choice. Check your answers against the Answer Key. Questions marked with an asterisk (*) include annotated answers.

DEFINING ABNORMAL BEHAVIOR

1. Which of the following criteria is *not* used to distinguish normal from abnormal behavior?
    a. emotional discomfort
    b. depression
    c. atypicality
    d. social unacceptability

*2. Which of the following statements is true?
    a. Most psychologists believe that atypicality is the most important criterion for distinguishing psychologically abnormal behavior.
    b. For an individual to be considered to be suffering from a psychological disorder, he or she must have all four criteria of abnormality.
    c. A behavior that is considered abnormal in one society may not be considered abnormal in other societies, eras, or cultures.
    d. Maladaptivity may manifest itself as anxiety, depression, or agitation.

CLASSIFYING BEHAVIORAL DISORDERS

3. The term _____ has historically been used to describe less severe disorders. The term _____ has been used to describe more severe disorders.
    a. psychological / psychiatric
    b. mood disorder / schizophrenia
    c. psychosis / neurosis
    d. neurosis / psychosis

4. The *DSM-IV-R* has what advantage when compared to DSM-II?
    a. specifying more precisely when a diagnosis should be made
    b. greater diagnostic validity
    c. being based completely on the social-learning model
    d. addressing disorders that have only psychological causes

ANXIETY DISORDERS

5. Recurring episodes of intense anxiety that have a sudden onset for no apparent reason describe _____.
    a. generalized anxiety disorder
    b. panic disorder
    c. obsessive-compulsive disorder
    d. agoraphobia

6. John attempts to control his anxiety by staying in the "safety" of his own home, the only place where he does not experience anxiety. John has _____.
    a. social phobia
    b. antisocial personality disorder
    c. panic disorder
    d. agoraphobia

7. An anxiety disorder characterized by a persistent, irrational fear of performing some specific behavior (such as talking or eating) in the presence of other people is called a(n) _____.
    a. specific phobia
    b. social phobia
    c. agoraphobia
    d. triskaidekaphobia

8. Kimberly constantly thinks her immaculate house is dirty and spends most of her time cleaning, scrubbing, and straightening up. She could be diagnosed as suffering from a(n) _____.
    a. thought disorder
    b. specific dirt phobia
    c. obsessive-compulsive disorder
    d. generalized anxiety disorder

9. A person with a _____ experiences anxiety in only certain specific situations, whereas an individual with _____ experiences chronic anxiety in a wide variety of situations.
    a. phobia / generalized anxiety disorder
    b. generalized anxiety disorder / phobia
    c. social phobia / simple phobia
    d. simple phobia / obsessive compulsive disorder

10. If you interpret your roommate's fear of asking a girl out for a date as a phobia resulting from the fact that the last three girls he asked out said no, your interpretation would be consistent with the _____ perspective concerning anxiety disorders.
    a. biological
    b. humanistic
    c. behavioral
    d. psychoanalytic

SOMATOFORM DISORDERS

11. A person who interprets every upset stomach as a sign of appendicitis would most likely be diagnosed as having _____.
    a. a health phobia
    b. somatization disorder
    c. depression
    d. hypochondriasis

12. Which type of somatoform disorder typically develops soon after a specific serious stress or conflict?
    a. multiple personality
    b. conversion disorder
    c. somatization disorder
    d. hypochondriasis

13. An individual with _____ would be most likely to receive unnecessary medications or unnecessary surgery.
    a. somatization disorder
    b. conversion disorder
    c. psychogenic amnesia
    d. hypochondriasis

14. The _____ perspective proposes that the somatoform disorders result from anxiety associated with unresolved conflicts being converted into physical symptoms.
    a. behavioral
    b. biological
    c. humanistic
    d. psychoanalytic

DISSOCIATIVE DISORDERS

15. Your careless smoking caused your family's home to burn down. You are most likely to develop _____.
    a. panic disorder
    b. dissociative identity disorders
    c. dissociative amnesia
    d. dissociative fugue disorder

16. The police in your hometown pick up a man found loitering at the bus station at night who does not know his name. Most likely that person is suffering from _____.
    a. paranoid schizophrenia
    b. dissociative identity disorder
    c. dissociative fugue disorder
    d. dissociative amnesia

17. Individuals like Eve from *The Three Faces of Eve* who display a number of separate personalities are suffering from _____.
    a. dissociative amnesia
    b. conversion disorder
    c. schizophrenia
    d. dissociative identity disorder

18. Which of the following terms does not belong?
    a. dissociative fugue disorder
    b. conversion disorder
    c. dissociative disorder
    d. dissociative identity disorder

19. A history of significant childhood trauma—primarily sexual abuse—is frequently associated with _____.
    a. generalized anxiety disorder
    b. dissociative identity disorder
    c. dissociative amnesia
    d. schizophrenia

*20. Freud's view that excessive application of defense mechanisms can lead to serious disorders is provided the best support by the _____ disorders.
    a. anxiety
    b. dissociative
    c. schizophrenic
    d. mood

MOOD DISORDERS

21. Which of the following categories of symptoms is *not* characteristic of the mood disorders?
    a. anxiety
    b. a marked change in activity level
    c. feelings of sadness, hopelessness, and despair
    d. insomnia or excessive sleep

22. People who become lethargic and sleep more than usual typify the mood disorder termed _____ disorder.
    a. major depressive
    b. bipolar
    c. conversion
    d. schizophrenic

23. Jeff alternates periods of euphoria and frantic activity with periods of deep depression and is suffering from _____.
    a. seasonal affective disorder
    b. obsessive-compulsive disorder
    c. major depression
    d. bipolar disorder

24. False perceptions that lack a sensory basis—such as hearing imaginary voices—are _____.
    a. associated with unresolved sexual conflicts
    b. illusions

    c. hallucinations

    d. delusions

25. If your therapist suggests that you should receive an increased exposure to artificial light, you most likely _____.

    a. suffer from major depressive disorder

    b. suffer from seasonal mania disorder

    c. suffer from seasonal affective disorder

    d. have a schizophrenic therapist

26. Which of the following neurotransmitters or hormones has *not* been associated with the mood disorders?

    a. dopamine

    b. melatonin

    c. serotonin

    d. norepinephrine

27. According to the cognitive-behavioral perspective, mood disorders are _____.

    a. caused by repressed love-hate relationships

    b. the result of the loss of a primary source of reinforcement, such as the loss of a loved one or of a loss of any kind

    c. the result of Pavlovian conditioning

    d. caused by a deficiency of brain chemicals

28. Twin studies with identical twins show a much higher concordance rate for _____ than _____.

    a. bipolar disorder / major depressive disorder

    b. major depressive disorder / bipolar disorder

    c. winter SAD / summer SAD

    d. summer SAD / winter SAD

SCHIZOPHRENIA

29. Which of the following is *not* a primary symptom of schizophrenia?

    a. emotional expression disturbances

    b. social withdrawal

    c. psychomotor disturbances

    d. thought disturbances

30. It is common for schizophrenics to invent new words or _____.

    a. neologisms

    b. divergent vocabulary

    c. echolalia

    d. word salad

31. How are the disturbances in emotional expression associated with schizophrenia characterized?

    a. by a blunted or fiat affect

    b. as inappropriate

    c. Neither of the above apply.

    d. Either of the above apply.

32. Well-organized delusional thought characterizes _____ schizophrenia.

    a. paranoid

b. residual

c. catatonic

d. disorganized

33. You observe a schizophrenic individual who remains in a bizarre position for several hours. That individual would be diagnosed as having _____ schizophrenia.

a. residual

b. disorganized

c. paralyzed

d. catatonic

*34. The _____ hypothesis suggests that schizophrenia is caused by either abnormally high levels of or an increased reactivity to a specific neurotransmitter.

a. endorphin

b. learned-helplessness

c. dopamine

d. norepinephrine

PERSONALITY DISORDERS

*35. Which of the following statements concerning personality disorders is true?

a. Manifestations of (symptoms) disappear during middle and old age.

b. The prognosis for overcoming any of the personality disorders is poor.

c. People with personality disorders are likely to request psychological treatment.

d. Personality disorders usually develop during the mid-to-late 20s.

36. The charming con man, who allows rich young women to fall in love with him and then steals their money, might well be diagnosed as having _____.

a. multiple personality.

b. paranoid schizophrenia.

c. antisocial personality disorder.

d. bipolar disorder.

37. What does psychoanalytic perspective concerning antisocial personality disorder suggest about these individuals?

a. They did not develop an id.

b. They did not develop an ego.

c. They did not develop a superego.

d. They have not learned to avoid punishment.

Answer Key

1. b	*2. c	3. d	4. a	5. b	6. d	7. b	8. c	9. a	10. c	11. d	12. b	13. a
14. d	15. c	16. c	17. d	18. b	19. b	*20. b	21. a	22. b	23. d	24. c	25. c	26. a
27. b	28. a	29. c	30. a	31. d	32. a	33. d	*34. c	*35. b	36. c	37. c		

Annotated Answers

2. The correct choice is **c.** Each society decides what is considered abnormal or disordered. For example, our society views hallucinations as a sign of a serious disorder (frequently schizophrenia), while some societies in Polynesia and South America view hallucinations as a great gift.

a. Atypicality alone is not sufficient to classify a behavior as abnormal.

b.   Although all disorders are considered atypical, any given disorder may show only one or a combination of maladaptivity, emotional discomfort, and social unacceptability.

d.   It is emotional discomfort (not maladaptivity) that may manifest as anxiety, depression, or agitation.

20.   The correct choice is **b**. The dissociative disorders involve a memory loss (dissociative amnesia and fugue) or a change in identity (dissociative identity disorder). According to Freud, all involve an extreme use of the defense mechanism of repression to deal with (or deny) anxiety-producing situations. Freud's view makes sense on an intuitive level, and the behavioral and biological perspectives do not offer well-developed or cohesive explanations for the dissociative disorders.

a.   Freud's explanation for the different anxiety disorders involves using defense mechanisms to deal with internal conflicts involving sexual and aggressive impulses, and proposes that different conflicts (Oedipal complex, anal fixation) result in different disorders. If you are a "true Freudian," these explanations may appear reasonable; however, the behavioral perspective proposing a conditioning model offers a simpler explanation.

c.   Freud's explanation of the schizophrenia centers around massive regression to the oral stage and receives little serious support today. The biological perspective is the focus of great attention today.

d.   Freud's explanation of the mood disorders stresses oral fixation that results in excessive self-hatred (depression) and self-love (mania). Research evidence does not support this view. As is the case with the mood disorders, the biological perspective has received far more experimental support.

34.   The correct choice is **c**. The dopamine hypothesis of schizophrenia has received strong experimental support.

a.   There is no endorphin hypothesis of schizophrenia.

b.   The learned-helplessness theory is related to the mood disorders.

d.   The monoamine theory is also related to the mood disorders.

35.   The correct choice is **b**. The prognosis for overcoming personality disorders is very poor, at least in part because these individuals do not tend to believe that there is anything wrong with the way they are functioning and tend to refuse treatment.

a.   Symptoms of personality disorders become less (not more) obvious in middle and old age.

c.   Individuals with personality disorders are likely to refuse (not request) psychological treatment.

d.   Personality disorders generally develop in childhood or adolescence (not in the mid-to-late 20s).

PART VI.   SUMMARY TABLES –

To test your understanding of the material discussed in this chapter, complete the following table. Check your answers with those supplied in Part IX.

SUMMARY OF BEHAVIORAL DISORDERS

Disorder	Type of Disorder	Description
Agoraphobia		
Antisocial personality		
Bipolar disorder		
Catatonic schizophrenia		
Conversion disorder		
Disorganized schizophrenia		
Generalized anxiety disorder		
Hypochondriasis		
Major depressive disorder		
Dissociative identity disorder		
Obsessive-compulsive disorder		

Disorder	Type of Disorder	Description
Panic disorder		
Paranoid schizophreniz		
Dissociative amnesia		
Dissociative fugue disorder		
Posttraumatic stress disorder		
Residual schizophrenia		
Seasonal affective disorder		
Specific phobia		
Social phobia		
Somatization disorder		
Undifferentiated schizophrenia		

THEORETICAL PERSPECTIVES OF BEHAVIORAL DISORDERS

Disorder	Psychoanalytic	Behavioral	Biological
Anxiety			
Somatoform			
Dissociative			
Mood			
Schizophrenia			
Antisocial personality			

– PART VII. THOUGHT QUESTIONS/CRITICAL THINKING –

Prepare answers to the following discussion questions.

1. The text defines a simple phobia as an irrational fear of a specific situation or object (for example, heights or spiders). The text defines a social phobia as an irrational fear of performing some specific behavior in the presence of other people (for example, talking, or eating). At one level it seems

appropriate to consider some social phobias to be simple phobias. Discuss why *DSM-IV-R* considers social phobias a separate disorder.

2. It is very common for people (both educated and uneducated) to incorrectly use the terms schizophrenia and multiple personality. Differentiate between the two disorders, and explain possible reasons why the terms are often confused or used incorrectly.

3. According to the psychoanalytic perspective, the anxiety, somatoform, and dissociative disorders develop as a result of an individual's inability to adequately cope with anxiety associated with internal conflicts or unacceptable urges. If you accept this proposal, it would seem that, at least in some instances, an individual has some choice (at an unconscious level) as to which disorder he or she will develop. You won't ever have a conscious choice as to which type of anxiety, somatoform, or dissociative disorder you might develop. However, if you did, which disorder would you choose to develop and which disorder would you be least likely to choose? Explain your selections. (You might want to determine how much disruption each disorder would cause in your life.)

4. Decide on a diagnosis as to what type of disorder each of the following individuals has. Cite specific information to justify your diagnoses.
   a. Linda, a 20-year-old college student, suffers from fatigue, frequent upset stomach, and difficulty sleeping. She is also having difficulty concentrating on her classes and can't seem to study for more than a few minutes at a time. She is worried about her grades, roommate, whether she will find a summer job, and so forth.
   b. Bill, who is in his 40s, is the local town's resident "crazy person." He spends much of his day stationed at an intersection in town where he directs traffic and often angrily lectures drivers for ignoring his commands to stop.
   c. Joy is a 32-year-old housewife who is depressed. She has finally decided to see a neurologist because of the headaches and blackouts from which she has suffered for a number of years. She fears that she may have inherited some defect from her mother that is responsible for her problems. Her mother was an alcoholic who suffered from blackouts, usually after a drunken incident during which she abused Joy.
   d. John is 29 years old and works in the same office as your mother. Your mother frequently discusses John's problems. He has been plagued with health problems for the entire year your mother has known him. John has a history of back problems, suffers from migraine headaches, and has been to three doctors about his "nervous stomach." None of the medications he has taken seem to have worked. It seems as though not a day goes by without John complaining about one of his health problems, and your mother feels sorry for him.

– PART VIII. APPLICATIONS –

1. Behavioral disorders (or mental health problems) may be contrasted with physical health problems that have biological causes (disease, injury, etc.). However, the distinction between behavioral and physical disorders is not always clear-cut. The somatoform disorders, which have primarily physical symptoms, are considered behavioral disorders. Additionally, there is mounting evidence for a physical basis for the mood disorders and schizophrenia (also considered to be behavioral disorders). Do you feel somatoform disorders should be considered behavioral or physical disorders? Why or why not? Do you feel that mood disorders and schizophrenia should be considered behavioral or physical disorders? Why or why not?

2. Decide on one or two possible psychological disorders that each of the following individuals would be most likely to develop. Cite evidence to support your choices.
   a. Bob, a 16-year-old adolescent, recently convinced his girlfriend to engage in sexual intercourse. He has mixed feelings concerning his behavior. Although he (and his girlfriend) found the experience to be satisfying, he is also experiencing guilt.
   b. As a young child, Cathy was subjected to recurrent sexual abuse by her older stepbrother.
   c. Tom, who was first described in application 2(c) in Chapter 14

– PART IX. SUMMARY TABLES SOLUTIONS –

SUMMARY OF BEHAVIORAL DISORDERS

Disorder	Type of Disorder	Description
Agoraphobia	Anxiety	Intense fear of being in places or situations from which escape might be difficult
Antisocial personality	Personality disorder	History of chronic and continual disregard for the rights of others and rules of society; a lack of remorse; extreme self-centered behavior
Bipolar disorder	Mood	Extreme mood swings, from immobilizing depression to euphoria and frantic activity
Catatonic schizophrenia	Schizophrenia	Extreme psychomotor disturbances, from stuporous immobility (waxy flexibility) to wild excitement and agitation
Conversion disorder	Somatoform	Manifested as sensory or motor-system disturbance for which there is no organic cause
Disorganized schizophrenia	Schizophrenic	Disorganization and regression in thinking and behavioral patterns
Generalized anxiety disorder	Anxiety	Chronic state of pervasive anxiety (free-floating anxiety)
Hypochondriasis	Somatoform	Complain about a variety of physical symptoms and fear that symptoms indicate serious disease
Major depressive disorder	Mood	Deep enduring depression that impairs ability to function effectively
Dissociative identity disorder	Dissociative	Alternates between an original or primary personality and one or more secondary or subordinate personalities
Obsessive-compulsive disorder	Anxiety	Reflected in persistent, unwanted, and unshakable thoughts and/or irresistible, habitual, repeated actions

SUMMARY OF BEHAVIORAL DISORDERS (continued)

Disorder	Type of Disorder	Description
Panic disorder	Anxiety	Experiences four or more panic attacks in a four-week period
Paranoid schizophreniz.	Schizophrenic	Dominant symptom is well-developed delusional thoughts
Dissociative amnesia	Dissociative	Sudden loss of memory (typically, for all events for a specific period of time), usually after a particularly stressful or traumatic event
Dissociative fugue disorder	Dissociative	Combines amnesia with a "flight" away from an intolerable situation
Posttraumatic stress disorder	Anxiety	Symptoms include reexperiencing a traumatic event, numbing of general responsiveness, and increased arousal
Residual schizophrenia	Schizophrenic	Label used when major symptoms are absent or markedly diminished
Seasonal affective disorder	Mood	Recurrent winter or summer depression
Specific phobia	Anxiety	Irrational fear of a specific situation or object
Social phobia	Anxiety	Irrational fear of performing some specific behavior in the presence of other people
Somatization disorder	Somatoform	Multiple and recurrent physical symptoms for which medical attention is sought, but that have no physical cause
Undifferentiated schizophrenia	Schizophrenic	"Catch-all" category for individuals who are schizophrenic but do not manifest the specific symptoms associated with the other subtypes of schizophrenia

THEORETICAL PERSPECTIVES OF BEHAVIORAL DISORDERS

Disorder	Psychoanalytic	Behavioral	Biological
Anxiety	Defense mechanisms used to control anxiety associated with internal conflicts involving sexual or aggressive impulses fail or are overused	Pavlovian conditioning, two-factor conditioning, and modeling are responsible	An autonomic nervous system that is more easily aroused or is hypersensitive
Somatoform	Unresolved sexual conflicts are converted into physical symptoms	Symptoms persists if reinforced and allow the person to escape or avoid anxiety	No evidence for biological factors
Dissociative	Repression is used to ward off unacceptable impulses (primarily sexual in nature)	Does not offer a comprehensive explanation Operant avoidance responses are reinforced by allowing the individual to avoid anxiety	No evidence for the biological perspective
Mood	Develops as a result of oral fixation No research evidence supporting this perspective	A loss of primary source of reinforcement Learned helplessness if an individual believes he or she has little control over rewards and punishments	Genetic factors associated with levels of specific neurotransmitters (norepinephrine, serotonin) in the brain
Schizophrenia	Develops as a result of oral fixation Currently, not a seriously considered explanation	Follows extinction of normal patterns of responding (due to inadequate reinforcers or rewards)	Abnormally high levels of or reactivity to the neurotransmitter dopamine
Antisocial personality	Failure to develop a superego	Failure to learn to avoid punishment and/or punishment has little meaning for these individuals	Higher brain centers that control impulsive actions are slow to develop

CHAPTER 16
TREATMENT OF BEHAVIORAL DISORDERS

– PART I. LEARNING OBJECTIVES –

When you finish studying this chapter, you should be able to do the following:

PSYCHOLOGICAL THERAPIES: PSYCHOANALYSIS

1. Describe the primary goal of psychoanalysis, and describe four techniques Freud developed to accomplish this goal.

2. Discuss the similarities and differences between Freud's psychoanalysis and modern psychoanalytic therapy.

COGNITIVE THERAPIES

3. Discuss the basic premise and approach of the cognitive therapies.

4. Describe the primary focus of Ellis's rational-emotive therapy (RET), and discuss how a self-defeating irrational belief system may be challenged.

5. Describe the primary focus of Beck's cognitive behavior therapy, and discuss techniques utilized to counteract negative self-images.

BEHAVIORAL THERAPIES

6. Discuss how the central thesis of behavioral therapy differs from traditional methods of therapy, and outline the basic techniques utilized by behavior therapies.

7. Describe two types of behavior therapy that are based on Pavlovian conditioning—Wolpe's systematic desensitization and aversion conditioning—and discuss situations in which each approach would be appropriate.

8. Describe three types of behavior therapy based on operant conditioning—positive reinforcement, extinction, and punishment—and discuss situations in which each approach would be appropriate.

9. Describe how modeling can be a helpful therapy technique, and give examples of two types of behaviors that can be acquired or altered through modeling.

10. Define a token economy, and discuss how it can be used to maintain adaptive behavior patterns.

FAMILY THERAPY

11. Discuss the premise upon which family therapy is based, and describe techniques that are used to change maladaptive patterns in disturbed families.

12. Discuss how couple therapy is similar to family therapy, and discuss why couple therapy often focuses on improving communication.

EVALUATING PSYCHOTHERAPY

13. Summarize the research concerning whether receiving psychotherapy is more beneficial than not receiving therapy.

14. Summarize research comparing the success rates of different types of psychotherapy, and discuss why this type of research may diminish in the future.

15. Describe four features that are shared by most types of psychotherapy.

BIOLOGICALLY BASED THERAPIES

16. Summarize the history of psychosurgery, and describe the lobotomy procedures and the effects this procedure has on an individual.

17. Summarize the history of electroconvulsive therapy (ECT), explain how it is thought to work, and discuss its current status.

18. Describe the effects that psychoactive drugs have had on the number of individuals hospitalized and the length of hospitalization since the 1950s.

19. List four major categories of psychoactive drugs, and describe the use of each category in controlling the symptoms of behavioral disorders.

– PART II. OVERVIEW –

A number of different psychological therapies for treating behavioral disorders exist. Freud's psychoanalysis attempts to help individuals first gain insight into their unconscious conflicts and then resolve these conflicts. Psychoanalysis uses the techniques of free association, dream analysis, and interpretation of resistance and transference. Contemporary psychoanalytically oriented therapists utilize a modified version of Freud's technique.

Cognitive therapies define behavioral disorders as arising from irrational or distorted beliefs or cognitions and attempt to replace these irrational cognitions with more appropriate beliefs. Ellis's rational-emotive therapy (RET) attempts to force individuals to confront and challenge irrational self-defeating belief systems. Beck's cognitive behavior therapy focuses on the negative self-images and self-labels of disturbed individuals. Cognitive behavior therapy attempts to alter these inappropriate beliefs by using "experiments" or real-life exercises that will contradict an individual's negative self-labels.

Behavioral therapies—based on the principles of Pavlovian conditioning, operant conditioning, and modeling—are designed to teach individuals appropriate behaviors to replace the inappropriate or disturbed behaviors they previously learned. Two behavior therapies based on Pavlovian conditioning are systematic desensitization (which is very effective in treating phobias) and aversive conditioning (which may be used to alter an individual's previously acquired positive response to a harmful substance, such as alcohol). Techniques based on operant conditioning are used to induce desired behaviors (positive reinforcement) and eliminate undesirable behaviors (extinction and punishment).

In addition to treating people individually, frequently an individual's problems are addressed in family therapy because the behavior and interaction of family members affect the functioning of other members of the family. Couple therapy is the most common approach for treating relationship problems within couples.

Many people with behavioral disorders recover without the benefit of therapy (spontaneous remission), but psychotherapy has been shown to be more effective and result in better outcomes than not receiving therapy. Research attempting to evaluate the relative effectiveness of the different types of therapies indicates that no one technique is significantly superior to the others. Most psychologists and psychiatrists agree that a combination of psychotherapy with drug therapy lead to the best outcome for most patients.

In addition to psychological therapies, a number of biologically based treatments for behavioral disorders exist. The lobotomy, which is the severing of connections between the frontal cortex and lower regions of the brain, and which was once used to "treat" schizophrenia, is the best-known psychosurgery technique. Although the lobotomy was successful in calming agitated patients, this technique did not generally have beneficial consequences for the individual. Today other more specific forms of psychosurgery exist and are used in some circumstances. Electroconvulsive therapy (ECT), which had its beginnings at about the same time as the lobotomy, is still in use today. ECT is used primarily to treat major depression when an individual does not respond to other treatments. Psychoactive drugs comprise the most commonly used biologically based technique currently used. Four different categories of psychoactive drugs are used to control (but not cure) a variety of psychological disorders: (1) antipsychotics (for schizophrenia), (2) antidepressants (for major depression), (3) antimanics (for bipolar disorder), and (4) antianxiety drugs (for anxiety and tension).

– PART III. KEY TERMS/MATCHING EXERCISES –

Match the following concepts and/or individuals with the appropriate descriptions. Check your answers against the Answer Key.

THERAPIES (OVERVIEW)

Concepts	Descriptions
_____ 1. cognitive therapy	a. Attempts to allow an individual to gain insight or conscious awareness of repressed conflicts so that the conflicts can be resolved
_____ 2. psychoanalysis	b. Assumes that distorted or irrational thoughts contribute to psychological difficulties
_____ 3. biomedical approach	c. Based on one or both assumptions that many psychological problems result from biological abnormalities, and that physiological intervention will reduce symptoms
_____ 4. psychological therapy	d. Based on the idea that because maladaptive behavior is learned, it can also be unlearned
_____ 5. behavioral therapy	e. Any nonbiological, noninvasive psychological technique or procedure used to improve a person's adjustment to life

Answer Key
   1. b   2. a   3. c   4. e   5. d

Individuals	Descriptions
_____ 1. Beck	a. Developed systematic desensitization to treat phobias
_____ 2. Ellis	b. Developed techniques of free association, dream analysis, and interpretation of resistance and transference
_____ 3. Freud	c. Believes that disturbed people typically have very negative self-images based on highly negative self-labels
_____ 4. Wolpe	d. Believes therapy should focus on the here and now and challenges individuals to find flaws in their irrational belief systems

Answer Key
  1. c   2. d   3. b   4. a

PSYCHOLOGICAL THERAPIES

Concepts	*Descriptions*
_____ 1. transference	a. Involves being encouraged to say whatever comes to mind
_____ 2. dream analysis	b. Treat(s) phobias by training individuals to relax when confronted with a fear-inducing stimuli
_____ 3. free association	c. Use(s) techniques based on positive reinforcement, extinction, and punishment and is also referred to as behavior modification
_____ 4. operant conditioning therapies	d. Process in which people relate to their therapist in a manner similar to the way they relate to other important people in their life
_____ 5. aversive conditioning	e. To Freud, the "royal road to the unconscious"
_____ 6. resistance	f. Experiential method(s) that involve(s) altering negative self-images and self-defeating behaviors
_____ 7. systematic desensitization	g. Viewed as a sign that the therapist is getting close to the "problem"
_____ 8. rational-emotive therapy	h. Involve(s) substituting a negative response for a positive response to an inappropriate or harmful stimuli
_____ 9. cognitive behavior therapy	i. Confrontative method that involves challenging irrational beliefs and substituting more logical thoughts

Answer Key
  1. d   2. e   3. a   4. c   5. h   6. g   7. b   8. i   9. f

BIOLOGICALLY BASED THERAPIES

Concepts	*Descriptions*
_____ 1. antianxiety drugs	a. Newer techniques that relieve specific symptoms of some psychological disorders as a result of the destruction of limited amounts of tissue located in specific brain structures
_____ 2. psychoactive drugs	b. Describe(s) lithium carbonate as useful in controlling the symptoms of bipolar disorder
_____ 3. antidepressants	c. Also referred to as major tranquilizers and most effective in managing the symptoms of schizophrenia
_____ 4. electroconvulsive therapy (ECT)	d. Also referred to as minor tranquilizers and used to reduce symptoms of anxiety and tension
_____ 5. lobotomy	e. Involve(s) disconnecting the frontal cortex from lower brain structures that mediate emotional responses
_____ 6. antipsychotic drugs	f. Since the 1950s, the most common form of biomedical treatment of psychological disorders
_____ 7. psychosurgery	g. Involves inducing a convulsive seizure that is associated with a reduction of the symptoms of depression
_____ 8. antimanics	h. Consist(s) of tricyclics, MAO inhibitors, SRIs and is primarily used to treat major depression

– PART IV. TRUE-FALSE STATEMENTS –

Fill in the blank before each statement with either a T (true) or an F (false). Check your answers against the Answer Key. Then go back to the items that are false and make the necessary change(s) to the statements to convert the items into true statements.

PSYCHOLOGICAL THERAPIES

_____ 1. Resistance occurs when an individual undergoing psychoanalysis begins to respond to the therapist in much the same manner as he or she responds to other important people in his or her life.

_____

_____

_____ 2. A's (activating events), B's (belief systems), and C's (emotional consequences) are related to Beck's cognitive behavior therapy.

_____

_____

_____ 3. Systematic desensitization is useful in stopping people from continuing to engage in "bad habits" such as smoking and alcohol abuse.

_____

_____

_____ 4. The behavior therapy techniques of positive reinforcement, aversive conditioning, and extinction are all based on operant conditioning.

_____

_____

_____ 5. Family therapy assumes that individual pathology is rooted in a disturbed family and that changing the interactions of the family will affect those individuals displaying pathology.

_____

_____

EVALUATING PSYCHOTHERAPY

_____ 6. Eysenck's (1952) finding that approximately two-thirds of disturbed people improve markedly whether they receive psychotherapy or not has been supported by additional research.

_____

_____ 7. Research examining the success rate of different types of psychotherapy has shown that no particular type of psychotherapy is significantly superior to the others.

_____

BIOLOGICALLY BASED THERAPIES

_____ 8. Today, psychosurgery is the most common biomedical treatment of psychological disorders.

_____

_____

_____ 9. Like lobotomies, discussion of electroconvulsive therapy is mostly "historical" in nature because both of these treatments are no longer in use.

_____

_____

Answer Key
   1. F   2. F   3. F   4. F   5. T   6. F   7. T   8. F   9. F

– PART V. MULTIPLE-CHOICE QUESTIONS –

Choose the best answer to each question. Circle your choice. Check your answers against the Answer Key. Questions marked with an asterisk (*) include annotated answers.

PSYCHOLOGICAL THERAPIES: PSYCHOANALYSIS

1. The basic aim of psychoanalysis can be described as to _____.
   a. weaken the id
   b. make the conscious unconscious
   c. make the unconscious conscious
   d. confront negative self images

2. Which of the following is not one of the therapeutic techniques of Freud's psychoanalysis?
   a. interpretation of transference
   b. emotive therapy
   c. interpretation of resistance
   d. free association

3. Sometimes an individual decides to terminate therapy at a time the therapist feels is premature and at a point when therapy is about to make significant progress. This patient's behavior illustrates _____.
   a. repression
   b. reaction formation
   c. transference
   d. resistance

4. It is not uncommon for clients to "fall in love" with their therapists. This type of client behavior illustrates _____.
   a. attachment
   b. resistance

c. transference

d. projection

*5. Which of the following is true of contemporary psychoanalytically oriented therapists?

 a. They pay more attention to a patient's current life and relationships.

 b. They tend to desire a longer duration of therapy.

 c. They sit out of view of a patient.

 d. They attempt to gain insight into the unconscious roots of a patient's problems.

COGNITIVE THERAPIES

6. According to Ellis's rational-emotive therapy (RET), psychological problems arise as a result of _____.

 a. specific activating events (A)

 b. the individual's belief system (B)

 c. emotional consequences (C)

 d. negative self-images

7. Rational-emotive therapy tends to focus on _____. Cognitive behavior therapy focuses on _____.

 a. thoughts / behavior

 b. behavior / thoughts

 c. irrational beliefs / negative self-images

 d. negative self-images / irrational beliefs

8. _____ is the therapist who would most likely instruct a 40-year-old secretary, who feels she is inferior and unworthy of a job with greater responsibility, to enroll in a course at her local community college.

 a. Beck

 b. Wolpe

 c. Watts

 d. Ellis

BEHAVIORAL THERAPIES

9. Developing a hierarchy of fears is a component of _____.

 a. aversive conditioning

 b. cognitive behavior therapy

 c. extinction technique

 d. systematic desensitization

10. Which of the following is involved with systematic desensitization involves?

 a. training one to relax when confronted with fearful stimuli

 b. interpreting fearful stimuli to be less fearful

 c. changing misconceptions regarding fearful stimuli

 d. uncovering repressed feelings regarding fearful events

*11. The Pavlovian conditioning behavioral therapy of _____ would effectively treat an individual suffering from a spider phobia, whereas the _____ technique would be appropriate to treat alcohol abuse.

 a. aversive conditioning / systematic desensitization

 b. systematic desensitization / aversive conditioning

 c. extinction / punishment

 d. punishment / extinction

12. Which of the following applies to virtual reality therapy?
    a. It has been successful in treating phobias such as fear of flying.
    b. It can be used in conjunction with systematic desensitization.
    c. It involves the application of Pavlovian conditioning techniques.
    d. All of the above apply

13. Whcih of the following is true of behavior modification?
    a. It is most successful in treating mood disorders.
    b. It refers to behavioral and cognitive therapies.
    c. It involves the application of Pavlovian conditioning techniques.
    d. It involves changing behavior by manipulating reinforcers.

14. The type of therapy in which a chronic drinker is given a drug that induces nausea when combined with alcohol is called _____.
    a. systematic desensitization.
    b. aversive conditioning.
    c. chemotherapy.
    d. counterconditioning.

15. Which type of behavioral therapy technique would be most appropriate in order to convert a nonassertive individual into an assertive person?
    a. positive reinforcement
    b. aversive conditioning
    d. client-centered therapy
    c. punishment

*16. Which of the following pairs of techniques and problem behaviors do *not* go well together?
    a. modeling and mouse phobia
    b. punishment and fingernail biting
    c. systematic desensitization and assertiveness
    d. aversive conditioning and cocaine abuse

17. Token economies are often a component of _____ therapy.
    a. extinction
    b. cognitive behavior
    c. aversive conditioning
    d. positive reinforcement

FAMILY THERAPY

18. Family therapy involves attempting to do which of the following?
    a. instruct family members in how to accept the disturbed family member "as he or she is."
    b. support the other family members during the disturbed member's "illness."
    c. change maladaptive patterns of interaction among family members.
    d. All of the above choices apply.

19. Which of the following is most common approach for treating relationship problems within a primary couple?
    a. couple therapy
    b. having one person receive individual therapy
    c. having both people receive individual therapy from the same therapist
    d. having both people receive individual therapy from different therapists

EVALUATING PSYCHOTHERAPY

20. Which statement is *false*?
    a. Whether a person receives individual or family therapy has little impact on the therapy's effectiveness.
    b. More experienced psychotherapists tend to achieve better results than less experienced psychotherapists.
    c. People who receive therapy are more likely to show marked improvement than similarly disturbed people who do not receive therapy.
    d. Behavior therapy is significantly more effective than cognitive therapy.

21. What is one reason why researchers have found little difference in the effectiveness of various psychotherapy approaches?
    a. All therapists are well trained.
    b. All therapists must take the same licensing exam.
    c. Most approaches began as one approach anyway.
    d Almost all styles of therapy share certain common features.

22. To which of the following does eclecticism refer to?
    a. the use of electroconvulsive therapy
    b. the therapist using a pragmatic application of a number of clinical techniques
    c. the use of magnetic resonance imaging
    d. a new type of cognitive therapy

23. Which of the following is *not* a common feature shared by almost all styles of therapy?
    a. focusing on an individual's early experiences
    b. providing a warm, supportive relationship
    c. providing a rationale for symptoms and treatment
    d. combating a client's demoralization

BIOLOGICALLY BASED THERAPIES

24. Following a lobotomy, what could a person could be expected to do?
    a. Show an inability to plan ahead.
    b. Be lethargic and unmotivated.
    c. Show memory loss.
    d. All of the above choices apply.

25. Electroconvulsive therapy is most effective for the treatment of _____.
    a. schizophrenia
    b. major depression
    c. bipolar disorder
    d. generalized anxiety disorder

*26. Which of the following to psychoactive drugs?
    a. They all tend to have a calming effect on an individual.
    b. They attempt to control the symptoms of psychological disorders.
    c. They are a second-line treatment modality used only if first choice treatments fail.
    d. They cure psychological disorders.

27. Depressed patients given both drugs and psychotherapy _____ compared to patients given drugs only.
    a. took much longer to recover

b. had a comparable relapse rate
   c. had a higher relapse rate
   d. had a lower relapse rate

28. Jeff is an out-patient who suffers from muscle tension, sleeplessness, and feelings of impending doom. What drug would Jeff's doctor possibly prescribe for him?
   a. Lithium
   b Thorazine
   c. Librium and Valium
   d. Mellaril

Answer Key

   1. c   2. b   3. d   4. c   *5. a   6. b   7. c   8. a   9. d   10. a   *11. b   12. d
   13. d   14. b   15. a   *16. c   17. d   18. c   19. a   20. d   21. d   22. b   23. a   24. d
   25. b   *26. b   27. d   28. c

Annotated Answers

   5. The correct choice is **a**. While Freud basically ignored a patient's current life and relationships and concentrated instead on early experiences, contemporary psychoanalytically oriented therapists emphasize a patient's current situation much more so than Freud did.
   b. Contemporary psychoanalysis tends to be briefer in duration than Freudian psychoanalysis.
   c. Freud had patients lie on a couch and remained out of their view (to reduce distractions); contemporary psychoanalysts have patients sit on a chair and face them.
   d. Both Freudian and contemporary psychoanalysts attempt to gain insight into the unconscious roots of a patient's problems.

   11. The correct choice is **b**. Systematic desensitization is perhaps the most effective treatment for phobias, and aversive conditioning is designed specifically to treat problems such as alcohol abuse.
   a. This choice has the two Pavlovian conditioning-based behavior therapies listed, but they are incorrectly associated with the problem behaviors.
   c. Both extinction and punishment are operant conditioning-based behavior therapy techniques.
   d. The explanation for **c** above applies.

   16. The correct choice is **c**. Systematic desensitization is a treatment for phobias (not nonassertiveness).
   a. Modeling is an appropriate treatment for phobias and for establishing other new adaptive behaviors.
   b. Punishment is an appropriate treatment for eliminating voluntary maladaptive responses such as fingernail biting.
   d. Aversive conditioning is designed to substitute a negative response for a positive response to an inappropriate or harmful stimulus (such as cocaine abuse).

   26. The correct choice is **b**. Psychoactive drugs attempt to control the symptoms of a variety of psychological disorders. For example, lithium carbonate controls the manic symptoms associated with bipolar disorder.
   a. Different psychoactive drugs vary considerably in their effects: some calm, some energize, and some promote an emotional lift.
   c. For some psychological disorders (such as schizophrenia and bipolar disorder) psychoactive drugs would be the treatment of choice. The text refers to electroconvulsive therapy as a second-line treatment modality.
   d. Psychoactive drugs do not cure psychological disorders but temporarily control or manage the symptoms of the disorders.

– PART VI. SUMMARY TABLES –

To test your understanding of the material discussed in this chapter, complete the following tables. Check your answers with those supplied in Part IX.

SUMMARY OF THERAPY TECHNIQUES

Therapy	Individual(s)	Cause(s) of Disorder(s)	Goal of Therapy	Methods of Therapy
Psychoanalysis				
Cognitive *Rational- emotive*				
Cognitive Behavior				
Behavioral				
Biologically based				

SUMMARY OF PSYCHOACTIVE DRUGS

Category	Types	Specific Drugs	Disorder(s) Prescribed for	Effect
Antipsychotics				
Antidepressants				
Antimanics				
Antianxiety				

– PART VII. THOUGHT QUESTIONS/CRITICAL THINKING –

Prepare answers to the following discussion questions.

1. The text discusses several general features common to most psychological therapies approaches. There are also a number of more specific features or techniques that are shared by some (but not all) approaches. Decide which of the therapy approaches described in the text (psychoanalysis, rational-emotive therapy, cognitive behavior therapy, and behavioral therapy) share each of the following emphases or techniques.
    a. An emphasis on an individual's past experiences
    b. Encourages a gaining of insight into the causes of an individual's difficulties or problems
    c. Therapist uses a confrontational approach or style.
    d. Utilizes specific situations or experiences to encourage an individual to alter behavior or reasoning

2. Imagine that your mother is currently hospitalized for a psychological problem and her doctor recommends that she receive electroconvulsive therapy (ECT). What questions would you ask the doctor before you would give your consent for the treatment?

3. While none of the psychotherapy approaches has been shown to be significantly superior to the other approaches, they do differ considerably in the theoretical orientation and techniques employed.

Additionally, no one type of therapy would be "right" for everyone. If you were to decide to enter therapy, which type of therapy would you most likely select? Why? Which type of therapy would you least likely select? Why?

– PART VIII. APPLICATIONS –

1. During the last couple of years many organizations providing psychological services (hospitals, independent clinics, stress units, etc.) have started to advertise their programs through newspapers, mass mailings, radio, and television. The following us a typical advertisement.

   > Do you have......feelings of hopelessness?......a sense of worthlessness?......constant fatigue?......sleep problems?......a loss of appetite? If your answer is yes to two or more of these questions, you may be suffering from depression. Here at the ABC Institute we specialize in the treatment of depression and other psychological problems. Our treatment is proven to be effective. The majority of our clients experience marked improvement after just a few short weeks of treatment. The effects of depression are devastating, and it is no longer necessary for you to continue to suffer. Call us at the ABC Institute today for a free evaluation of your problem.

   Assume that you answered yes to several of the questions mentioned in the advertisement. Prepare a list of questions that you would want to know the answers to before you decide to enter treatment at the ABC Institute. Explain the reasons why you would ask each question.

2. Imagine that a close friend of yours is experiencing each of the following psychological difficulties:
   a. His main problem concerns interpersonal relationships. He has difficulty in maintaining friendships, frequently gets into disagreements with friends, and is often disappointed by the actions of his friends.
   b. She is a chronic procrastinator and, as a result, is in danger of flunking out of college.
   c. He is afraid to drive his car after dark.
   d. She is very anxious and insecure and tends to feel that she cannot compete effectively with others in college, in relationships, and in life in general.
   e. He had an unhappy childhood and believes that if his childhood had been happier, his life would be better today.

   Select one or two types of therapy that you would recommend to your friend. Explain the reasons why you selected each therapy.

– PART IX. SUMMARY TABLES SOLUTIONS –

SUMMARY OF THERAPY TECHNIQUES

Therapy	Individual(s)	Cause(s) of Disorder(s)	Goal of Therapy	Methods of Therapy
Psychoanalysis	Freud	Unconscious conflicts and repressed urges, most of which are rooted in childhood experience	To help individuals gain insight or conscious awareness of repressed conflicts and then to resolve those conflicts	Free association, dream analysis, and interpretation of resistance and transference
Cognitive *Rational-emotive*	Ellis	Self-defeating irrational beliefs	Challenge or dispute irrational beliefs and then substitute more logical or realistic thoughts	Confrontation, persuasion, role playing, interpretation, behavior modification, and reflection of feelings
Cognitive Behavior	Beck	Irrational beliefs concerning negative self-images and self-labels	Help the client restructure his or her thinking, especially negative self-labels	Experiential method to disprove a client's misguided self-impressions
Behavioral	Wolpe Bandura	Result from learning	Help clients unlearn maladaptive behavior while learning more adaptive behavior	Systematic desensitization, aversive conditioning, positive reinforcement, extinction, and punishment
Biologically based	de Egas Moniz Watts Cerletti Bino	Result from biological abnormalities	Elimination of symptoms through physiological intervention	Psychosurgery, electroconvulsive therapy, and psychoactive drugs

SUMMARY OF PSYCHOACTIVE DRUGS

Category	Types	Specific Drugs	Disorder(s) Prescribed for	Effect
Antipsychotics	Also called major tranquilizers Phenothiazine derivatives	Thorazine Clozapine	Schizophrenia	Blocks dopamine receptor sites (CNS)
Antidepressants	Tricyclics, mono-amine oxidase (MAO) inhib-itors, serotonin reuptake inhi-bitors (SRIs)	Elavil Nardil Marphan Prozac	Major depression and severely depressed individuals	Increases level of or sensitivity to nor-epinephrine and serotonin (CNS)
Antimanics	Inorganic salts	Lithium carbonate (Lithane, Lithonate)	Bipolar disorder	Increases reuptake of norepinephrine and serotonin (CNS)
Antianxiety	Also called minor tranquilizers Propanediols and benzodiazepine	Miltown Librium Valium Xanax	Anxiety and tension (especially generalized anxiety disorder)	Relaxes skeletal muscles

CHAPTER 17
SOCIAL PSYCHOLOGY

– PART I. LEARNING OBJECTIVES –

When you finish studying this chapter you should be able to do the following:

SOCIAL PERCEPTION

1. Define social perception, and list three factors that influence it.

2. Describe the importance of first impressions on social perception, and discuss differences in the formation and maintenance of positive and negative first impressions.

3. Define person schemas, and explain how person schemas influence social perception.

4. Define implicit personality theories, and describe how central traits and the halo effect are associated with implicit personality theories.

ATTRIBUTION THEORIES

5. Discuss the basic premise of attribution theory, and differentiate between dispositional and external causes.

6. Describe Jones' correspondent inference theory approach to understanding attribution, and discuss three variables related to making correspondent inferences.

7. Describe Kelley's covariation principle approach to understanding attribution, and discuss three dimensions that are analyzed in making attributions.

8. List and describe three factors that cause attribution errors to be made in the inferences people draw concerning the behavior of others.

ATTITUDES

9. Define attitude, and discuss the three-component model of attitudes.

10. Discuss five types of experiences that influence the attitudes people develop.

11. List and describe three functions that attitudes serve.

12. Summarize the research concerning the consistency between attitudes and behavior, and discuss three variables influencing whether attitudes are predictive of behavior.

13. Describe two consistency theories (balance theory and cognitive dissonance theory) that explain how attitudes are changed.

14. Define persuasion, and discuss three elements (the communicator, the message, the audience) that are important in persuasive communication.

PREJUDICE

15. Define prejudice, stereotypes, and discrimination; discuss the interrelationships among these three terms.

16. Define and differentiate between outgroups and ingroups, and discuss three factors that may influence the development of prejudice.

17. Describe the prejudiced or authoritarian personality, and discuss common features in the manner in which individuals with these personalities were reared.

IMPLICIT ATTITUDES

18. Define implicit attitudes and describe how they differ from explicit attitudes.

19   How are implicit attitudes measured?

20. Are implicit attitudes and explicit attitudes typically in agreement? Can you provide an example of when they might not be?

SOCIAL INFLUENCE ON BEHAVIOR

21. Define conformity, and differentiate between informational and normative social influences.

22. Summarize Sherif and Asch's research concerning conformity, and discuss several factors that increase an individual's tendency to conform.

23. Define compliance by contrasting it with conformity, and describe two techniques that increase compliance.

24. Define obedience by contrasting it with conformity and compliance, and summarize Milgram's study of obedience.

25. Discuss three reasons why people may respond to social influence in the form of destructive obedience.

INTERPERSONAL BEHAVIOR: ATTRACTION AND AGGRESSION

26. Discuss four factors that influence interpersonal attraction.

27. Discuss Buss' theory that attractiveness features have evolved to ensure that we are attracted to potential mates that ensure greater reproductive success.

28. How do the attractiveness features described by Buss differ for men and women? Do these differences make sense in evolutionary terms?

29. Describe the biological perspective concerning aggression, and summarize the research regarding this biological perspective.

30. Describe the psychosocial perspective concerning aggression, and discuss three major areas this perspective focuses on.

– PART II. OVERVIEW –

Social psychology is concerned with how a variety of social factors influence thoughts, beliefs, feelings, and behaviors. Social perception relates to how one forms judgments about the qualities of people one meets. The primacy effect results in people's first impressions of an individual having a strong and frequently lasting influence on their perception of the individual. Both person schemas and implicit personality theories result in one inferring a person's overall personality or traits from a limited amount of information. In addition to having such a "personality profile" of individuals, people also attempt to understand the reasons behind the behavior of others. According to attribution theory, people attribute another's behavior to either dispositional causes (or internal traits) or external causes (such as environmental or situational factors). The tendency exists to attribute the behavior of others to dispositional causes, while we frequently explain our own behavior by referring to external causes.

Attitudes are learned, relatively enduring predispositions to respond in a consistent way to certain people, groups, ideas, and situations. Attitudes serve a variety of functions—from providing one with a frame of reference and information concerning others to identifying with or gaining approval from one's peers. The attitudes and behaviors of a person are related but may not be consistent in specific situations. Two theories related to attitude change and overall cognitive consistency are balance theory and cognitive dissonance theory. Balance theory proposes that the attitudes of other people (who we like or dislike) play a significant role in determining whether we maintain or modify our attitudes. Cognitive dissonance theory proposes that we experience discomfort when we are aware of a conflict between two attitudes or an attitude and behavior. This conflict is then reduced by our changing our attitude. Persuasion involves direct attempts to change another person's attitudes. The attitude of prejudice is discussed in depth.

Implicit attitudes are attitudes you hold that are not available to your consciousness. Often implicit attitudes differ from our explicit attitudes when they are socially undesirable. For example, your implicit attitudes about race and religion may differ from your explicit and public attitudes about these subjects. Implicit attitudes are measured using the Implicit Association Test.

Conformity, compliance, and obedience all relate to altering feelings, beliefs, and behavior as a result of social influence. Conformity refers to simply modifying one's behavior so that it is consistent with the behavior of others. Compliance refers to modifying one's behavior in response to direct requests from others to do so. Finally, obedience refers to modifying one's behavior in response to direct commands or orders from people perceived as having power to do so. Research examining conformity (Sherif and Asch), compliance, and obedience (Milgram) shows that social influence is very strong and frequently difficult to resist.

This chapter concludes with a discussion of interpersonal behavior. Interpersonal attraction focuses on factors that influence the people we choose to like and love. Four general factors that influence interpersonal attraction are proximity, similarity, reciprocity, and physical attractiveness. Interpersonal aggression is defined as any physical or verbal behavior intended to hurt another person. Biological factors (which have been linked to human aggression) include levels of prenatal androgens, structures in the limbic system, and genetic factors (from twin studies). The psychosocial perspective concerning aggression has focused on three areas: the association between frustration and aggression, social learning, and the influence of mass-media violence.

– PART III. KEY TERMS/MATCHING EXERCISES –

Match the following concepts with the appropriate descriptions. Check your answers against the Answer Key.

SOCIAL PERCEPTION AND ATTRIBUTION THEORIES

Concepts	Descriptions
_____ 1. covariation principle	a. Propose(s) that people tend to believe that behavior is caused by either dispositional or external causes
_____ 2. person schemas	b. Tendency to overestimate dispositional causes associated with the behavior of others, and to overestimate external causes to one's own behavior
_____ 3. false consensus bias	c. Suggest(s) several factors that determine whether people make dispositional attributions
_____ 4. social perception	d. Generalized assumptions about certain classes of people
_____ 5. attribution theory	e. Belief that we control events in our lives that are in fact controlled by external causes
_____ 6. implicit personality theories	f. Suggest(s) that one considers the situation, the persons involved, and the stimuli toward which a behavior is directed when making attributions
_____ 7. primacy effect	g. Tendency to infer other positive (or negative) traits from one's perception of one central trait
_____ 8. illusion of control	h. Refer(s) to the first information received about a person that often seems to count the most
_____ 9. halo effect	i. Often organized around central traits that one tends to associate with many other characteristics
_____ 10. fundamental attribution error	j. Assumption that one's own attitudes and behaviors are shared by most people
_____ 11. correspondent inference theory	k. Describe(s) the ways we perceive, evaluate, categorize, and form judgments about the qualities of people we encounter
_____ 12. implicit atitude	l. an influence on your behavior that may not be available to your conscious awareness.

Answer Key

1. f   2. d   3. j   4. k   5. a   6. i   7. h   8. e   9. g   10. b   11. c   12. l

ATTITUDES AND PREJUDICE

Concepts	Descriptions
_____ 1. cognitive dissonance theory	a. Negative, unjustifiable, and inflexible attitude toward a group and its members based on erroneous information
_____ 2. ingroup bias	b. Tendency to carefully select what information to reveal concerning personal attitudes
_____ 3. impression management	c. Individuals perceived as different as a result of their not sharing the same characteristics as one's own
_____ 4. authoritarian personality	d. Preconceived and oversimplified beliefs and expectations about the traits of members of a particular group that do not account for individual differences
_____ 5. persuasion	e. Propose(s) that other people play a significant role in determining whether one maintains attitudes or changes them
_____ 6. prejudice	f. Measured by the F Scale and associated with prejudicial attitudes
_____ 7. attitudes	g. Propose(s) that an individual experience(s) a state of discomfort whenever two related cognitions are in conflict
_____ 8. discrimination	h. Associated with a tendency to see one's own group in a favorable light
_____ 9. outgroup	i. Learned, relatively enduring predispositions to consistently respond in favorable or unfavorable ways to people, groups, ideas, or situations
_____ 10. balance theory	j. Behavioral consequence of prejudice
_____ 11. stereotypes	k. Three important elements related to this concept are the communicator, the message, and the audience

Answer Key

1. g   2. h   3. b   4. f   5. k   6. a   7. i   8. j   9. c   10. e   11. d

SOCIAL INFLUENCE ON BEHAVIOR

Concepts	Descript
_____ 1. compliance	a. Tend signif
_____ 2. normative social influence	b. Tend assoc
_____ 3. door-in-the-face technique	c. Asso requ
_____ 4. conformity	d. Ten a re
_____ 5. obedience	e. Ref acc
_____ 6. informational social influence	f. Ref bel
_____ 7. stereotype threat	g. As or
_____ 8. foot-in-the-door technique	h. Te

3. According
acceptable ma

INTERPERSONAL BEHAVIOR: ATTRACTION AND AGGRESSION

Concepts	Descriptions
_____ 1. reciprocity	a. Principle stating that when one receives expressions of liking and loving, the tendency is to respond with similar expressions
_____ 2. frustration-aggtression hypothesis	b. Any physical or verbal behavior intended to hurt another person
_____ 3. mere exposure effect	c. Suggests that your best friend might live next door to you
_____ 4. similarity	d. Explains why we are attracted to people in close proximity to us
_____ 5. interpersonal aggression	e. Psychosocial perspective concerning aggression that links frustration and aggression
_____ 6. proximity	f. Refers to the observation that people are attracted to others who often share common beliefs, values, attitudes, interests, and intellectual ability

– PART IV. TRUE-FALSE STATEMENTS –

Fill in the blank before each statement with either a T (true) or an F (false). Check your answers against the Answer Key. Then go back to the items that are false and make the necessary change(s) to the statements to convert the items into true statements.

SOCIAL PERCEPTION AND ATTRIBUTION THEORIES

_____ 1. Negative first impressions are more easily altered in response to additional information than are positive first impressions.

_____ 2. The halo effect would predict that you perceive a well-mannered child as more attractive than his less-polite identical twin.

correspondent inference theory, if you observe a person behaving in a socially ner, you would not make a correspondent inference.

_____ 4. The fundamental attribution error occurs when a person falsely believes that he or she has control over an event in his or her life.

_____

_____

ATTITUDES AND PREJUDICE

_____ 5. LaPiere's study involving a Chinese couple found a high level of consistency between individuals' attitudes and behaviors.

_____

_____

_____ 6. Balance theory suggests that if you like your roommate, you would also like his or her boyfriend or girlfriend.

_____

_____

_____ 7. Providing accurate information that contradicts a prejudiced individual's viewpoint is an effective way to alter that person's negative attitude.

_____

_____

SOCIAL INFLUENCE ON BEHAVIOR

_____ 8. The less familiar a person is with an attitude object, the more likely he or she is to conform.

_____

_____

_____ 9. Conformity involves simply modifying behaviors so that they are consistent with those of others; compliance involves modifying behavior in response to direct requests from others.

_____

_____

INTERPERSONAL BEHAVIOR: ATTRACTION AND AGGRESSION

_____ 10. Proximity, similarity, the halo effect, and physical attractiveness are four primary variables contributing to interpersonal attraction.

_____

_____

_____11. Berkowitz suggests that frustration will not result in aggression unless suitable environmental cues are present.

_____

_____

_____12. Sociobiologists support the psychosocial perspective concerning aggression.

_____

_____

Answer Key
1. F   2. T   3. T   4. F   5. F   6. T   7. F   8. T   9. T   10. F   11. T   12. F

– PART V. MULTIPLE-CHOICE QUESTIONS –

Choose the best answer to each question. Circle your choice. Check your answers against the Answer Key. Questions marked with an asterisk (*) include annotated answers.

SOCIAL PERCEPTION

1. Darley and Latané (1968) found that one would be more likely to help another person in trouble if _____.
   a. paid to do so
   b. the other person was of the same sex
   c. he or she was the only bystander
   d. there were several bystanders

2. To what are first impressions most directly related to?
   a. impression management.
   b. the halo effect.
   c. the mere exposure effect.
   d. the primacy effect.

3. A person believes that elementary schoolteachers are nurturing people. This is an example of
   a. a person schema
   b. an attribution
   c. prejudice
   d. an implicit personality theory

*4 A friend tells you about the clumsy person who sits next to him in class who is always dropping her pencil and stepping on your friend's feet. As a result of _____, you expect that the person is also not very bright.
   a. person schemas
   b. prejudice
   c. implicit personality theories
   d. balance theory

5. Which term is *not* directly associated with the other three terms?
   a. halo effect
   b. person schemas
   c. implicit personality theories
   d. central trait

ATTRIBUTION THEORIES

6. The theory that describes how one decides if another person's behavior is a result of internal or external factors is the _____ theory.
   a. decision
   b. attribution
   c. balance
   d. social influence

7. An assumption that behavior is determined by internal causes, such as personal attitudes or goals, is referred to as _____.
   a. consensus
   b. fundamental attribution
   c. situational attribution
   d. dispositional attribution

8. When would you be most likely to attribute a person's behavior to a correspondent inference or dispositional cause?
   a. when that behavior is focused on achieving a unique outcome that would unlikely occur as the result of some other behavior
   b. when that behavior is fairly common
   c. when that behavior illustrates conformity
   d. when that behavior is socially desirable

9. According to Kelley's covariation principle, which of the following is **not** one of the three potential causes of a behavior we examine when making an attribution?
   a. persons involved
   b. stimuli or objects toward which the behavior is directed
   c. consistency of the behavior
   d. situation or context

*10. If your professor believes that anyone who doesn't find psychology as fascinating as he or she does must be an idiot, your professor would be _____.
   a. committing the fundamental attribution error
   b. a "victim" of the false consensus bias
   c. prejudiced
   d. using a person schema

ATTITUDES AND PREJUDICE

11. Which of the following is included in the definition of attitudes?
   a. Attitudes involve predispositions to respond in a consistent way.
   b. Attitudes are learned.
   c. Attitudes are enduring.
   d. All of the above are included in the definition.

12. If a child earns a nod of approval from a parent when he or she makes a racially derogatory comment, he or she is likely to develop a negative attitude toward the group through _____.
   a. direct experience.
   b. Pavlovian conditioning
   c. operant conditioning
   d. observation

13. At times the attitudes we express allow us to identify with or gain approval from our peers. This statement describes the _____ function of attitudes.
    a. social identification
    b. social adjustment
    c. conformity
    d. normative social influence

14. According to _____, the attitudes of other people play a significant role in determining whether we maintain our attitudes or change them.
    a. balance theory
    b. attribution theory
    c. the covariation principle
    d. cognitive dissonance theory

15. When people that we dislike do not agree with us, we probably will be in a state of _____.
    a. nonbalance
    b. imbalance
    c. balance
    d. dissonance

16. According to cognitive dissonance theory, people are motivated to _____.
    a. achieve consistency between attitudes and behavior
    b. behave inconsistently
    c. avoid unconscious conflicts
    d. avoid people who are similar to themselves

17. According to cognitive dissonance theory, which individual would most likely undergo a change in attitude concerning the death penalty (which he or she was originally opposed to)?—an advertising/public relations expert who wrote a brief _____.
    a. anti–death penalty piece as a favor for a friend
    b. anti–death penalty piece for a client and was paid to do so
    c. pro–death penalty piece as a favor for a friend
    d. pro–death penalty piece for a client and was paid to do so

18. A used-car salesman tells you, "That's a fine car at an outstanding price." This salesman is not effective in persuading you to buy the car, in large part, because of which of the following?
    a. There is little prestige associated with being a used-car salesman.
    b. The salesman is unattractive.
    c. You doubt that the salesman is trustworthy.
    d. You doubt that the salesman has any expertise concerning cars.

19. Attempts to change attitudes are often most successful if there is _____ discrepancy between the individual's original attitude and the attitude that is being encouraged.
    a. a small
    b. a moderate
    c. a large
    d. no

*20. Preconceived and oversimplified beliefs and expectations about the traits of members of a particular group that do not account for individual differences defines _____.
    a. person schemas
    b. an outgroup

c. prejudice

d. stereotypes

21. We divide our world into two groups of people, "us" and "them." You and I belong to the _____.

    a. outgroup

    b. ingroup

    c. minority group

    d. known group

22. The slogan from the youth movement of the late 1960s and early 1970s, "Don't trust anyone over 30," is an example of which of the following?

    a. the ingroup bias

    b. the outgroup bias

    c. discrimination

    d. social perception

23. Attitudes are composed of beliefs, feelings, and behaviors. Regarding prejudiced attitudes, these three components—in order—relate to _____, _____, and _____.

    a. discrimination, stereotypes, prejudice

    b. prejudice, stereotypes, discrimination

    c. stereotypes, prejudice, discrimination

    d. ingroup, outgroup, compliance

24. Overt acts of prejudice tend to increase during which periods?

    a. isolation between the groups

    b. voluntary cooperation

    c. forced cooperation

    d. frustration

25. Which personality trait is *not* included in the profile of the authoritarian personality?

    a. high self-esteem

    b. emotional coldness

    c. rigidity

    d. intolerance

SOCIAL INFLUENCE ON BEHAVIOR

*26. Changing your behavior to be consistent with the behavior of a group because you believe that the group is more knowledgeable than you illustrates _____ influence.

    a. social identification

    b. normative social

    c. understanding

    d. informational social

27. In Sherif's experiment that asked subjects to estimate how far a light moved in group-testing situations, subjects' estimates became progressively more similar. Following the group test, when tested alone subjects made judgments similar to those made in the group situations, indicating the _____ influence.

    a. social identification

    b. normative social

    c. social adjustment

    d. informational social

28. Who would be *least* likely to exhibit conforming behavior in Asch's experiment involving line-comparison judgments?
    a. an individual with low self-esteem
    b. an architectural draftsman
    c. a college freshman in a group of college seniors
    d. the last individual to answer in a group of seven subjects

29. Which of the following are individuals who conform to negative stereotypes associated with their group exemplifying?
    a. a negative person schema
    b. a stereotype threat
    c. an ingroup bias
    d. compliance

30. A career woman would like her husband to help a little more with the housework. If she first requests that her husband do 50 percent of the work, she would be using the _____ technique.
    a. settle-for-less
    b. door-in-the-face
    c. foot-in-the-door
    d. foot-in-the-mouth

31. Milgram's study examined _____.
    a. obedience
    b. the authoritarian personality
    c. conformity
    d. compliance

32. A teenage gang member murders a member from a rival gang but denies being to blame because "The gang leader told me to do it." This teenager's statement would support the _____ explanation of destructive obedience.
    a. diffusion of responsibility
    b. graduated demands
    c. visible symbols of power
    d. reduced personal accountability

INTERPERSONAL BEHAVIOR: ATTRACTION AND AGGRESSION

33. Probably the most basic reason you will not fall in love with and marry a Russian citizen is _____.
    a. conformity
    b. proximity
    c. reciprocity
    d. similarity

34. Regarding interpersonal attraction, which of the following old adages is most correct?
    a. Birds of a feather flock together.
    b. Don't take any wooden nickels.
    c. Two's company, three's a crowd.
    d. Opposites attract.

35. What did cross-cultural study of sex differences in mate selection find?
    a. Men and women both place very high values on physical attractiveness.
    b. Women place greater value on physical attractiveness than men.

c. Men place greater value on physical attractiveness than women.

d. Men and women in industrial societies place less value on physical attractiveness than men and women in more primitive societies.

36. Which of the following does Lorenz believe?
    a. All species have an "aggressive instinct."
    b. There is survival value associated with aggression directed toward members of the same species.
    c. Unlike most other species, humans do not have an innate inhibition that prevents them from killing other humans.
    d. All of the above choices are correct.

*37. Which of the following describes the most recent revision of the frustration-aggression hypothesis?
    a. In order for frustration to result in aggression, a readiness to act aggressively and environmental cues must both be present.
    b. Frustration can produce a number of possible responses other than aggression.
    c. Aggression is always a consequence of frustration.
    d. Frustration always leads to aggression.

38. Regarding the effect of television violence on children, which of the following is the consensus of opinion among psychologists?
    a. No consensus has been reached.
    b. Violence on TV has a cathartic effect and reduces aggressive behaviors.
    c. Violence on TV has a negative effect on boys but not on girls.
    d. Violence on TV does lead to aggressive behavior.

Answer Key

1. c	2. d	3. a	*4. c	5. b	6. b	7. d	8. a	9. c	*10. b	11. d	12. c	13. b
14. a	15. c	16. a	17. c	18. c	19. b	*20. d	21. b	22. a	23. c	24. d	25. a	*26. d
27. d	28. b	29. b	30. b	31. a	32. d	33. b	34. a	35. c	36. d	*37. a	38. d	

Annotated Answers

4. The correct choice is **c**. Implicit personality theories are assumptions about personality traits that go together. Clumsy is a "bad intellectual" trait that would be associated with a lack of intelligence.
    a. Person schemas relate to generalized assumptions about certain classes of people, whereas implicit personality theories are based around the traits of individuals.
    b. Prejudice involves negative attitudes toward an entire group.
    d. Balance theory is associated with attitude changes and not with social perception.

10. The correct choice is **b**. The false consensus bias is the tendency to assume that most people share your attitudes and behaviors and to conclude that a person who does not share your attitudes and behaviors is abnormal. Thus, someone who doesn't find psychology fascinating has something wrong with them (they're an idiot).
    a. The fundamental attribution error involves attributions concerning the behavior of another person: specifically, overestimating dispositional and underestimating external causes.
    c. Prejudice is a negative attitude toward an entire group and not an assumption concerning the personality traits of an individual.
    d. Person schemas are generalized assumptions about *classes* of people (for example, lawyers) and not people who just happen not to find psychology fascinating.

20. The correct choice is **d**. This is the definition of stereotypes.
    a. Person schemas is a related term; however, stereotypes may be more specific than the generalized assumptions of a person schema. Additionally, person schemas refer to classes of people (lawyers) while stereotypes refer to groups of people (blacks).
    b. Outgroups are the "them" in the "us versus them" category. They are frequently subject to prejudice.
    c. The definition of stereotypes relates to the belief component of a prejudicial attitude. Prejudice also involves feeling and behavior components.

26. The correct choice is **d**. This question relates to conformity and describes the informational social influence of conformity. If you're at a fancy dinner party and do not know which fork to eat your salad with, you will probably wait until others start to eat and then use the same fork as they.
    a. Social identification refers to a function of attitudes that provides us with information about other people's attitudes.
    b. The normative social influence of conformity relates to altering our behavior because we think it is to our advantage (such as gaining the approval of others, and avoiding disapproval) without an actual change in our beliefs. Even if you really believe that it is correct to eat your salad with your fingers, you would probably still use a fork at a fancy dinner party.
    c. Understanding refers to a function of attitudes that provides a frame of reference that helps us structure and make sense out of the world and our experiences.

37. The correct choice is **a**. This statement summarizes Berkowitz's (1978) view of the frustration-aggression hypothesis.
    b. This statement summarizes Miller's (1941) view of the frustration-aggression hypothesis.
    c. This choice (and choice **d**) are the two sides of Dollard's (1939) original view of the frustration-aggression hypothesis.
    d. See **c** above.

– PART VI. SUMMARY TABLES –

To test your understanding of the material discussed in this chapter, complete the following tables. Check your answers with those supplied in Part IX.

ATTRIBUTION THEORY

Attribution of Causes	Theories	
	Correspondent Inference	Covariation Principle
Dispositional		
External		

TYPES OF SOCIAL INFLUENCE

Type	Definition	Example of Experiments	Influencing Factors
Conformity			
Compliance			
Obedience			

– PART VII. THOUGHT QUESTIONS/CRITICAL THINKING –

Prepare answers to the following discussion questions.

1. Discuss the advantages (or benefits) and disadvantages (or costs) of person schemas and implicit personality theories. Refer to the discussion of heuristics in Chapter 10. Are person schemas and implicit personality theories heuristics? Why or why not?

2. Prejudiced attitudes between two groups frequently exist bilaterally as opposed to unilaterally. For example, some soldiers may be prejudiced toward sailors and sailors toward soldiers, and some whites may be prejudiced toward blacks and blacks toward whites. Discuss principle(s) of social psychology that would explain this observation.

3. Discuss how you would approach each of the following situations. Explain why you would use the approaches you selected.
   a. You are a consultant hired by the president of a local company that has been negatively affected by economic conditions. This company is experiencing major labor-management conflicts.
   b. You have been appointed chairperson of your dormitory to collect contributions for the victims of a natural disaster in a nearby state.
   c. Your younger brother will be a college freshman next fall at a college where he does not know any other students. Based on the material in this chapter, what advice would you give him that would result in a successful (both academically and interpersonally) adjustment to college?

4. Try to be completely honest here. When you first read about Asch's line-comparison judgment experiment and Milgram's obedience experiment, what did you think about the individuals who were the subjects in these experiments? Did you attribute their behavior to dispositional or external causes? Did you fall victim to the fundamental attribution error? Now that you have read the discussion of factors influencing conformity and obedience, predict what you think your behavior would have been had you been a subject in the Asch and Milgram studies.

5. The text describes three types of social influence. These three influences may be viewed as blending together. Conformity is modifying one's behavior to be consistent with the behavior of others. Compliance is modifying one's behavior as a result of a direct request from others. Obedience is modifying one's behavior in response to a command or order from a person perceived as having power or authority. Describe an example of conformity, compliance, and obedience that could be observed in each of the following situations:
   a. junior-high-age adolescents at school
   b. the employees in an office
   c. a group of individuals who live in a neighborhood (or apartment, or dormitory).

– PART VIII. APPLICATIONS –

1. Ideally, naturalistic observation would be the research method I would choose for this application, but due to time constraints we're going to develop a new research method—the naturalistic interview. The fundamental attribution error is to overestimate external causes and underestimate external causes when accounting for the behavior of others (and to do the opposite when accounting for our own behavior). Select two or three individuals with whom you have frequent contact. Over the next few days, casually slip into your conversation a number of questions asking your friends to make attributions concerning the behavior of others (for example, "Why do you think she piles so much food on her plate?") and themselves ("Why did you go to the movies last night?"). Make sure that you ask each person a number

of questions concerning both themselves and others. Remember their answers and write them down as soon as you get a chance. When you have finished your data collection, examine the answers to determine whether or not you see evidence of the fundamental attribution error.

2. You decide to design an experiment illustrating conformity for the lab section of general psychology that you are in charge of. You are interested in showing that larger groups result in an increased tendency to show conformity than smaller groups. So that your students will be less likely to "see through" your experimental procedure, you decide to do the experiment the week before the class reads the social psychology chapter in the text. Assume that you can come up with an acceptable reason for the students to come to the lab at different times (in order to give you a number of smaller groups). You would also probably hand out written material for the class to read. For all but one of the students, this written hand-out would be instructions for the "script" they should follow as confederates in the experiment. The remaining student—the subject—would read material concerning an experiment or lab exercise that he or she will falsely believe to be the focus of the lab session. You may choose either to design an experiment replicating Asch's line-comparison judgment task or some other situation (suggestions: trying to talk the instructor into having class outdoors because it's such a nice day; complaining about the lab instructor for being unreasonable).

   a. What is your hypothesis?
   b. Write a paragraph explaining exactly what procedure you will use to conduct the experiment
   c. Identify the independent variable.
   d. Identify the dependent variable and explain how it will be measured.
   e. Identify the experimental group(s).
   f. Identify the control group.
   g. Explain how you would assign subjects to the experimental and control groups.
   h. Provide any necessary operational definitions.
   i. Evaluate your experiment with regard to the APA's ethical guidelines. Even though this experiment is only a classroom exercise and not a "real" experiment, you must adhere to the guidelines.
   j. How would you compare the experimental and control groups on their performance on the dependent variable? Using only descriptive statistics, how would you present the results (that is, would you calculate means, percentiles, etc.)?
   k. Predict what differences in behavior you would find if your hypothesis was confirmed by the results of the experiment.

– PART IX. SUMMARY TABLES SOLUTIONS –

ATTRIBUTION THEORY

| | *Theories* | |
Attribution of Causes	**Correspondent Inference**	**Covariation Principle**
Dispositional	Socially undesirable behaviors Focused on a unique outcome (or noncommon effect) Free will	Behavior is typical for the individual (low distinctiveness). Behavior is different from that of others (low consensus).
External	Socially acceptable behaviors Focused on a common outcome Presence of social or other influence (lack of free will)	Behavior unusual or atypical for the individual (high distinctiveness) Behavior similar to that of others (high consensus)

TYPES OF SOCIAL INFLUENCE

Type	Definition	Example of Experiments	Influencing Factors
Conformity	Behavior or beliefs are modified so that they are consistent with those of others.	Sherif: stationary light Asch: line-comparison judgments	Increased tendency to conform when majority group is unanimous, perceive group members acting independently, size of group is larger, unfamiliar with attitude object, low self-esteem, and believe group members have higher status
Compliance	Behavior is altered in response to direct requests from others.	Cialdini et al.: college students asked to interact with delinquent youths	Foot-in-the-door technique Door-in-the-face technique
Obedience	Behavior is altered in response to commands or orders from people perceived as having power or authority.	Milgram: subjects instructed to shock another individual for incorrect responses	Increased tendency to be obedient as a result of diminished personal accountability, authority figure has highly visible symbols of power or status, and if individual is presented with a series of graduated demands

APPENDIX
ELEMENTARY STATISTICS

– PART I. LEARNING OBJECTIVES –

When you finish studying this chapter, you should be able to do the following:

DESCRIPTIVE STATISTICS

1. Discuss the function of measures of central tendency, and describe three measures of central tendency.

2. Discuss the function of measures of variability, and describe three measures of variability.

3. Describe the normal distribution, and explain how z-scores are related to the normal distribution.

4. Discuss how correlation is used to describe the relationship between two variables, and describe the Pearson product-moment correlation coefficient.

5. Explain how regression is related to correlation, and discuss how regression is used.

INFERENTIAL STATISTICS

6. Discuss how a sample is used to estimate characteristics of a population.

7. Explain why researchers need to use hypothesis testing, and differentiate between the null hypothesis and the alternative hypothesis.

8. Discuss how *t*-tests allow researchers to interpret the results of their experiments, and describe Type I and Type II errors.

9. Discuss how analysis of variance is similar to the *t*-test, and discuss when it is necessary to use analysis of variance.

10. Describe factor analysis, and list two areas of psychology in which factor analysis has been extensively used.

– PART II. KEY TERMS/MATCHING EXERCISES –

Match the following concepts with the appropriate descriptions. Check your answers against the Answer Key.

DESCRIPTIVE STATISTICS: MEASURES OF CENTRAL TENDENCY AND VARIABILITY

Concepts	Descriptions
_____ 1. range	a. Table that shows how many individuals actually received each possible score on a test
_____ 2. mode	b. Measure of variability that is computed by subtracting the lowest score from the highest score
_____ 3. standard deviation	c. Measure of variability that is the average of the squared distances of the scores from the mean
_____ 4. frequency distribution	d. Measure of central tendency that is computed by adding up all the scores and dividing by the number of scores
_____ 5. mean	e. Measure of central tendency that is the middle score in a list of scores that have been arranged in increasing order
_____ 6. variance	f. Measure of variability that is the square root of the average of the squared distances of the scores from the mean
_____ 7. median	g. Measure of central tendency that is the most frequently occurring score in a group of scores

Answer Key

  1. b   2. g   3. f   4. a   5. d   6. c   7. e

DESCRIPTIVE STATISTICS: NORMAL FREQUENCY DISTRIBUTION, CORRELATION, AND REGRESSION

Concepts	Descriptions
_____ 1. probability	a. Graph used to visualize the relationship between two variables
_____ 2. scatter plot	b. Proportion of cases that fit a certain description
_____ 3. z-scores	c. Measure of the degree to which two variables covary
_____ 4. regression	d. Used to predict a score on a variable from the individual's score on another variable
_____ 5. normal distribution	e. Bell-shaped curve in which scores near the mean are most common
_____ 6. Pearson product-moment correlation coefficient	f. Measure of correlation that is used most often and varies from −1.0 to +1.0
_____ 7. correlation coefficient	g. Standard deviation scores

Answer Key

  1. b   2. a   3. g   4. d   5. e   6. f   7. c

INFERENTIAL STATISTICS AND ADVANCED STATISTICAL TECHNIQUES

Concepts	Descriptions
_____ 1. analysis of variance	a. Incorrectly concluding that the independent variable has no effect when it does
_____ 2. working hypothesis	b. Incorrectly concluding that the independent variable has an effect when it has none
_____ 3. Type II error	c. Statistical procedure that is conceptually similar to the *t*-test and examines differences between the means of two or more groups
_____ 4. factor analysis	d. Statistical technique used to determine if there is a significant difference between the means of two groups
_____ 5. null hypothesis	e. Highly sophisticated correlational technique used to identify the basic factors underlying psychological phenomena
_____ 6. Type I error	f. Predicts that the independent variable will have an effect on the dependent variable
_____ 7. *t*-test	g. Predicts that the independent variable will have no effect on the dependent variable

Answer Key
   1. c   2. f   3. a   4. e   5. g   6. b   7. d

STATISTICAL SYMBOLS

Concepts	Descriptions
_____ 1. s^2	a. Variable that can take on many values
_____ 2. Σ	b. "Add up these scores"
_____ 3. x	c. Mean
_____ 4. f	d. Number of scores
_____ 5. z	e. Frequency
_____ 6. X	f. Variance
_____ 7. r_{xy}	g. Standard deviation
_____ 8. N	h. Standard deviation score
_____ 9. s	i. Pearson product-moment correlation coefficient

Answer Key
   1. f   2. b   3. a   4. e   5. h   6. c   7. i   8. d   9. g

– PART III. TRUE-FALSE STATEMENTS –

Fill in the blank before each statement with either a T (true) or an F (false). Check your answers against the Answer Key. Then go back to the items that are false and make the necessary change(s) to the statements to convert the items into true statements.

DESCRIPTIVE STATISTICS

_____ 1. A distribution of scores that is asymmetrical and unbalanced is said to be a normal distribution.

_____ 2. The variance and standard deviation reflect the degree of spread or fluctuation of scores around the mean.

_____ 3. A z-score of +2.0 corresponds to a score two standard deviations above the mean.

_____ 4. In a distribution of scores, the mean is unaffected by extreme scores.

_____ 5. A scatter plot is used to visualize a frequency distribution.

INFERENTIAL STATISTICS AND ADVANCED STATISTICAL TECHNIQUES

_____ 6. In a random sample, everyone in the specified population has the same chance of being in the sample.

_____ 7. If tests of statistical significance indicate that the null hypothesis would only happen five percent of the time or less by chance, then psychologists would conclude that it was not a chance event but a real effect.

_____ 8. Researchers try to minimize the probability of making Type II errors.

_____ 9. Factor analysis is a highly sophisticated correlational procedure.

Answer Key
1. F   2. T   3. T   4. F   5. F   6. T   7. T   8. F   9. T

– PART IV. MULTIPLE-CHOICE QUESTIONS –

Choose the best answer to each question. Circle your choice. Check your answers against the Answer Key.

DESCRIPTIVE STATISTICS

1. _____ statistics are used to summarize the results of research. _____ statistics are used to draw conclusions about the research.
   a. Central tendency / Variability
   b. Descriptive / Inferential
   c. Inferential / Descriptive
   d. Regression / Correlational

2. Descriptive statistics include all of the following concepts except _____.
   a. measures of variability
   b. correlation
   c. hypothesis testing
   d. measures of central tendency

3. A type of average calculated by dividing the sum of scores by the number of scores is the _____.
   a. mean
   b. median
   c. mode
   d. range

4. In the distribution of scores 1, 1, 2, 3, 5, 6, the median is _____.
   a. 1
   b. 2
   c. 2.5
   d. 3

5. In a distribution of scores it is possible to have more than one _____.
   a. median
   b. standard deviation
   c. mean
   d. mode

6. Why is the standard deviation a better estimate of the variability of a distribution than the range?
   a. It is easier to compute.
   b. It is about the same as the mean, anyway.
   c. It relies on the median.
   d. It is less influenced by extreme scores.

7. To calculate a z-score for an individual score, you need to know the _____ of the distribution of scores.
   a. median and variance
   b. variance and standard deviation
   c. mean and standard deviation
   d. median and standard deviation

8. In a normal distribution of scores, more individuals would fall between z-scores from _____ than in the other three choices.
   a. 0 to +1.0
   b. +1.0 to +2.0

c.   +2.0 to +3.0

d.   +1.0 to +3.0

9. According to the normal distribution statistic, _____ percent of Wechsler IQ scores fall between 85 and 115.

a.   50

b.   68

c.   84

d.   98

10. What does the correlation coefficient describes?

a.   The probability that scores vary together

b.   The Pearson product-moment score

c.   The relationship between individual scores

d.   The degree of relationship between variables

11. Most likely there is a _____ correlation between a person's time on a half-mile run and their time on a mile run.

a.   zero

b.   positive

c.   negative

d.   unsystematic

12. The Pearson product-moment correlation measure of correlation can take on any numerical value from −1.0 to +1.0. The size of the correlation represents the _____ of the relationship, and the sign of the correlation represents the _____ of the relationship between two variables.

a.   degree / direction

b.   direction / range

c.   range / degree

d.   direction / degree

13. Regression is most closely related to _____.

a.   variability

b.   factor analysis

c.   correlation

d.   hypothesis testing

14. If you know an individual's score on one variable (e.g., height), you would use _____ to predict his or her score on a second variable (e.g., weight).

a.   estimation

b.   regression

c.   the median

d.   the correlation coefficient

INFERENTIAL STATISTICS

15. Why is a random sample representative?

a.   Everyone in the specified sample has an equal chance of being chosen.

b.   It is scientific

c.   It is used by experts.

d.   It leaves nothing to chance.

16. Inferential statistics, such as the *t*-test, actually test the _____.
   a. experimental hypothesis
   b. working hypothesis
   c. null hypothesis
   d. either the null or working hypothesis

17. You conduct an experiment and calculate a *t* ratio and find that the chance probability of obtaining a *t* as large as you found is 10 percent. Which of the following would you conclude?
   a. You had miscalculated the *t* ratio because it is always at the .05 level or less.
   b. The null hypothesis was incorrect.
   c. There is a real difference between the groups.
   d. There is no real difference between the groups.

18. A statistic commonly used to decide if there is a statistically significant difference between the means of two groups is the _____.
   a. z-score
   b. Pearson product-moment correlation coefficient
   c. *t*-test
   d. F-test

Read the following and then respond to questions 19–21:

You conduct an experiment on the effects of caffeine on resting heart rate. You have four groups of subjects who receive different dosages of caffeine (no caffeine, low dose, medium dose, and high dose).

19. Which of the following is the null hypothesis?
   a. The higher the dosage of caffeine, the higher the heart rate.
   b. Caffeine groups will have different heart rates than the no-caffeine group.
   c. The three caffeine groups will not differ on heart rate.
   d. The four groups will not differ on heart rate.

20. You should use a(n) _____ to analyze the results of your study.
   a. factor analysis
   b. analysis of variance
   c. *t*-test
   d. correlation

21. If you incorrectly interpret the results of your study and make a Type I error, what would you do?
   a. Reject the null hypothesis when it is, in fact, false.
   b. Not reject the null hypothesis when it is, in fact, false.
   c. Reject the null hypothesis when it is, in fact, true.
   d. Not reject the null hypothesis when it is, in fact, true.

22. A statistical technique that attempts to find clusters of tests that correlate with one another is _____.
   a. covariance
   b. factor analysis
   c. regression
   d. F-test

Answer Key

1. b   2. c   3. a   4. c   5. d   6. d   7. c   8. a   9. b   10. d   11. b   12. a
13. c   14. b   15. a   16. c   17. d   18. c   19. d   20. b   21. c   22. b

CPSIA information can be obtained at www.ICGtesting.com
Printed in the USA
268778BV00004B/8/P